BRITISH HISTORY

A SOURCE BOOK

This is a Flame Tree Book
First published in 2003
This edition published 2006

07 09 10 08 06

1 3 5 7 9 10 8 6 4 2

FLAME TREE PUBLISHING
Crabtree Hall, Crabtree Lane, Fulham,
London, SW6 6TY, United Kingdom
www.flametreepublishing.com

Flame Tree is part of
The Foundry Creative Media Company Limited

ISBN 1 84451 456 0

A copy of the CIP data for this book is available from the British Library

Printed in China

BRITISH HISTORY

A SOURCE BOOK

Gerard Cheshire, David Harding, Lucinda Hawksley,
Brenda Ralph Lewis, Jon Sutherland, Helen Tovey

INTRODUCTION: PROFESSOR ERIC EVANS

FLAME TREE
PUBLISHING

CONTENTS

Each chapter is divided into entries and organized chronologically

INTRODUCTION

BRITISH HISTORY is an endlessly fascinating subject which can be studied on several levels. Firstly, there is the story of the emergence of a nation in the ninth and tenth centuries from divided and frequently warring local kingdoms. Anglo-Saxon England appeared stable and usually prosperous, until the Norman Conquest of 1066 instituted not only a political but a social revolution, witnessing, as it did, the brutal replacement of one stable landed elite by another, foreign one. Norman and its successor, Angevin rule, proved immensely durable. In various guises, it would survive for more than 400 years; 1066 was to be the last occasion of a successful invasion by a foreign power.

It is possible, but nowadays rather unfashionable, to present the history of post-conquest Britain in terms of general success and increasing influence. Thus, the civil wars of the mid-fifteenth century were ended by the Battle of Bosworth in 1485 which installed a new Tudor dynasty. The Tudors gave the

English more efficient government and, with the removal of papal influence from the state during the reign of Henry VIII, a new and increasingly self-confident independence. Passing rapidly over the troubled, short reigns of Edward VI and Mary I, we can dwell on the shrewd and, when necessary, consummately ruthless rule of Elizabeth I, the so-called Virgin Queen, who consolidated a viable Protestant rule in England and saw off an invasion threat from the immensely powerful Philip II of Spain in 1588. Elizabeth also used Parliament when needed, whom she flattered that she was consulting for its advice (when really she wanted its money). The seventeenth century witnessed titanic struggles between the Stuart monarchy and propertied Englishmen represented in Parliament. This century saw civil wars, a brief and troubled republic, the restoration of the monarchy and then monarchical wings decisively clipped by the bloodless and so-called 'Glorious Revolution' of 1688.

Since that date, no year has passed without a session of Parliament and monarchs have had to acknowledge clear and defined limits to their power.

The eighteenth and nineteenth centuries witnessed the gradual emergence of a genuine parliamentary government and a reduced (but never a derisory) role for the monarchy. Britain could present itself as the most 'enlightened' nation in Europe and was certainly, by the end of the eighteenth century, the richest. Success in the Revolutionary and Napoleonic Wars saw Britain, from 1815, established as unchallengeably the most powerful nation in the world. The long reign of Victoria (1837–1901) can be represented as the apogee of British power and influence. British leaders felt that they could offer huge benefits to the world. Britain seemed to provide a stable, progressive parliamentary government in which power changed hands peacefully as decided by a large, if still all-male electorate. A constitutional monarch of immense prestige, Victoria was a Queen-Empress from 1876 and was related, by the 1880s, to virtually every other royal house in Europe. A peaceful reign, Britain fought only one brief European war in the century from 1815–1914, which naturally she won. Economic prosperity was aided by a beneficent Empire, grounded in the

need for trade, but always ready to educate subject races into the advantages of Protestant religion and a close association with the mother country. Whatever the rest of the world may have thought, British self-confidence and certainty of its own superiority appeared impregnable. The golden and diamond jubilees of Victoria's accession in 1887 and 1897 were occasions of lavish and triumphal imperial self-congratulation.

Those who picture British history over a millennium as a natural progression, have more trouble with the twentieth century. Two cataclysmic world wars were both won, but at an enormous, unsustainable cost. These wars (in which British colonies and Commonwealth associates played an important part) witnessed the beginnings of the end of Empire. Although British withdrawal from its colonial possessions from the late 1940s to the late 1970s was, in general, a relatively dignified and peaceful affair, it proved difficult to answer the shrewd, and cutting, accusation of the far-from-hostile American critic, Dean Acheson, that by the 1960s, Britain had lost an empire and failed to find a role. Assimilation with a wider European framework has proved a problematic and controversial affair and no substitute for ruling an empire on which the sun never set. Few would argue that the British have been either eager or successful Europeans since entering the Common Market in 1973. Europe, as a political issue, had brought the Conservatives (once the most successful, democratic political party in the western world) to a pitiful, bickering rump by the beginning of the twenty-first century. Whether New Labour, its successor (however temporarily), as 'the natural party of government', owes anything at all to its roots a century before as a Labour party of, and for, working people and 'the left-out millions', is a matter of high dispute.

Nowadays, though, few want to present British history in this linear way. 'Dominant narratives' are out of fashion. There is no agreement on which events or developments are most important. More historians are now interested in looking at the past from different perspectives. Some have made careers looking at history in a 'bottom up' way and trying to reconstruct the lives, struggles and cultures of those who lacked power and, frequently, the literacy to leave written records of their own. Social history, the dominant perspective of the 1960s and 1970s, has been transformed into cultural history, from the 1980s, with a greater emphasis on shifting perspectives and multiple identities. What it is to be English, let alone British, has been the subject of fierce contention. Certainly, British history can no longer be presented as 'southern English, centrist, moderated by occasional, apologetic glances north and west'. The secure certainties of an imperial power have given way to an anguished introspection, not only about identity, but the nature of history itself.

This volume does not aim to answer deep, philosophical questions about the nature of the subject History, still less probe the future to discern where it is heading. Its aim is less ambitious but, arguably, more satisfying. It gives readers brief, succinct answers to questions about the leading figures, movements and developments in British history over almost two millennia. From this rich assortment of factual information, readers can be led into further and deeper enquiry. If this book proves either a secure starting point for detailed later investigation, or merely the reliable answer to a particular historical query which has puzzled the reader, it will have served its purpose.

PROFESSOR ERIC EVANS

CULTURE

3000 BC	Construction of Stonehenge
AD 7th century	Edinburgh Castle built
AD 10th century	Westminster Abbey built
1066	Tower of London built
1400	Death of Geoffrey Chaucer
15th century	Renaissance begins
1593	Death of Christopher Marlowe
1616	Death of William Shakespeare
1723	Death of Christopher Wren
1633	Buckingham Palace built
1675	St Paul's Cathedral built
1703	Death of Samuel Pepys
1705	Blenheim Palace built
1727	Death of Isaac Newton
1759	Death of George Frederick Handel
1768	Royal Academy built
18th century	Kew Gardens laid out
1784	Death of Samuel Johnson
1796	Death of Robert Burns
1815	Brighton Pavilion built
1824	Death of Lord Byron
1848	Pre-Raphaelite Movement begins
1850	Death of William Wordsworth
1851	Crystal Palace built for the Great Exhibition
19th century	Arts and Crafts Movement
1870	Death of Charles Dickens
1871	Royal Albert Hall built
1896	Death of William Morris
1901	Death of Oscar Wilde
1918	Death of Wilfred Owen
1927	BBC established
1944	Death of Sir Edward Lutyens
1958	Death of Ralph Vaughan Williams
1960s	Rise of the Beatles
1976	Death of Benjamin Britten
1999	Millennium Dome constructed

STONEHENGE (c. 3000 BC)

Remains of a stone circle in Wiltshire, England. The exact origins of Stonehenge are a mystery. Archeological evidence has proved that the site has been used for religious and sacred rituals, including sacrifice, but no definitive initial purpose for the site can be given with certainty. There is also no rigid evidence as to how, and by whom, the monument was erected, but it was constructed in alignment with the orbit of the sun: at the summer solstice the sun rises directly overhead. Stonehenge is also strongly associated with Druidism, a religion that was prevalent in Britain in pre-Christian times.

◼ *see* Avebury

AVEBURY (c. 2600 BC)

Ancient stone circles in south-west England. Avebury is the largest known 'stone circle' in the world. It is composed of an outer ring and two inner circles, with the tallest stones over 20 ft in height. Thirty-six stones are still standing, but there are believed to have been at least four times as many in previous centuries. As with Stonehenge, Avebury's exact origins are a mystery, but it is known to have been a sacred site.

◼ *see* Stonehenge

◄ *LEFT: Avebury stone circle*

GLASTONBURY TOR

Sacred hill in south-west England, traditionally in the legendary Isle of Avalon. The Tor stands on the ley lines – geographical lines that connect ancient sacred sites – and is one of several rumoured burial sites of King Arthur. On it stands St Michael's Chapel, an important early Christian church. Glastonbury Tor was a sacred Celtic site and has many ancient rituals associated with it. Archeological evidence has found links to sacred rituals dating back to 500 BC.

◆ *see* King Arthur

EDINBURGH CASTLE (c. AD 7TH CENTURY)

Historic Scottish building. The oldest parts of Edinburgh Castle date back to Edwin of Northumbria, from whom the city takes its name. The first historical mention of the castle as a royal residence is the death of Queen Margaret (1093). She was later canonised and a chapel bearing her name built at the castle. In 1174 the castle was won by Henry II, but passed back to the Scots in 1186. The first Scots Parliament met here in 1215. Edward I took the castle in 1291 and looted many of its treasures. It was won back again in 1313, after which all but St Margaret's Chapel was destroyed by Robert Bruce so the English could never take it again. Despite this, battles continued to

▲ *ABOVE: Edinburgh Castle*

rage for centuries between the two nations over the site and subsequent buildings. In 1566 James VI (James I of England) was born here. The castle's dungeons were used to house foreign prisoners during the Napoleonic Wars.

◆ *see* Robert Bruce, Edward I, Henry II, James VI of Scotland, Malcolm III, Mary, Queen of Scots, Napoleonic Wars

BEDE, THE VENERABLE (c. AD 673–735)

English religious writer and historian. Bede lived in what is now county Durham. Orphaned at the age of seven, he was subsequently looked after by a religious order. At 19 he became a deacon and was a priest by 30. He knew Latin, Greek and possibly Hebrew. His works include De Orthographia, De Natura Rerum and, the most famous, Ecclesiastical History of the English Nation – written in Latin, this was first translated into English by Alfred the Great.

◆ *see* Alfred the Great

WESTMINSTER ABBEY (c. AD 10TH CENTURY)

Historic religious building. Reputedly there has been a place of worship here since the 700s. William I was crowned in Westminster Abbey, setting a precedent for future monarchs. This royal connection saved the building from destruction during the Dissolution of the Monasteries (the religious order settled here was dissolved). In the Civil War the abbey housed Cromwell's soldiers, and was partially destroyed. Christopher Wren assisted with its restoration. The abbey contains many illustrious memorials, including ones to Isaac Newton and David Livingstone. The area known as Poets' Corner contains many graves of, or memorials to, great writers; these include Charles Dickens and William Shakespeare.

◆ *see* Dissolution of the Monasteries, William I, Christopher Wren

▲ ABOVE: A scene from the Bayeaux Tapestery, probably the most celebrated of tapestries.

BAYEUX TAPESTRY (c. 11TH CENTURY)

Long strip of embroidered linen (not actually a tapestry). The Bayeux Tapestry depicts the events that led to the Norman Conquest: the defeat of England's king, Harold, by the William the Conqueror of Normandy (later William I of England). It was made in the French town of Bayeux and commissioned by a half-brother of William.

⬦ see Norman Conquest, William I

TOWER OF LONDON (c. 1066)

Most complete medieval fortress in Britain. The Tower of London was begun by William I, as a symbol to the people of Britain that he was not to be challenged. The first, temporary, fort was augmented by a stone tower, from which the building takes its name. King Stephen was the first monarch to live in the Tower, but successive monarchs also made it their residence and added to the building, as well as excavating a large ditch, or moat, all around the fort. At one time a royal menagerie of exotic animals was kept at the Tower, including elephants and big cats – in 1835 they were moved to London's new zoo. From the 1100s, the Tower was used as a prison. After 1285, prisoners were transported to the dungeons through Traitors' Gate. The most famous prisoner to have been taken through the gate was Princess Elizabeth, later Elizabeth I. Others to have been imprisoned here include Edward III, Henry VI and Guy Fawkes. Those to have been executed at the Tower include Lady Jane Grey and Anne Boleyn. The Tower is no longer used as a royal residence. The Tower, and its Yeoman Warders (better known as 'Beefeaters'), is now one of London's premier tourist attractions.

see Anne Boleyn, Edward III, Elizabeth I, Henry VIII, Princes in the Tower, William I

WINDSOR CASTLE (1066)

The monarch's official residence in Windsor, south-east England. The original castle at Windsor was made of earth and was not a permanent structure.It was built by William I to guard the main route to London. The first stone castle, built on the same site, was erected during the reign of Henry II. It was added to through the reigns of several successive monarchs, including the construction of the impressive St George's Chapel.

see Prince Albert, Ascot, Charles I, Edward VII, Henry II, Queen Victoria, William I

▲ *ABOVE: Windsor Castle*

CHAUCER, GEOFFREY (c. 1340–1400)

English poet. Chaucer was born into a wealthy family. As an adult he became a soldier and fought in France, where he was captured. He was ransomed by the king of England who later gave him a diplomatic post. While in this position he visited various European countries. He was the first poet to write in English, rather than Anglo-Norman or Latin. As well as the famous Canterbury Tales his works include The Book of the Duchess and Troilus and Criseyde. Many other works, including The Romance of the Rose, have been attributed to him, but authorship is unproven.

RICHMOND PALACE (14TH CENTURY)

Ruined historic building, in which many British monarchs lived. Richmond Palace was destroyed in the late 1300s, but rebuilt during the reign of Henry V (1413–22). It was the favourite residence of Henry VII and his son, Henry VIII, was born here. The palace was ruined again after Charles I's execution.

◆ *see* Charles I, Henry V, Henry VII, Henry VIII

RENAISSANCE (15TH CENTURY)

Period of great change in every sphere of society, considered by scholars to be the beginning of modern history. The term Renaissance comes from the French and literally means rebirth. It was a movement that began in the north of Italy in the fifteenth century and spread throughout Europe; it continued to expand for the next two centuries. The cultural changes affected every area of life, including the arts, architecture, sciences and philosophy. In art and architecture, the movement saw a return to the classical influence of ancient Greece and Rome, and a move away from the rigidity of the austerely religious medieval world – a central figure of the Italian Renaissance was

Leonardo da Vinci. In Britain the movement was particularly prominent during the reign of Elizabeth I – a world in which William Shakespeare was a key Renaissance figure – and into the Stuart dynasty. Charles I, a committed patron of the arts, was a key part of the continuing movement, which at his death was crushed into submission under Cromwell's puritanical government. The Restoration of Charles II to the throne in 1660 led to a new period of rebirth, in which the arts once again flourished.

see Charles I, Charles II, Oliver Cromwell, Restoration, William Shakespeare

HOLBEIN, HANS (c. 1497–1543)

German artist who worked in Britain. Holbein first visited Britain in the 1520s. He also worked in Switzerland and Italy, as well as his native Germany. In 1533, he was employed as a court painter by Henry VIII, for whom he worked until his death. Holbein's most famous works include The Ambassadors and his pre-marriage portrait of Anne of Cleves: Henry later divorced Anne, reputedly because she proved to be less attractive than her portrait.

see Henry VIII

HOLYROODHOUSE, PALACE OF (c. 1500)

The British monarch's official residence in Scotland, located in Edinburgh. The palace became a royal residence in the 1500s, after centuries of fighting over Edinburgh Castle between the Scots and English. The first monarch to live here was James IV of Scotland. Mary, Queen of Scots also lived here, for six years, after her arrival in Scotland (from France) in 1561. The palace stands at one end of Edinburgh's Royal Mile, with Edinburgh Castle at the opposite end.

see Edinburgh Castle; Mary, Queen of Scots

TALLIS, THOMAS (c. 1505–85)

English musician. Tallis was a gentleman of the royal chapel and began his career under Mary I. He retained his post when her half-sister Elizabeth succeeded and, with William Byrd, became the foremost music printer of the time.

see William Byrd

HAMPTON COURT PALACE (c. 1520S)

Tudor palace designed by Christopher Wren. The site, on the banks of the Thames, was owned by Cardinal Wolsey. In 1529, Henry VIII seized Wolsey's land and his newly built house. Subsequent monarchs, including Elizabeth I, lived at Hampton Court until the death of George II. George III turned it into 'grace and favour' apartments, a tradition that continues today. Hampton Court, which was opened to the public by Queen Victoria, is famous for its gardens – partially designed by Capability Brown – and large maze. The palace was damaged by fire in the 1980s, but quickly restored. It is reputed to be one of Britain's most haunted buildings.

see Capability Brown, Elizabeth I, George II, Henry VIII, Thomas Wolsey, Christopher Wren

▲ ABOVE: Hampton Court Palace

GIBBONS, ORLANDO (1538–1625)

English composer. Gibbons was a choirboy at King's College, Cambridge and later the organist at Westminster Abbey. He was a favourite of the young Charles I and played in his court. Gibbons wrote over 40 pieces of church music, mainly anthems and madrigals. He also wrote music for the viol and virginal.

see Charles I, Westminster Abbey

BYRD, WILLIAM (1543–1623)

Elizabethan musician. Byrd and his collaborator Thomas Tallis were key figures in the rise of the arts at the court of Elizabeth I. At the age of 20, Byrd became organist at Lincoln Cathedral and went on to hold the monopoly over music printing, with Tallis.

see Elizabeth I, Thomas Tallis

MARLOWE, CHRISTOPHER (c. 1564–93)

English playwright and poet, contemporary of Shakespeare. Marlowe took the dramatic world by storm with Tamburlaine the Great. His other plays include The Jew of Malta and Dr Faustus. Amongst his poems are 'The Passionate Shepherd' and 'Hero and Leander'. The details of his life are shady and it has been suggested he was a 'secret agent' for Elizabeth I. He died in a brawl in a pub in Deptford (reputedly over money), where he was living in an attempt to escape the plague.

see Elizabeth I, Plague, William Shakespeare

SHAKESPEARE, WILLIAM (1564–1616)

England's foremost playwright, also a poet. William Shakespeare lived during the reign of Elizabeth I, of whom he was a favourite, and achieved great fame and popularity in his lifetime. He was married to Anne

Hathaway, with whom he had three children. They lived in Stratford-upon-Avon, the town in which he was born, but he moved to London in c. 1591, leaving his family behind in Stratford. The town is now a popular tourist attraction, based on its Shakespearean associations. He returned to Stratford in later years, as a rich man. He remained there for the rest of his life, and is buried in the town's Holy Trinity Church – the same place in which he was baptised. As well as being a writer, Shakespeare became an actor after moving to London. In 1597, he also became a shareholder in the Globe Theatre (which was being built on the south bank of the Thames) and subsequently acted on its stage. Many of his own plays were also performed at the Globe. Among his works are the comedies, The Two Gentlemen of Verona, The Merry Wives of Windsor, Much Ado about Nothing and A Midsummer Night's Dream; the tragedies, Romeo, and Juliet, Hamlet, Othello and Macbeth and the history plays, Henry V and King John. In total, he wrote 35 plays (although

▲ *ABOVE: Shakespeare, at the height of his career, looks out on the life of London*

some scholars contest they were all his own work). His works also include 154 sonnets and the poems 'Venus and Adonis' and 'The Rape of Lucrece'.

▶ *see* Elizabeth I, Christopher Marlowe

JONSON, BEN (1572–1637)

English playwright, actor and poet, buried in Westminster Abbey. Jonson spent his life in and out of gaol for being too outspoken in his writings. In 1598 he killed another actor in a dual and was tried for murder – he defended himself, escaping execution by a legal loophole. Although best known for his comedies, Jonson also wrote tragedies. His works include the play Every Man in his Honour – in which one of the parts was acted originally by Shakespeare.

▶ *see* William Shakespeare

▲ *ABOVE: Ben Jonson*

JONES, INIGO (1573–1652)

London-born architect, influential in bringing Italian-style architecture to England. He designed the Queen's House at Greenwich, followed by the Banqueting House in Whitehall. He was also instrumental in the re-design of Covent Garden and its splendid Palladian church, St Paul's (or 'The Actors' Church'). Jones also worked on properties outside London, including Wilton House, in Wiltshire.

▶ *see* Charles I, James I

MILTON, JOHN (1608–74)

English poet and writer; famous for
Paradise Lost and Paradise Regained.
Amongst his works are Samson
Agonistes and Areopagitica (calling for
freedom of the press). He wrote many
controversial pamphlets: attacking the
monarchy; calling for relaxation of the
divorce laws; and on matters of religion.
He went blind in 1651 but continued to
write, dictating his works. Milton was an
outspoken follower of Oliver Cromwell,
who gave him a job in his government.
After the Restoration Milton's works
were publicly burned.

see Oliver Cromwell, Restoration

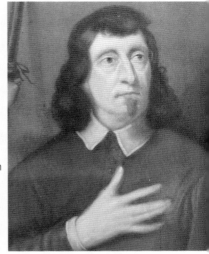

▲ ABOVE: John Milton

DRYDEN, JOHN (1631–1700)

English poet, playwright and satirist. Dryden came from a family of
Cromwellian supporters, although his own allegiance shifted after the
Restoration. Dryden was the first poet to hold the official title of Poet
Laureate (awarded in 1668). His poems include 'Annus Mirabilis' (about the
Great Fire of London), 'Heroic Stanzas on the Death of Oliver Cromwell' and
'Astraea Redux' (on Charles II's return). His plays include Marriage à la
Mode and The Indian Queen. He is buried in Westminster Abbey.

see Charles II, Oliver Cromwell, Great Fire of London, Poet Laureate,
Restoration

23

WREN, CHRISTOPHER (1632–1723)

English architect in the time of Charles II. As well as being one of
England's most revered architects, Wren was also Professor of Astronomy
at Oxford University and one of the founders of the Royal Society.
Perhaps best known for St Paul's Cathedral, he designed many other
famous buildings, including Kensington Palace, the Admiralty building in
Whitehall, Chelsea Hospital, the Royal Observatory at Greenwich and
parts of Hampton Court Palace.

⚫ *see* Cambridge University, Charles II, Great Fire of London, Hampton Court
Palace, St Paul's Cathedral

BUCKINGHAM PALACE (1633)

Official London home of the British monarch. Built in 1633 by Lord Goring
and called Buckingham House, it has since been remodelled several
times. The house became royal property in 1761, when it was acquired by
George III. His son,
George IV, turned it
into a palace, under
the guidance of the
architect John Nash. It
was unfinished when
George died and, in
1830, Nash was
dismissed and
replaced by Edmund
Blore. Queen Victoria
was the first monarch

▲ *ABOVE: Buckingham Palace*

to make the palace her official residence. She required Blore to make several changes, including the addition of more nurseries. Marble Arch, which now stands at one end of Hyde Park (a triumphal arch after the battles of Trafalgar and Waterloo) was part of Nash's Buckingham Palace. It was moved during Victoria's reign, however, because it was too narrow for a carriage to pass through. Buckingham Palace is surrounded by St James's Park, Green Park and Hyde Park.

◆ *see* Hyde Park, St James's Park, Queen Victoria

PEPYS, SAMUEL (1633–1703)

English diarist. Pepys is famous for his extensive diaries, covering the years 1660–69, which show life in London during the time of the Plague of 1665 and the Great Fire of London in 1666. His diaries were not intended for publication. He worked as a secretary in the household of Sir Edward Montagu; he also worked as a clerk for the Navy and the Admiralty. His diary ends in 1669, the year his eyesight failed.

◆ *see* Great Fire of London, Plague

NEWTON, ISAAC (1642–1727)

English physicist and mathematician, most famous for developing his theory of gravity. Among his discoveries, Newton demonstrated that white light is made up of several different colours of light, made headway in the study of differential calculus, created the basis for celestial mechanics and invented the world's first reflecting telescope. In 1687 his book Mathematical Principles of Natural Philosophy was published and secured his contemporary reputation as Britain's foremost physicist. The book contained his theories of the law of gravitation, famously discovered by Newton after watching an apple fall from a tree.

◆ *see* Enlightenment

▶ *RIGHT: Henry Purcell*

PURCELL, HENRY (1659–95)

English composer. Although he began composing at a young age, little of Purcell's work prior to 1680 has survived. In his position as royal composer, Purcell wrote a great deal of state and ceremonial music; he is also known for his songs (including 'Nymphs and Shepherds'), anthems, church music and operas, especially Dido and Aeneas. He also wrote the music for many plays – a significant and popular form of entertainment in the Restoration years, as theatricals had been banned during the time of Cromwell. Amongst the playwrights with whom Purcell worked were William Congreve and John Dryden.

◆ *see* Charles II, Oliver Cromwell, John Dryden, Mary II, Restoration, Westminster Abbey, William III

VANBRUGH, JOHN (1664–1726)

English architect and playwright. Vanbrugh began his career in the army, under the command of the Duke of Marlborough (for whom he later designed Blenheim Palace). He was captured by the French and, for two years, was imprisoned in the Bastille; during this time he started writing his play The Provok'd Wife. As well as Blenheim Palace, Vanbrugh designed Castle Howard, in Yorkshire.

◆ *see* Blenheim Palace

POET LAUREATE (1668)

Originally an honorary name given to many poets, the first Poet Laureate in its modern meaning was John Dryden (1668). For the first time a Poet Laureate became a salaried member of the Royal Household. Formal duties originally included writing poems on specific occasions, such as a royal birth or death, or an occasion of national importance. Today the role is less defined. Poet Laureates have included Wordsworth; Alfred, Lord Tennyson; Cecil Day-Lewis; John Betjeman; Ted Hughes and Andrew Motion.

◄ *see* John Betjeman, John Dryden, William Wordsworth

ST PAUL'S CATHEDRAL (1675)

London's premier Protestant cathedral. In Roman times, a temple stood here; since c. 604 the site has been home to a cathedral dedicated to St Paul. The present building, designed by Sir Christopher Wren, was begun in 1675, although it wasn't completed until 1710. It was built to replace the third cathedral, which had been destroyed in the Great Fire. One of St Paul's most outstanding features is its huge dome, inside which is the famous Whispering Gallery – if you whisper against the wall at one side of the gallery, it can be heard all the way round on the opposite side. In the 1950s, a chapel in the cathedral was renamed the American Chapel, in honour of those Americans who died in World War II.

◄ *see* Great Fire of London, Christopher Wren

▲ *ABOVE: St Paul's Cathedral*

HANDEL, GEORGE FREDERICK (1685–1759)

German composer and musician who moved to the London court of George I. His great early works composed during this time include the opera Agrippina and the oratorio Resurrection. In 1710, Handel moved to England, where he was lauded. He remained in London for the rest of his life, making only occasional trips back to Germany. Two of his most famous works were composed while in England: The Water Music and Messiah. Handel wrote 50 operas and 23 oratorios. He is buried in Poets' Corner in Westminster Abbey.

◆ *see* George I, Westminster Abbey

HOGARTH, WILLIAM (1697–1764)

English painter, caricaturist and engraver; also social reformer. Hogarth defined his age with story-telling series of engravings, such as The Harlot's Progress and The Rake's Progress. His engravings and caricatures, although humorous, show the grim side of London: gin palaces, violence and cruelty. His paintings include fine portraiture. After marrying the daughter of renowned artist Sir James Thornhill, Hogarth became influential in Thornhill's academy (forerunner to the Royal Academy). He gave strong support to British artists, in a world where foreign art was the vogue.

KEW GARDENS (c. 18TH CENTURY)

Royal Botanic Gardens. Kew Gardens encompass more than 300 acres of land. The first known botanic garden in the area was laid out in 1759. This small plot was extended and

▶ *RIGHT: Kew Gardens*

remodelled several times; in the 1770s it was restructured by Capability Brown. Today Kew Gardens boasts a scientific research centre for botany as well as the gardens that are open to the public. One of its most famous landmarks is the great conservatory.

♦ *see* Capability Brown

BLENHEIM PALACE (1705)

English stately home, constructed between 1705 and 1722. The land and sufficient money to build on it were given to the Duke of Marlborough by Queen Anne. The palace, which was designed by John Vanbrugh, is named after Marlborough's great military victory, the Battle of Blenheim (1704), fought in Germany against the French and Bavarians. The magnificent grounds, which encompass over 2,000 acres, were landscaped by Capability Brown. Winston Churchill (a descendant of the duke) was born in Blenheim Palace.

♦ *see* Capability Brown, John Churchill, Winston Churchill, John Vanbrugh

JOHNSON, SAMUEL (1709–84)

English lexicographer, poet and critic – the inventor of the Dictionary. Johnson's family was impoverished and lack of funds led him to abandon his degree at Oxford. His title of 'Dr' comes from two honorary doctorates awarded to him after the publication of his Dictionary in 1755. This brought him fame, but not financial security. His circumstances were only relieved in 1762 when George III awarded him an annual pension. In 1763 Johnson met James Boswell, who later became his

▶ *RIGHT: Dr Samuel Johnson awaiting an audience*

biographer. In 1764 he founded 'The Club' with the painter Joshua Reynolds, frequented by the actor David Garrick and by Charles James Fox. Johnson is buried in Westminster Abbey.

see Oxford University

BROWN, LANCELOT 'CAPABILITY' (1715–83)

English landscape gardener, who also worked as an architect. Lancelot 'Capability' Brown is the most famous landscape gardener Britain has ever known. He developed a distinct method of design that came to be known as the 'English Style'; his work can be seen at some of Britain's most prominent buildings, including Blenheim Palace and Hampton Court. Brown's nickname came from one of his favourite expressions, that of describing a building as having 'capability' for improvement.

see Blenheim Palace, Hampton Court Palace

ADAM, ROBERT (1728–92)

Scottish architect. Robert Adam was one of the Adams Brothers, with his architect siblings, William, John and James. Robert studied at Edinburgh University, then travelled through Italy to study the buildings there. The brothers then established an architecture practice in London. In 1762 Robert became sole architect to the king; he resigned after six years in office to become an MP. The Adams style, particularly in interiors, has become an enduring characteristic of British architecture.

BURNS, ROBERT (1759–96)

Scottish poet. Burns was the son of an impoverished Ayrshire farmer. He wrote his first poems while working as a farm labourer. They were published in 1786, making him suddenly famous. With the money he made he bought a farm for himself and his wife Jean Armour – although his best known lover is Mary Campbell, to whom he wrote many poems. Burns' most famous poem is 'Tam O'Shanter'; he also wrote songs, including 'Auld Lang Syne'.

ROYAL ACADEMY (1768)

Oldest fine-art academy in England. The Royal Academy of Arts was founded by George III. Its first president was Sir Joshua Reynolds. The Academy served as an art school and an exhibition venue – today, its Summer Exhibition remains one of the art year's most prestigious events. The first Royal Academy building was in Pall Mall; today it is housed in Burlington House on Piccadilly. It houses some of the finest artworks in Britain.

◀ *see* George III

WORDSWORTH, WILLIAM (1770–1850)

English poet; leading figure of the Romantic movement. Wordsworth was born in the Lake District, where he spent the majority of his life. His love for nature and the natural world is the most prominent feature in his works, which includes such classics as 'The Prelude' and 'Daffodils'. This almost obsessional love of nature has led to his being described as a pantheist. Wordsworth's unmarried sister, Dorothy, was his lifelong companion, even following his marriage to Mary Hutchison (1802). Dorothy's journals are believed by many scholars to have inspired some of William's best works. The Wordsworths are strongly associated with their great friend, Coleridge.

◀ *see* Samuel Taylor Coleridge

▶ *RIGHT: William Wordsworth*

COLERIDGE, SAMUEL TAYLOR (1772–1834)

English Romantic poet; also a philosopher and playwright. An idealist, Coleridge left Cambridge early to join the army. Rescued from a miserable military existence by wealthy friends, he befriended the poet Robert Southey, with whom he dreamed of founding a 'Pantisocratic' community in America. Coleridge's first poems were published in 1794. He met Wordsworth in 1797 and in 1798 they published the joint volume Lyrical Ballads, which included Coleridge's masterpiece The Rime of the Ancient Mariner. His other works include 'Kubla Khan' and 'Osirio'. Coleridge was married with four children (he is also reputed to have been in love with Wordsworth's sister-in-law, Sara).

◆ *see* Cambridge University, William Wordsworth

BRUMMEL, BEAU (1778–1840)

Regency 'dandy'. George Bryan Brummel was distinguished for his fashion sense and renowned for his ready wit while still at Eton. He led the fashion in Regency London and was a favourite of the Prince Regent. In 1816, however, after quarrelling with him, Brummel fled to France, unable to pay a gambling debt. He died there, in poverty.

◆ *see* George IV

BYRON, LORD (1788–1824)

British poet, associate of Shelley, known for his wild lifestyle. He published his first poetry volume in 1807, and gained fame with Childe Harold's Pilgrimage (1812). Byron travelled widely and spent years living in Italy after a scandalous separation from his wife in 1816. Always an idealist, Byron espoused the Greek cause of liberation from Turkey. While commanding a section of the Greek army he died of rheumatic fever. His body is buried in Westminster Abbey, but his heart is buried in Greece.

ARTS AND CRAFTS MOVEMENT (LATE 19TH CENTURY)

English artistic movement. Two formative exponents of the movement were William Morris and John Ruskin. The Arts and Crafts Movement began as a reaction to the effects of the Industrial Revolution. By the end of the nineteenth century, the majority of furniture sold in Britain was mass-produced in factories. Many critics complained that it had lost its beauty and craftsmanship through the methods of mass production. Arts and Crafts devotees wanted a return to artistic expertise and hand-made goods. The movement also saw a reaction against the excessively ornate style typical of the Victorian era. The movement took its name from the Arts and Crafts Exhibition Society, which was set up in 1887 to exhibit the work of artisans. Among the founding members of the exhibition were William Morris and the designer Walter Crane.

◆ *see* Industrial Revolution, William Morris

DICKENS, CHARLES (1812–70)

Nineteenth-century English writer and favourite of Queen Victoria. Dickens had a financially unstable childhood, during which his father was imprisoned for debt. Consequently, Dickens, aged 12, was sent out to work, rudely interrupting his education. At the age of 16 he began working as a journalist. Shortly after his 21st birthday he produced Sketches by Boz, published as a magazine series: a method of publication he used for most

▶ *RIGHT: Charles Dickens*

of his works, reaching a much wider audience than novel readers alone. Dickens' first bestseller, Pickwick Papers, was written while he was still in his early twenties. His many later novels include David Copperfield, A Christmas Carol, Nicholas Nickleby, Oliver Twist and A Tale of Two Cities. An amazingly prolific author, Dickens died aged just 58, in the middle of writing The Mystery of Edwin Drood. He is buried in Poets' Corner, Westminster Abbey. Charles Dickens remains one of Britain's best-loved writers, and his works are regularly dramatised in films, on television and on the stage.

◆ see Queen Victoria

BRIGHTON PAVILION (1815)

English stately building, designed by John Nash. The Royal Pavilion at Brighton was built for the Prince Regent (later George IV), who made the seaside town highly fashionable by his patronage. The pavilion was hugely expensive and derided by opponents of the Regent for its extravagant architecture. The style was actually inspired by the Moghul palaces of India and looks strikingly unusual alongside the rest of the town's buildings. The Pavilion is one of Brighton's most popular tourist attractions.

◆ see Beau Brummel, George IV

◀ LEFT: Brighton Pavilion

ELIOT, GEORGE (1819–90)

Pen name of Mary Ann Evans, English novelist. Like the Brontë sisters, Eliot chose to wrote under a pseudonym to assist publication in a male-dominated industry. Her most famous novels include Middlemarch, Silas Marner and Daniel Deronda.

MORRIS, WILLIAM (1834–96)

English artist, founder of the Arts and Crafts Movement. Morris was a painter, designer and craftsman, as well as a political activist (Socialist), poet and novelist. In addition Morris was a businessman, setting up Morris & Co, which produced textiles, furniture, stained glass and ceramic tiles. Early in his career, he was strongly associated with the Pre-Raphaelite Movement, especially Dante Rossetti, and with the painter Edward Coley Burne-Jones. In his later career, Morris established the Merton Abbey workshops based on Utopian ideals of shared labour and shared finances. Morris was married to Jane Burden, who became famous as a Pre-Raphaelite model.

◊ see Arts and Crafts Movement, Pre-Raphaelites

PRE-RAPHAELITE MOVEMENT (1848)

English artistic movement of the nineteenth century. The Pre-Raphaelite Brotherhood was founded by Dante Gabriel Rossetti, William Rossetti, Frederick George Stephens, William Holman Hunt, Thomas Woolner, James Collinson and John Everett Millais. William Rossetti, brother of Dante (and of the poet Christina) was the only non-artist member of the group. He was a writer who came up with the movement's short-lived magazine, Germ. The brotherhood strove for an artistic ideal they felt had disappeared at the time of Raphael. Although trained at the Royal Academy, they were opposed to the methods taught by the Academy.

They were especially concerned with techniques of lighting and developed a new style of painting – covering the canvas with a white background before painting the picture on the top, giving their works a spectacular luminosity. The prominent critic John Ruskin was an influential supporter of the group, helping to bring them to the notice of the conservative art world who, at first, were furiously opposed to them. Other artists associated with the movement include Edward Burne-Jones, William Morris, Arthur Hughes, Henry Wallis and Elizabeth Siddal (wife of Dante Rossetti). Key pictures of the movement include Rossetti's The Girlhood of Mary Virgin, Holman Hunt's The Light of the World and Millais' Lorenzo and Isabella.

◆ see William Morris, Royal Academy

GREAT EXHIBITION (1851)

Exhibition to show the greatness of the British Empire. The Great Exhibition of 1851 was a special project of Queen Victoria's husband, Prince Albert. It was held in the Crystal Palace in Hyde Park between May and October 1851. The brainchild of Henry Cole (later to become Chairman of the Society of Arts), the exhibition was intended to extol the glorious achievements of Britain and its Empire. It was held at the

height of the Industrial Revolution with exhibits brought from all over Britain and her colonies, including new inventions, works of art and jewels. The Koh-i-Noor diamond was among the treasures on display. People came from all over Britain, as

▲ ABOVE: The Great Exhibition at Crystal Palace

36

well as all over the world, to visit the Crystal Palace – in total, over six million people flocked to Hyde Park during the five months of the exhibition. The hundreds of thousands of pounds raised by the exhibition went towards building museums in the South Kensington area of London

see Prince Albert, Crystal Palace

CRYSTAL PALACE (1851)

Building constructed for the Great Exhibition (1851). The Crystal Palace was a fantastic building of glass and iron, designed by Joseph Paxton. Two thousand workers were needed to construct it. It stood originally in Hyde Park, but was moved after the exhibition to the area of south-east London now known as Crystal Palace. The building burned down in 1936.

see Great Exhibition

BALMORAL (1852)

Scottish castle, the Highland home of Queen Victoria. In 1852 the queen bought the land (10,000 acres) from the Earl of Fife. The castle was built shortly afterwards, paid for by Prince Albert. It became the queen's favourite home and started a fashion in England for all things Scottish. The castle, on the banks of the River Dee, was constructed from Scottish granite. Its tallest tower is over 30 m (100 ft) high. Queen Elizabeth, the Queen Mother lived here.

see Elizabeth Bowes-Lyon, Queen Victoria

▲ ABOVE: Balmoral

WILDE, OSCAR (1854–1901)

Irish writer and exponent of aestheticism, who lived in England. Wilde wrote: one novel, The Picture of Dorian Gray; plays, including The Importance of Being Earnest and An Ideal Husband; poems and children's stories. His plays, ostensibly drawing-room comedies, dealt with the prejudices of Victorian England. He was married to Constance and they had two sons. In 1895 he was accused of homosexuality – then a criminal offence – by the 8th Marquess of Queensberry (father of his lover, Lord Alfred Douglas). Wilde was imprisoned with hard labour. On his release, he fled England for Paris, where he died. He was granted a posthumous pardon in the 1990s.

▶ RIGHT: Oscar Wilde

MACKINTOSH, CHARLES RENNIE (1868–1923)

Scottish artist, strongly associated with Glasgow. Mackintosh trained as an architect – one of his best-known buildings is the Glasgow School of Art – but was also fascinated by interior decor. His architectural projects (such as Hill House near Glasgow) were created homogenously, with Mackintosh designing the interiors as well. His catalogue of works includes watercolours of landscapes, sketches of nature and textile designs. Mackintosh was a member of the Glasgow Four, with J. Herbert MacNair and the artist sisters Frances and Margaret Macdonald. In 1900 Mackintosh married Margaret. The group exhibited in Britain and in Europe, alongside the Viennese Secessionists.

LUTYENS, SIR EDWARD (1869–1944)

English architect. Lutyens began his tuition with the architect Ernest George. In later years he became strongly associated with the landscape gardener Gertrude Jekyll, with whom he often worked in partnership. His work was classical in style, greatly influenced by architecture of the Baroque era. He is famous for, among other achievements, the planning and creation of New Delhi in India (then part of the British Empire); for the Cenotaph in Whitehall, London; for the Monument to the Missing of the Battle of the Somme, at Thiepval, France; and for Queen Mary's Dolls' House, which is housed in Windsor Castle

see Windsor Castle

ROYAL ALBERT HALL (1871)

Concert venue in Kensington, London. Prince Albert proposed the building of a Hall of Arts and Sciences, to be paid for out of the profit made by the Great Exhibition. As he died before the building was finished, Queen Victoria renamed it the Royal Albert Hall, in memory of him. The highly ornate Albert Memorial stands opposite it. The Hall is used for a host of musical events, despite its well-documented echo, including the annual Proms concerts.

see Prince Albert, Great Exhibition, Proms, Queen Victoria

▶ *RIGHT: Royal Albert Hall*

WILLIAMS, RALPH VAUGHAN (1872–1958)

Composer whose music is described as quintessentially 'English'. Vaughan Williams studied in Cambridge, Berlin and Paris (with Ravel). He travelled round Britain recording traditional songs and carols. In World War I he volunteered for the Field Ambulance Service, after which he became Professor of Composition at the Royal College of Music. His works were diverse and include symphonies, hymns and music for the ballet and opera; they include The Sea, London and Pastoral. In 1938 he was awarded the Order of Merit.

◄► *see* World War I

BROOKE, RUPERT (1887–1915)

English poet. Brooke's first book of poems was published in 1911, the year he travelled through Europe. In 1913, following a nervous breakdown, he visited North America, Canada and the Pacific. He enlisted as soon as war broke out, but died of blood poisoning while in Turkey. Brooke's youth, good looks and patriotic poetry made him a symbol of Britain's lost generation. His works include 'The Soldier', 'The Old Vicarage, Grantchester' and Lithuania (a play).

◄► *see* World War I

BAIRD, JOHN LOGIE (1888–1946)

Scottish inventor, amongst those credited with creating television. In 1925 Baird transmitted his first television picture, but his claims were disbelieved by the newspapers. He gave his first demonstration of television in 1926 and in 1928 transmitted a signal between London and New York. His main rival was Marconi, whose television service the BBC adopted in 1936.

◄► *see* British Broadcasting Corporation

ELIOT, T. S. (1888–1965)

American poet, playwright and critical essayist who moved to England in 1915. Eliot worked as a schoolteacher, a bank clerk, a book reviewer, a book editor and a director of Faber and Faber publishers. His first published poem was 'The Love Song of J. Alfred Prufrock' (1915). His first volume of poetry was published in 1917. He was friends with Ezra Pound and Virginia Woolf. His poetry includes The Waste Land and Old Possum's Book of Practical Cats (on which the musical Cats is based). Amongst his plays are Murder in the Cathedral (about Thomas Becket) and Sweeney Agonistes. Eliot was awarded the Nobel Prize for Literature in 1948

see Thomas Becket

▶ *RIGHT: T. S. Eliot*

OWEN, WILFRED (1893–1918)

English poet, famous for his war poetry. Owen, who worked as a tutor before the war, was invalided out in 1917 with shell shock. He was returned to the fighting in 1918 and killed seven days before the Armistice. He was awarded the Military Cross. Most of Owen's poetry was not published until after his death, when his works were tirelessly lauded by his great friend and fellow poet, Siegfried Sassoon. His poems include 'Anthem for Doomed Youth' and 'Dulce et Decorum Est'.

see World War I

WALTON, WILLIAM (1902–83)

English composer. Walton has become one of the best-known composers of the twentieth century, mainly through his composition of music for films, most notably Lawrence Olivier's Henry V.

BETJEMAN, JOHN (1906–84)

English poet. Betjeman also worked as a teacher, journalist, broadcaster and expert critic of architecture. His first volume of poetry was published in 1931. Among his most famous works are: 'A Subaltern's Love Song', 'Myfanwy', 'Slough' and his autobiography, Summoned by Bells. He became Poet Laureate in 1972.

◆ see Poet Laureate

BRITTEN, BENJAMIN (1913–76)

English composer. Edward Benjamin Britten was born in Suffolk. He was only four years old when he wrote his first musical composition and began studying music in earnest aged 11. He attended the Royal College of Music from 1930 and became successful as a composer of theme tunes for the radio and film industries. His most famous works include the operas Billy Budd, Peter Grimes and Gloriana, written on the occasion of the coronation of Queen Elizabeth II.

◆ see Elizabeth II

BRITISH BROADCASTING CORPORATION (BBC) (1927)

Radio and television broadcasting company. The BBC came out of the British Broadcasting Company, founded in 1922. The BBC was set up in 1927 and given broadcasting monopoly (which ended in the 1950s with the advent of commercial television and radio). The corporation was financed by licence fees from radio owners and money from the government. In 1936, the BBC started the world's first television service. Today the BBC's World Service broadcasts across the globe.

BEATLES, THE (1960S)
English pop band. The Beatles, Paul McCartney, John Lennon, George Harrison and Ringo Starr, came from Liverpool. They had their first hit in 1962 with 'Love Me Do'. In 1963, they reached number one in the UK with 'Please Please Me'. In 1964, the Beatles became the first UK band to take America by storm; in doing so they changed the face of international music forever. The 'Mersey Sound' became popular throughout the world and the songwriting duo of Lennon and McCartney created an entirely new brand of music. The last single before their acrimonious split in 1970 was 'Let It Be'.

MILLENNIUM DOME (1999)
Exhibition centre in south-east London. The Millennium Dome was built to celebrate the year 2000. It opened on 31 December 1999 and closed

exactly a year later. Despite the hype and spectacular exhibits, the Dome was unsuccessful. It did, however, regenerate the formerly downtrodden area in which it was built.

◄ LEFT:
The Millennium Dome

INDUSTRY

▲ *ABOVE: Hadrian's Wall*

HADRIAN'S WALL

Roman defence against tribes from the north. Twenty years before the Antonine wall was built, Publius Aelius Hadrianus had Hadrian's Wall constructed to mark the northern boundary of the Roman Empire some eighty miles farther south, between Maryport and Wallsend. The fortified wall, built AD 122–26 was eventually abandoned by the crumbling Roman Empire in around AD 383. Although now only a fragmented ruin, the wall still runs approximately 185 km (115 miles) roughly east to west.

◨ *see* Antonine Wall, Romans

ANTONINE WALL (AD 142)

Barrier constructed to mark the northern frontier of the Roman territory in England. The wall was built in AD 142 under the orders of the emperor Antonius Pius and ran between the rivers Clyde and Forth. It was intended to keep out marauders from the north. It was guarded for some 60 years.

◨ *see* Hadrian's Wall

COINAGE, DEBASEMENT OF (1540S)

Reduction in standard and content of metal in coins. During the reign of Henry VIII, Britain suffered a monetary depression due to extreme levels of inflation triggered by unprofitable trade with other countries. Henry's solution was to debase the value of coinage. This meant effectively declaring lower denominations of coin worthless apart from their bullion (weight) value. The idea behind debasement was to stimulate sharp rises in the prices for exported goods and so recover the economy of Britain.

see Henry VIII

EAST INDIA COMPANY (1600)

Company established to secure a monopoly on trade routes between England and the Far East. The East India Company came into being in around 1600 and lasted for 258 years, helping to finance the expansion of the British Empire. Links with India were being forged in Elizabethan times, so it made sense to establish an official trading relationship between the two countries as a way of seeing off competition from other dominant European nations, including France and the Netherlands. In 1784, Tory prime minister William Pitt introduced the India Act, which forced the company to form a committee responsible to Parliament in London, thereby ensuring that the Crown still had a significant say in the rule of India, which by then was virtually run by the East India Company.

see Robert Clive, Seven Years' War

▶ *An East India Company ship in 1787*

COALBROOKDALE

Centre of the Industrial Revolution in Britain. The Industrial Revolution
was literally fuelled by coal, which heated the boilers of the steam
engines and fired the furnaces. England had vast reserves of coal at that
time and Abraham Derby (1678–1717), based at Coalbrookdale on the river
Severn, pioneered the use of coke for smelting iron.

◆ *see* Industrial Revolution

AGRICULTURAL REVOLUTION (18TH CENTURY)

The Agricultural Revolution began in earnest with an invention thought
up by English agriculturalist Jethro Tull (1674–1741). In around 1701 he
built a machine that he called a 'seed drill', which was designed to solve
the problems inherent with sowing seed by hand. The seed drill, which
was pulled by horses, inserted seed into the soil in even rows across a
tilled field. Hand sowing had always resulted in a random distribution of
seed over the field with the additional problem of the seed remaining on
the surface, less likely to germinate and vulnerable to hungry birds. Tull's
machine changed this and made it possible to weed and harvest the
crop with far less wastage. Before long various other machines were seen
out in the fields, each designed for performing a different agricultural
task: ploughing, tilling, scything and threshing. Improvements in
efficiency, combined with various changes in farming management,
all contributed to the revolution in agriculture.

◆ *see* Industrial Revolution

INDUSTRIAL REVOLUTION (18TH CENTURY)

Period in the eighteenth century which saw great technological advance.
The period of industrialisation in Britain, now known as the Industrial
Revolution, lasted for some 100 years. As well as automating many tasks

by use of machines, it saw a change in society. Millions of people migrated from rural areas to find work in urban environments, ultimately creating the urban working class.

The Agricultural Revolution had already primed Britain for the change to begin by depriving many rural workers of their jobs. When industrial pioneers began inventing new industries there were plenty of people waiting to be employed. The cotton spinning factories of Richard Arkwright (1732–92), established over the latter third of the eighteenth century, are a good example of this. His machines saw the utilisation of water power, followed by steam power, the main driving force of the Industrial Revolution.

James Watt (1736–1819) had improved upon Thomas Newcomen's (1663–1729) steam engine in the 1760s. It was used initially for pumping flood water from mines which, in turn, provided the coal for fuelling the Industrial Revolution. By the early 1800s steam engines were also pulling the materials and products of industry along railway tracks and urban areas were black with their pollution. The iron and steel industry became the backbone of the Industrial Revolution, providing raw materials for the most impressive machines.

◘ see Agricultural Revolution

▲ ABOVE: George Stephenson's 'Rocket' is admired

CANALS

Man-made waterway orginally intended to facilitate transportation of goods to industrial towns. The fundamental feature of any canal is that it comprises sections of level waterway, making them extremely efficient transport routes for bulk materials, because the effort

required to move a cargo over still water is relatively little compared with other methods. The first major canal to be constructed in Britain was the Bridgewater Canal. It became a key player in the burgeoning Industrial Revolution because it enabled the transportation of large quantities of coal from collieries in Worsley to factories in Manchester. In turn, manufactured goods could be cheaply moved to Liverpool docks and distributed via cargo ship. This pioneering work enabled the eventual construction of a waterway network some 4,000 km (2,500 miles) in length and spanning the greater part of Britain.

 *see* Duke of Bridgewater

ARKWRIGHT, RICHARD (1732–92)

English inventor. In 1768 Richard Arkwright contrived a machine for spinning the new material cotton. He called his device a 'spinning frame'. It was just one of various pioneering introductions he made to the textiles industry during his lifetime. Three years after perfecting the spinning frame he set up a spinning factory in which the machinery was driven by water power. Two years before his death he installed a steam engine in his Nottingham factory.

see Industrial Revolution

◀ *LEFT: The first major canal to be constructed in Britain was the Bridgewater Canal*

BRIDGEWATER, FRANCIS EGERTON, 3RD DUKE OF (1736–1803)

English pioneer of canal construction. With the onset of the Industrial Revolution in England it became vital that materials and fuel could be shipped from one place to another efficiently. In 1762 work began on the Bridgewater Canal, the brainchild of Francis Egerton 3rd Duke of Bridgewater. The canal ran from Liverpool to Worsley via Manchester and was engineered by James Brindley (1716–72). It included an aqueduct spanning the Irwell Valley.

◆ *see* Canals

STAMP ACT (1765)

Imposition of tax by the British on the American colonies. In 1765 the British Parliament reacted to the threat of revolt in North America with the Stamp Act, a form of taxation designed to raise funds from its American colonies to pay for their defence. The colonies refused to use the tax stamps issued to them and a blockade of British merchant shipping forced the British government to repeal the act in 1766. Ironically the Stamp Act only served to precipitate the American Revolution (1775–83).

◆ *see* American Revolution

OWEN, ROBERT (1771–1858)

Welsh social reformer. Robert Owen was one of the first people to promote the ideas of socialism. Socialism is essentially a movement aiming to remove any class structure from society by giving communities private ownership of the means of production, distribution and exchange of goods. The members of the community should therefore enjoy social equality. Robert Owen set out to show that socialism could be put into practice by establishing a model community in New Lanark, Scotland. The success of this project led to the establishment of the co-operative movement, but socialism has never secured a true foothold in Britain.

see New Lanark

DAVY, HUMPHREY (1778–1829)

English chemist, inventor of the Davy lamp. The transition from eighteenth to nineteenth centuries was a period which saw marked advances in scientific understanding of the chemical world. Humphrey Davy was at the forefront of this field and made some important discoveries. Utilising the invention of electrolysis, he was able to isolate and discover no fewer than seven new elements between 1807–08.

STEPHENSON, GEORGE (1781–1848)

British engineer, inventor of the steam train. Although James Watt had improved the steam engine in the 1760s it was 50 years before it

▲ *ABOVE: George Stephenson with the first steam locomotive, Rocket*

became efficient and reliable as a source of power for vehicles. Vehicles need to be able to pull their own weight effectively before they can be considered a viable means for transporting passengers or goods. George Stephenson set about the problem of building a steam-powered locomotive in the early 1800s. By 1814 he had completed his first locomotive, Blucher. In 1829 he had perfected his experiments and designed Rocket, capable of 47 kph (29 mph).

◆ *see* James Watt

FARADAY, MICHAEL (1791–1867)

English chemist and physicist. Michael Faraday is generally regarded as the 'father of electricity'. In fact he was one of many scientists of his era for whom electricity was a central fascination. In 1821 he began his own experiments with electromagnetism, resulting in the invention of a device for generating electricity, the dynamo. He then built an apparatus which converted electrical energy into motive force, the very first prototype model of an electric motor.

NEW LANARK (1800)

Utopian industrial community. In 1800, at the age of 29, Robert Owen became the manager of a mill in a place called New Lanark, Scotland. Owen used his position to create a model community which fulfilled his socialist ideals. He achieved this by improving working and housing conditions for the employees in his charge and provided schools for their children. Others became inspired by his vision of 'villages of co-operation' and he stimulated the creation of the co-operative movement, which was established in 1844.

◆ *see* Robert Owen

FACTORY ACTS (1802)

Series of Acts to protect the lot of factory workers. The Industrial Revolution caused the urbanisation of Britain. Millions of people migrated to urban environments to find the only work available to them. These people were vulnerable to exploitation by factory owners, knowing that jobs were difficult to come by elsewhere. Eventually empathetic politicians intervened by introducing a series of Factory Acts to make sure that the working class was not abused. Beginning with the Health and Morals of Apprentices Act (1802), employers began having to comply with regulations, facing prosecution for not doing so. Other acts determined the minimum age at which children could legally be expected to begin work and the weekly hours an employee might be expected to put in. Legislation establishing the basic rights of women and children in particular were much needed in the textile mills.

◆ *see* Industrial Revolution

BRUNEL, ISAMBARD KINGDOM (1806–59)

English pioneering engineer. Among the great nineteenth-century engineers Isambard Kingdom Brunel stands pre-eminent. The son of mass-production pioneer Marc Isambard Brunel (1769–1849), he was born with the credentials to go far and he certainly made the most of his 53 years. At the age of just 27 he became the chief engineer for the Great Western Railway and only four years later was building the first of his big ships, the Great Western. His achievements also include the steam ships Great Britain and Great Eastern, Clifton Suspension Bridge and the Thames tunnel project, in partnership with his father.

▲ *ABOVE: Isambard Kingdom Brunel*

CORN LAWS

Laws introduced to control the import and export of corn. At the end of the Napoleonic Wars in 1815, and during the early stages of the Industrial Revolution, the government of Lord Liverpool introduced the most famous Corn Law. It prohibited the import of any foreign corn until the domestic price reached 80 shillings a quarter – in effect a famine price. This law proved immensely controversial since it was represented as advantaging the landed interest and making the price of bread for the working man much higher than it needed to be. The law was modified in 1828 and 1842 and, after pressure from the largely middle-class Anti-Corn Law League, abolished by the government of Robert Peel in 1846.

BELL, ALEXANDER GRAHAM (1847–1922)

Scottish-born US inventor. In 1876 the world was introduced to a revolutionary device for transmitting speech from one place to another

via electrical signals through a wire. Alexander Graham Bell had perfected the telephone by assembling together the necessary components, begun in part by other scientists. Bell's inventive genius was to realise the potential in scientific developments around him and then turn his ideas into working devices with practical applications.

▶ *RIGHT: Alexander Graham Bell inaugurates the New York–Chicago telephone, 18 October 1892*

LONDON UNDERGROUND (1863)

System of railways under London. By 1863 London was already such a densely packed city that there was only one solution for putting in new railway lines – to go

underground. The first section of the London Underground system, known as the Tube, was between Farringdon and Paddington. The carriages were open topped and pulled by a steam locomotive, so the ride must have been extremely unpleasant with the choking, filthy fumes. That pioneering first section was built by the Metropolitan Railway Company, having been conceived by politician Charles Pearson. It had seven stations in all and the ride from one end to the other took thirty-three minutes.

KEYNES, JOHN MAYNARD (1883–1946)

British economist. In the years between the two world wars the economy of Britain was not buoyant, and the British Empire was in decline. In 1936 the economist John Maynard Keynes published his General Theory of Employment, Interest and Money. In it he proposed a solution to the worsening unemployment problem. The idea was that government should counteract the causes – lack of demand for goods and decreased national income – by increasing expenditure from the national purse. This policy became dubbed 'Keynesian economics' and is opposed by 'monetarism' which proposes cuts in government spending by way of a solution.

◀ *LEFT: The London Underground*

DREADNOUGHT (1906)

First battleship powered by steam turbines. Constructed in just 366 days, HMS Dreadnought had 10 12-inch guns, a maximum speed of 21 knots and was a massive 22,000 tons. For Britain battleships were a major component of national power and Dreadnought represented the move towards greater armour and increased offensive power, with larger guns and more destructive capability. Dreadnought represented a major move forward and all ships of a similar type took this name.

GENERAL STRIKE (1926)

Nationwide workers' strike. The early twentieth century was witness to the creation and rise of trades unions in the British work place. Trades unions came into being as a means for working men and women to collectively influence the way they were treated by their employers. In 1926 a royal commission, known as the Samuel Report, recommended a cut in the wages of coal miners as a means of making the industry more competitively buoyant on the world stage. The Trade Union Congress (TUC) responded by calling a nationwide workers strike known as the General Strike. The mine owners also demanded that their employees work longer

▲ *ABOVE: Improvised transport during the General Strike*

hours and sympathies ran so high that over two million people boycotted work across the country. The country coped with the standstill for nine days before all but the miners returned to work. The miners continued their lone strike for almost seven months, but ultimately without success.

NEW TOWNS (1945)

Post-war style of town reconstruction. Following World War II Britain had a housing shortage problem on its hands which required the building of new towns. The hearts of many British cities were either destroyed by bombs or in a state of urban decay. This left millions of people refugees in their own homeland. The most immediate solution was to build entire towns from scratch, using the American model of regular street patterns and series of self-contained neighbourhoods. Classic examples of this are Milton Keynes and Stevenage. In 1976 the new town planning policy was dropped in favour of inner-city rejuvenation projects.

OIL CRISIS (1970S)

Worldwide recession due to inflated oil prices. In 1960 a body was established called the Organisation of Petroleum-Exporting Countries (OPEC). Its members included most of the Arab nations in the Middle East. Through OPEC these countries were able to co-ordinate the price and supply policies of oil to consumer countries. In 1967 the Arab–Israeli

▲ ABOVE: Sheikh Yamani, the Saudi Arabian oil minister at a press conference in 1979

war began and Western involvement prompted Arab nations to react. By the early 1970s they had triggered a worldwide recession by demanding inflated prices for oil. This became known as the 'oil crisis' as it threatened the infrastructure of consumer countries. By the 1980s demand for their oil had lessened and the crisis ended.

CONCORDE (1976)

Supersonic aeroplane. In 1976 the Anglo-French Concorde project succeeded in bringing the first and only supersonic airliner into commercial service. Only allowed to reach supersonic speed whilst over oceans and unpopulated territory, due to the sonic 'boom', Concorde continued flying with a clean safety record until one crashed near Paris in 2000.

▲ ABOVE: Concorde was the first commercial aeroplane to fly at supersonic speeds

CHANNEL TUNNEL (1994)

Tunnel linking England and France. Officially opened in 1994, the first contact between the French and English sections of the Channel Tunnel was made in 1990. Boring began in 1987 from points near Dover and Calais some 50 km (31 miles) distant. The 'Chunnel' actually comprises twin rail tunnels and a smaller service tunnel.

POLITICS

12th century	Exchequer founded
13th century	Parliament founded
1215	Magna Carta sealed
1605	Gunpowder Plot foiled
1606	Death of Guy Fawkes
1607	First British colony established in Jamestown, Virginia
1642–49	English Civil War
1647	Levellers party established
1658	Death of Oliver Cromwell
1660	Restoration of the monarchy
1667	Civil List established
1670s	Whig party established
1704	Gibraltar becomes British colony
1707	Act of Union between England and Scotland
1829	Metropolitan Police instituted
1830s	Conservative Party established
1832	Great Reform Act gave millions the vote
19th century	Liberal party established
19th & 20th centuries	Home Rule in Ireland
1900	Labour Party established
1905	Sinn Fein established
1916	Easter Rising in Dublin
1919	IRA formed
1919	Amristat Massacre, India
1920	Northern Ireland established
1931	Commonwealth established
1949	NATO established
1952	Treaty of Rome signed
1956	Suez Crisis
1965	Death of Winston Churchill
1972	Bloody Sunday
1985	Anglo-Irish Agreement
1998	Devolution
1998	Good Friday Agreement
1998	Scottish Assembly created
1998	Welsh Assembly created

CHANCELLOR, LORD

British Cabinet post, chief law officer of the government, speaker of the House of Lords and privy councillor. Probably the most powerful lord chancellor in British history was Cardinal Wolsey in the sixteenth century. The position highlights the peculiarity of the British political system. The judiciary and executive (Cabinet) are meant to be separate but the lord chancellor is head of one and sits in the other. In the House of Lords, the lord chancellor sits on the woolsack.

◆ *see* House of Lords, Thomas Wolsey

WITAN, THE

Council for Anglo-Saxon kings seen as a precursor of the modern Parliament. The council, established in the ninth century, gave the king advice on state matters. Its members included bishops and major landowners. It was to be a check and balance on the monarch's power, and proceeded with government business at times when there were no kings.

◆ *see* Anglo-Saxons, Canute

DANEGELD (AD 991)

Money paid by the English in exchange for peace with the Danes during the tenth and eleventh centuries. The money was raised from taxation; the first payment in AD 991 was for £20,000. Several kings used the levy, seeing it as a useful way of raising revenue.

◆ *see* Danelaw, Ethelred the Unready, Vikings

CHANCERY

Long-standing court and administrative department of the British political and legal system. A Chancery division of the High Court still exists to this day. Established after the invasion of William the Conqueror in the eleventh century, the Chancery was increasingly influential between the fourteenth and sixteenth centuries. Because it had jurisdiction over its own activities, the court's officers could sue and be sued within the Chancery.

ODO, BISHOP OF BAYEUX (11TH CENTURY)

French bishop and half-brother of William the Conqueror. Odo was also thought to be the man to commission the Bayeux Tapestry. After the Norman Conquest of England in 1066, Odo was made Earl of Kent. When William was out of England, Odo acted as the King's regent. His relationship with William was not always good. He was imprisoned in 1082 until William's death in 1087. He returned to France in 1088 and died on a crusade with Robert, Duke of Normandy.

◘ *see* Norman Conquest, William I

CURIA REGIS

Royal court of the Norman and Angevin monarchies. Curia Regis was the period's most important executive and legislative body and it also served as a court for all matters relating to the king, meeting three times a year, at Easter, Pentecost and Christmas. The court's influence had declined by the thirteenth century, with government expanding and the rise of specialist departments such as the Chancery.

◘ *see* Chancery, Privy Council

GWENT, KINGDOM OF

Kingdom in south-east Wales secured by the Normans. Just 20 years after the Battle of Hastings, the Normans had, under William Fitz Osbern, established their rule as far west as Gwent. Several castles were built to protect the new administrative region.

EXCHEQUER (12TH CENTURY)

Financial and accounting office for medieval England. It obtained its name because accounts were calculated by means of counters on a chequered table in its Westminster headquarters. The Exchequer consisted of an Upper Exchequer and Lower Exchequer and was established in the twelfth century. The Lower department dealt with receipts received by government; the Upper Exchequer was also known as Exchequer of Account. Its power waned when the Treasury became the most important central financial department in the time of Elizabeth I.

PARLIAMENT (13TH CENTURY)

Legislature of the British political system. Parliament consists of the Monarchy, the House of Lords and the House of Commons. Its base is in Westminster, London. It emerged from the Curia Regis in the thirteenth century. Parliament has taken many forms during the hundreds of years

since. There has been the Barebones Parliament, the Long Parliament, the Short Parliament and the Model Parliament. Throughout this time its meetings were irregular, nothing like today's Parliament, and it met for special occasions such as to raise taxes for wars. Even after the events of the Glorious Revolution, Parliament's powers were still limited. Because of the power of the

◀ *LEFT: The Houses of Parliament*

monarch, and the fact that the vote was extended only to landowners, Parliament's powers were limited up until the nineteenth century. But as the franchise extended, through the Reform Acts in the nineteenth centuries, the Lower House, the House of Commons, became more representative of the country as a whole and Parliament's power increased. The single most important act as far as the House of Commons was concerned was the 1911 Parliamentary Act which assured its supremacy over the House of Lords. Its prominence was helped in the latter half of the century by the beginning of radio broadcasts in 1978 and live television broadcasts from the House of Lords in 1986 and the House of Commons in 1989. In the past decade there has been speculation that its powers have been waning as the country's most important law-making body and has instead just become a rubber-stamping body whose importance has been bypassed by the desire of politicians to make announcements to the media before Parliament.

MONTFORT, SIMON DE (1208–65)

English baron who opposed the power of the royals and led the opposition to Henry III. De Montfort was born in France but came to England in 1230 and claimed the title of Earl of Leicester through his English grandmother. He was married to the sister of Henry III, Eleanor. Initially he served the king but later emerged as leader of the reforming barons and helped draw up the Provisions of Oxford to allow constitutional reform. However, this did not head off conflict and the barons went into armed revolt. In 1264 he captured Henry and his son Edward, becoming the virtual ruler of England. He summoned a parliament, which included, for the first time, women. However Edward escaped and defeated and killed Simon.

◆ *see* Henry III

MARSHAL, WILLIAM

British nobleman, advisor to the monarch in the thirteenth century. Marshal was a key advisor to King John at the time of the signing of the Magna Carta, where he counselled caution. He was the monarch's chief advisor from 1213. Prior to that he had been on the crusades with Richard I from 1183 to 1187. He also served under Henry III and expelled Louis of France from Britain.

🔷 *see* King John

MAGNA CARTA (1215)

The Great Charter sealed at Runnymede on 15 June 1215 by King John and barons that has become one of the most important constitutional documents in British political history. Angered by the king's foreign policy and his dictatorial approach, the barons tried to get codified constraints on Royal power. One of the provisions of the Magna Carta secured the right of justice for everyone. It failed, though, to prevent the first Barons' War. Copies of the original document can still |be found in Salisbury and Lincoln Cathedrals and the British Library.

🔷 *see* King John

▲ *ABOVE: King John signing the Magna Carta*

PROVISIONS OF OXFORD (1258)

Constitutional reform in the thirteenth century. It granted executive power to the king who was to be supported by a council of 15. It made provision for Parliament to meet three times a year and local government became a responsibility of the council.

◆ *see* Henry III, Simon de Montfort

PARIS, TREATY OF (1259)

Treaty between the French and English monarchies which formalised the loss of large parts of the Angevin empire under King John. The two kings signing the treaty were Louis IX of France and Henry III of England. Henry, by signing the treaty, renounced his claims to large parts of France.

◆ *see* Henry III, King John

MODEL PARLIAMENT (1295)

Parliament summoned in November 1295 in order to allow Edward I to obtain money for wars. It got its name because of the make-up of the Parliament that was supposed to be the most representative ever assembled, at that stage. By today's standards it does not impress in those terms as it was made up only of earls, barons, bishops and knights. Around 150 men attended the Parliament in total.

◆ *see* Edward I

GLENDOWER, OWEN (1354–1416)

Landowner and symbol of the struggle for Welsh independence from England. Glendower (or Owain Glyndwr in Welsh) styled himself as the Prince of Wales and sought to forge an alliance with the French to throw off English rule. A dispute over land in 1400 in North Wales sparked off a 15-year revolt against Henry IV. One of his policies was to create a Welsh university and church. Although the revolt was ultimately unsuccessful, Glendower became a national hero.

◆ *see* Henry IV

▶ *RIGHT: The Star Chamber*

STAR CHAMBER (15TH–16TH CENTURIES)

Court of law in the fifteenth and sixteenth centuries. It was used first by Henry VII as a way of settling disputes arising from the Wars of the Roses. It was also used by Wolsey and Cromwell who tried to get those in dispute to use it in the first case rather than as a last resort. However it proved itself to be an unpopular institution. This arose from use as a way of maintaining Royal influence. This was particularly marked during the time of Charles I, especially in the time when he did not convene a Parliament. The chamber was eventually abolished by the Long Parliament.

◄ *see* Henry VII

TROYES, TREATY OF (1420)

Agreement between the French and British monarchies to establish claims and succession to the thrones of each country. The treaty was signed on 21 May 1420 during the Hundred Years' War. The terms of the treaty allowed for the French king, Charles VI, to betroth his daughter Catherine to Henry V. It also made Henry regent of France. Henry died two years later of dysentery, leaving his son Henry VI, who was only a year old, to take advantage of the terms set out in the Treaty of Troyes. Henry VI was also the son of Catherine despite the brief marriage. Henry VI turned out to be a weak and ineffective leader who eventually ended up in the Tower before being murdered in 1471.

◄ *see* Hundred Years' War

NEVILLE, RICHARD (1428–71)

English politician, known as the 'Kingmaker'. Originally he supported Richard, Duke of York, but after his defeat was forced to flee abroad. He then returned and helped Edward, Duke of York, become king. He wielded enormous power in his post as lord chamberlain until he fell out of the king's favour. He was then instrumental in restoring the deposed Henry VI to the throne,

see Edward IV, Henry VI, Wars of the Roses

POLE, EDWARD DE LA (1472–1513)

Nobleman. De La Pole, a Yorkist and Earl of Suffolk, had designs on becoming king. He fled the country after his ambition was thwarted. Although he returned to Britain, he quickly returned to the Continent in 1501. The Archduke of Burgundy handed him to the English. Imprisoned in the Tower, he was executed by Henry VIII.

MORE, THOMAS (1478–1535)

English author and politician. More came to prominence during the reign of Henry VIII, serving as lord chancellor. He fell out with the king, however, over the issue of religious policy, deeply disapproving of his marriage to Anne Boleyn. He was executed in 1535.

see Henry VIII

◀ LEFT: Statue of Thomas More

CROMWELL, THOMAS (1485–1540)

Tudor statesman. Cromwell oversaw England's religious separation from Rome in his position as Henry VIII's closest advisor. Cromwell arranged the divorce of the king from Catherine of Aragon in 1533. Subsequently he also dissolved the monasteries and ensured that their wealth was transferred to the Crown in the late 1530s. He had risen to this position from humble origins, beginning his career in the employ of Cardinal Wolsey. His fall from grace occurred after he persuaded Henry VIII to marry Anne of Cleves, whom the ageing king found unattractive. He was executed in 1540 on trumped-up charges of treason.

◆ *see* Henry VIII, Thomas Wolsey

CRANMER, THOMAS (1489–1556)

Archbishop of Canterbury (1533–56). Cranmer exerted enormous influence on the religious practice of England in the Tudor era and subsequently for years to come. As Archbishop, he declared Henry VIII's marriage to his first wife, Catherine of Aragon, void and then sanctioned the monarch's marriage to Anne Boleyn. By doing so he also sanctioned England's split from Rome's papal orthodoxy and the Protestant dominance. When Mary I, a devout Catholic, came to the throne in 1553, Cranmer was burned at the stake.

◆ *see* Henry VIII, Mary I

COUNCIL OF THE NORTH (16TH AND 17TH CENTURIES)

Political body that administered government policy and law in the sixteenth and seventeenth centuries in the north of England, including Cumberland, Durham, Northumberland and Yorkshire. It was originally established by Richard III, but dissolved in 1509. Henry VIII's lord chancellor, Cardinal Wolsey, re-established the council in 1525. Twelve years later it became a permanent body. With its close connections to government policy it became identified with the more unpopular edicts passed down from on high at an especially turbulent time in English history. The council was finally abolished by the Long Parliament in 1641.

 *see* Henry VIII

HOUSE OF COMMONS

Directly elected lower chamber of the British parliamentary system. The origins of the House of Commons can be traced to the thirteenth century when 'commoners', i.e. non-baronial representatives were summoned to Parliament. In the sixteenth century, the Commons acquired its permanent meeting place in Westminster. Its power increased enormously because of the Glorious Revolution that began in 1688 when control over taxation and free speech were won by the Commons. With the franchise being extended throughout the nineteenth century, its power and importance increased still further although the Lords often stymied many of its reforms. In the modern age, its importance has fluctuated. When there are small parliamentary majorities, it becomes very significant. There has been plenty of criticism, though, that its powers have waned over the last decade. Over 650 MPs are elected, and debates have been televised since 1989.

 *see* House of Lords

▶ RIGHT: The House of Commons

71

HOUSE OF LORDS

The unelected upper chamber of the British parliamentary system and the highest court of appeal in the country. The term was first used in the sixteenth century. The House of Lords was abolished as a result of the Civil War but was later restored. Its membership increasingly grew as peerages were awarded for political service and no longer relied on family titles. During the 1800s, the house clashed with the Commons many times on the Reform Bills. In 1911 its powers were denuded with the Parliamentary Act which limited the Lords' actions, removing its veto on pecuniary bills giving it only a power to delay bills. The House of Lords has been subject to reform over the past few years with Tony Blair's Labour abolishing almost all of the hereditary peers.

◆ see House of Commons

PRIVY COUNCIL (16TH CENTURY)

Governing body of the realm. Now largely ceremonial, and membership is granted to those who have obtained high office. It first emerged in the sixteenth century. Members in that time were drawn from those holding high state office. It used to meet wherever the Sovereign happened to be located. From the 1700s the Cabinet took over control and functions of the council. Although largely ceremonial it still holds powers used to administer legal disputes from Britain's overseas dependencies, including capital punishment cases.

FIELD OF THE CLOTH OF GOLD (1520)

Meeting near Calais between Henry VIII and Francis I of France. It was meant to be an attempt at demonstrating the good relationship between the two countries, though both nations and leaders were suspicious of each other. It was also an extravagant party. Over 4,000 people and 2,000 horses travelled with Henry VIII and a further 1,000 with his wife, Catherine of Aragon, across the Channel. The cost to the Crown has been put at £15,000.

◆ *see* Henry VIII

DUDLEY, ROBERT, EARL OF LEICESTER (1532–88)

Nobleman and confidant of Elizabeth I. Dudley was a favourite of the queen's and, at one time, was thought of as a suitable and possible husband for her. He was the fifth son of the Duke of Northumberland. Dudley became a privy councillor in 1559 and advocated a pro-Protestant foreign policy. He was married twice. When his first wife, Amy, died, rumour at the time held him responsible for her death. He married again in 1578.

◆ *see* Elizabeth I

BOTHWELL, JAMES HEPBURN, EARL OF (1535–78)

Third husband of Mary, Queen of Scots. Although a Protestant, Bothwell opposed any alliance with England. He was involved in the murder of Mary's second husband, Lord Darnley, in 1567 and soon afterwards he divorced his wife and married Mary who made him the Duke of Orkney. Opponents of the marriage forced Mary to abdicate in favour of her son James VI. Bothwell fled to Denmark where he was captured and imprisoned until his death in 1578.

◆ *see* Lord Darnley, Mary Queen of Scots,

DUDLEY, LORD GUILDFORD (D. 1554)

Husband of Lady Jane Grey. Dudley was a son of the Duke of Northumberland who, in 1553, organised his marriage to Lady Jane Grey in an attempt to stop Mary I, a devout Catholic, claiming the throne. The plot failed as Mary became queen and had Dudley executed the following year, along with Lady Jane Grey.

🔲 *see* Lady Jane Grey

BABINGTON, ANTHONY (1561–86)

Leader in a plot to assassinate Elizabeth I in 1586. Twenty-five year old Babington was a supporter of the Catholic Mary Stuart. He planned to mobilise English Catholics with the help of a Spanish invasion. Supporters of the queen intercepted a letter detailing his plans. Babington was subsequently tried and executed.

🔲 *see* Elizabeth I, Mary, Queen of Scots

BACON, FRANCIS (1561–1626)

Lawyer, statesman and philosopher in the Elizabethan Age. Bacon, born in 1561, was originally a lawyer who worked his way up to the post of Attorney General by 1613. By 1618 he had been appointed Lord Chancellor, but was impeached in 1621 on charges of corruption. A

friend of Thomas Hobbes, Bacon's works include Essays, The Advancement of Learning and Novum Organum and were influential in the Humanist tradition for more than a century.

🔲 *see* Elizabeth I

◀ *Contemporary painting of Sir Frances Bacon*

CECIL, ROBERT (1563–1612)

Statesman and minister to Elizabeth I. Cecil oversaw the transition from a Tudor to a Stuart monarchy when James I became king in 1603. In 1605, in recognition of his duties, James made him Earl of Salisbury. For the next three years he was the king's chief secretary, then from 1608 he became the lord treasurer. However, his influence with the monarch decreased in later life as James I became increasingly annoyed at his failed attempts to get more money from Parliament.

◆ *see* Elizabeth I, Gunpowder Plot, James I

FAWKES, GUY (1570–1606)

Co-conspirator in the Gunpowder Plot to blow up the Houses of Parliament on 5 November 1605. His deed is remembered in Britain every year on Guy Fawkes Night, 5 November. Fawkes was a staunch Roman Catholic and joined a group of three other conspirators. He was executed in 1606 after he betrayed his fellow conspirators under torture.

◆ *see* Gunpowder Plot, James I

CROMWELL, OLIVER (1599–1658)

Political leader, statesman and soldier. Lord Protector of England during the Commonwealth. Cromwell's Puritan ideals introduced radical change in England during the Civil War and subsequent Republic. Despite his overthrow of Charles I, Cromwell did not want to be ruler of England, but was attempting to establish a 'society of saints'.

Born in Cambridgeshire and educated at Sidney Sussex College, Cambridge, Cromwell rose from relatively humble beginnings to become the most powerful man in England. He was elected to the Long Parliament for Cambridge City and made his name as a radical. He then proved himself to be a natural military tactician when the Civil War broke out in 1642. Dissatisfied with the way war was being fought, he established the New Model Army, which helped to inflict a decisive defeat on the Royalists at Naseby in 1645. Once the royal forces had been subdued and Charles I executed in January 1649, Cromwell set about establishing his position. He ordered the massacres of civilians in Drogheda and Wexford and repelled further Royalist forces from Scotland summoned by Charles II. He established the Long Parliament and Barebones Parliament. The latter being a failure, Cromwell installed himself as Lord Protector. Although increasingly autocratic, a degree of religious tolerance (he allowed the Jews back into Britain, although this was also for commercial reasons) allowed his rule to be, by and large, sanctioned by the country. His death in September 1658, though, revealed the extent to which the political consensus revolved around him. His successor, his eldest son Richard, was deposed within six months.

see Barebones Parliament, Charles I, Richard Cromwell, English Civil War

BRITISH EMPIRE (17TH-20TH CENTURIES)

Land and territory ruled over by Britain from around 1600 to the 1930s. At its height, after World War I, the empire covered over 25 per cent of the world's population and area. It lasted three-and-a-half centuries – almost as long as the Roman Empire.

North America, Asia, Africa, the Caribbean and Australia were the areas affected by Britain's expansion as a world power during the seventeenth to twentieth centuries. By the time Britain began its process of colonisation, Spain and Portugal, two of the imperial powers of the fifteenth and sixteenth centuries, had colonised much of South America. Britain was concerned with opening up new trade routes rather than being driven by the religious zeal that marked the imperial concerns of other countries. At first Britain's empire found its wealth from the slave trade but by the time this was made illegal in 1807, it had grown sufficiently for Britain to rely on other forms of commerce.

Initially colonisation began in North America, in New England, Maryland and Virginia. A settlement in Jamestown, Virginia, in 1607 can be viewed as the beginning of the continental British Empire. Its rule of Ireland from the twelfth century, it is argued, was the original starting point. Canada became part of the Empire after British forces were victorious in the Seven Years' War with France between 1756–63.

The first great setback for the seemingly invincible Empire was its defeat by American forces during the American Revolution in 1776. This led to the loss of 13 American state colonies and the establishment of the United States of America. Despite this, the Empire continued to expand in other corners of the globe. The Napoleonic wars saw Britain claim French territory in the Caribbean. But it was the Victorian age that saw the largest expansion; this was the time of the European scramble for Africa. Britain took control of Kenya in 1888 and Uganda in 1890. There was also a scramble for territory in Asia, with Britain taking control of Hong Kong in 1841. By this time its reach had extended to the South Pacific. A year earlier, Britain had staked its claim to New Zealand.

London formerly ruled India, at the very centre of the Empire, from 1877, but its influence had been strong there since the formation of the East India Company in 1600. The company had effectively ruled India until violent protests in 1857.

In most of their dominions, notably in Australia, Canada, New Zealand and South Africa, the British allowed some forms of autonomous government. But with British power diminishing in the time between the two World Wars, and the changing times leading to resistance to its rule across the globe, the Empire eventually became the Commonwealth, a union that exists today.

◆ *see* Commonwealth, Seven Years' War, Queen Victoria

THE WHIG PARTY

Important political grouping in the seventeenth, eighteenth and early nineteenth centuries. It eventually developed into the Liberal Party of the nineteenth century. The name Whig emerged in the late 1670s to describe those members of Parliament who wished to keep James, Duke of York, from succeeding to the throne on the death of his elder brother, Charles II. They failed in this objective but recovered their position in the late 1680s as leading supporters of the Glorious Revolution of 1688, which ended the reign of James II. They were intermittently powerful in the reigns of William III and Anne before they became dominant under the Hanoverian monarchy which began in 1714. They always professed to support the political liberties of Englismen and religious toleration and looked back for inspiration to the Glorious Revolution since it witnessed the emergence of a 'balanced constitution' and strict limits to the powers of the monarchy. In the eighteenth century, rival groups of Whig politicians, headed by immensely wealthy aristocratic politicians, vied for power. Out of power for almost fifty years after 1783, they returned in 1830 to pass the first parliamentary reform Act under Earl Grey in 1832.

see William Pitt the Elder, William Pitt the Younger.

GUNPOWDER PLOT (1605)

Catholic conspiracy to blow up the Houses of Parliament and James I in November 1605. The attempt proved unsuccessful after a letter warning a Catholic MP of the plot was intercepted. Robert Catesby led the group. The others included Robert Winter, John Wright and the most famous of them all, Guy Fawkes. They hid around 30 barrels of gunpowder in a cellar under the House of Lords. Guy Fawkes was arrested on 4 November when he was discovered next to the barrels. Catesby was a fanatical Roman Catholic and was shot once the plot was uncovered. All those

◀ LEFT: The conspirators of the gunpowder plot

involved were executed. The event is marked each year in Britain with Guy Fawkes (Bonfire) night when millions of people set off fireworks in memory of the failed plot.

🔄 see Guy Fawkes, James I

CLARENDON, EDWARD HYDE (1609–74)

Statesman, politician. Clarendon was a long-time supporter of the monarchy including through the period of the English Civil War. He served in the Short Parliament in 1640 and Long Parliament from 1640–60. Following failed attempts to reconcile differences between Charles I and Parliament he went into exile in France in 1646. Clarendon became Charles II's closest advisor and helped to negotiate the return of the monarchy. On his return to England he became Lord Chancellor. His downfall was brought about by the Dutch War; he was forced into exile in France, where he died.

🔄 see Charles II, Long Parliament, Short Parliament

LILBURNE, JOHN (c. 1614–67)

Leader of the Levellers. The Levellers were a group of fundamentalist, democratic, republicans active during the English Civil War. They found considerable support in Oliver Cromwell's New Model Army but Cromwell himself found their views too radical. John Lilburne had served time in prison (1638–40) for distributing Puritan pamphlets. Having served in the parliamentary army he was elected to lead the Levellers in advocating ambitions for a democratic republic. He spent his time in and out of prison, his views considered dangerous and rebellion-inciting.

🔄 see Levellers

CROMWELL, RICHARD (1626–1712)

Son of Oliver Cromwell, Lord Protector of England (1658–59). Richard, as Oliver Cromwell's eldest son, succeeded his father on his death in 1658. Unlike his father, though, his time in office was short and he was dismissed by the Long Parliament in 1659. He managed to escape to France a year later. However, he returned to England 20 years on and lived out his life in seclusion.

◆ *see* Oliver Cromwell

ELEVEN YEARS' TYRANNY (1629–40)

Term used to describe the years after which Charles I dissolved Parliament and ruled without its guidance. After a number of confrontations with Parliament, Charles felt that the challenge to his 'divine right' was unforgivable and refused to convene Parliament. Although there was little overt oposition to this during the 11 years, the simmering resentment eventually gave rise to the English Civil War.

◆ *see* Charles I, Divine Right of Kings, English Civil War

DANBY, THOMAS OSBORNE, EARL OF (1631–1712)

British politician under Charles II. Danby was chief minister to the king between 1673–78. He was instrumental in instigating the Glorious Revolution in 1689 and his efforts were rewarded as he took up his position again for William III in 1690.

◆ *see* Glorious Revolution

◀ *LEFT: Thomas Osbourne, The Earl of Danby*

SHIP MONEY

Tax imposed from 1634 on maritime towns by Charles I to meet naval expenses. The tax was extended in 1635 to take in inland towns also. The tax was widely unpopular and came at a time when Parliament was not convened for 11 years. This became known as the 'Eleven Years' Tyranny'. Several refused to pay the tax including an ardent Parliamentarian, John Hampden, but in court, judges backed the Crown. However, it was eventually abolished and made illegal by the Long Parliament, whose members included Hampden.

◆ *see* Charles I, Long Parliament

LONG PARLIAMENT (1640–60)

Parliament assembled by Charles I. At a time of turbulence in British politics, Charles II tried to use the Parliament to push through reforms that ultimately led to the outbreak of the Civil War in 1642. During its existence competing factions held sway over the Long Parliament. By the mid-1640s, the New Model Army dominated the Parliament. It was purged in 1648 and what became known as its Rump, those members who retained their position after the purge, helped to establish the Commonwealth. In the 1650s the Rump itself was expelled by Cromwell and Parliament was not recalled until 1659. In 1660 it reconvened only to dissolve itself to be succeeded by the Convention Parliament. This led in turn to the restoration of the monarchy.

◆ *see* Charles II, Short Parliament

SHORT PARLIAMENT (1640)

Parliament convened by Charles I between April and May 1640. The king wanted to raise funds for the Bishops' Wars that were prompted by his attempts to impose Anglicanism on Scotland. Because a parliament had not been convened for so long, its members were apt to discuss other measures before they would concede to granting money for the king. An angry Charles I then quickly dissolved the Parliament.

▶ *see* Charles II, Long Parliament

LEVELLERS (1647)

Democratic party during the English Civil War. Among the allies of Cromwell's Parliamentarians, or Roundheads, were the Levellers, led by John Lilburne, a democratic party campaigning for the Republic, male suffrage and religious toleration. The Levellers found widespread support in the New Model Army – Cromwell's fighting force – but Cromwell disagreed with their demands for radical reforms and executed their leaders in 1649. From then on the Levellers' movement lost its political momentum, although it continued to exist until 1688.

▶ *see* John Lilburne

PRIDE'S PURGE (1648)

Purge of the Long Parliament in 1648 named after Thomas Pride, a colonel during the Civil War. The purge left just the Rump Parliament. It expelled around 140 MPs from the Parliament (there were only just over 150 in total) and paved the way for the vote that led to Charles I being brought to trial. Pride also happened to be a judge at the subsequent trial and also signed the King's death warrant. Some of those purged from the Parliament were arrested.

▶ *see* Charles I, Rump Parliament

MONMOUTH, JAMES SCOTT, 1ST DUKE OF (1649–85)

Illegitimate son of Charles II who tried to claim the English throne. Monmouth made his name as a military commander and was thought to be extremely popular as the Protestant candidate for the throne. However, his claim was never legitimised and he in 1685 led a rebellion to try and remove James II. It ended in disaster with his troops being slaughtered. He was captured, tried and executed.

◆ *see* James II

CONVENTION PARLIAMENT

Two Parliaments convened in the seventeenth century without the summons of the sovereign. The first Parliament was between April and December 1660 and recalled Charles II to the throne. The second was in February 1689. This met after the overthrow of James II.

◆ *see* Cavalier Parliament, Oliver Cromwell, English Civil War

RESTORATION (1660)

Reinstatement of the English monarchy in 1660 following the Declaration of Breda, in which Charles II was offered the monarchy in return for certain concessions such as greater religious liberty. Charles II was made king after the collapse of the Protectorate. Following the downfall of Richard Cromwell, there was much confusion over the immediate political future of England. With the Rump Parliament discredited, the Convention Parliament sought ways of returning Charles II from nine years of exile. He eventually returned to the country in May 1660 after receiving assurances about his constitutional position and safety. The new political order was cemented

▲ *ABOVE: Charles II and Queen Catherine of Braganza ceramic 1662* by the work of the Cavalier Parliament. Charles II, in 1662, married Catherine of Braganza, a Portuguese princess. Although there were no offspring, he fathered several illegitimate children, sparking a battle for the Crown upon his death in 1685. The same period was marked by a rebirth in English culture, especially in the writing of plays and poetry.

see Charles II, English Civil Wars

CAVALIER PARLIAMENT (1661–1679)

English Parliament during the period of Restoration. During the Interregnum, the period of Republican government between 1649 and 1660, Cromwell sought a parliament that could balance his, the army's and the legislature's interests. He failed, but three years after his death the Cavalier Parliament was convened, consolidating the restoration of the monarchy.

see Oliver Cromwell, English Civil War, Interregnum

CORPORATION ACT (1661)

Act of Parliament that excluded people from municipal office who refused to take communion in the Church of England. The act was finally repealed in 1828. It formed part of the Clarendon Code that sought to restore the supremacy of the Anglican Church.

see Charles II, Clarendon Code

HARLEY, ROBERT (1661–1724)

British Tory politician. Harley served as chief minister to Queen Anne and negotiated the longed-for end to the War of the Spanish Succession in the Treaty of Utrecht (1713). His luck changed under George I, when he was imprisoned under charges of Jacobite sympathies.

see Queen Anne, War of the Austrian Succession, Jacobites

CABAL, THE (1670S)

Advisory group to Charles II in the early 1670s, which has been viewed as the precursor to the modern Cabinet. Made up of noblemen, the Cabal took its name from the initials of the surnames of its members, Clifford, Arlington, Buckingham, Ashley and Lauderdale. Unlike the Cabinet, the Cabal had no formal power or status. It advised the king on matters such as foreign affairs.

◆ *see* Charles II

DOVER, TREATY OF (1670)

Pact between the British and the French to help France conquer Holland. Charles II and Louis XIV negotiated the treaty. The British would gain territory from the pact also. Charles also agreed to convert to Roman Catholicism as part of the deal. Two years after the treaty, a third Dutch War began, lasting two years. Peace was finally concluded by the Treaty of Westminster, signed in 1674.

◆ *see* Anglo-Dutch Wars, Charles II

TEST ACTS (1673)

Three acts of the seventeenth century which tried to exclude Nonconformists from high office in the civil and military arenas. From the date of the first act, 1673, all office holders had to swear allegiance to the monarch, affirm the monarch's supremacy as head of the Church of England, repudiate tenets of Roman Catholicism and receive the Anglican Communion. From 1678 all Roman Catholics were excluded from Parliament, except James II. The third act, in 1681, demanded that all government officials in Scotland had to be Protestants.

◆ *see* Roman Catholicism

WALPOLE, ROBERT (1676–1745)

British Prime Minister. He first became an MP in 1701 and held numerous offices under Queen Anne. He was imprisoned for corruption in 1712. In the early years of the Hanoverian dynasty, he was not in favour but his reputation revived when he took leading responsibility in restoring confidence in Britain's developing financial system after the stock market collapse known as the South Sea Bubble (1720). He became First Lord of the Treasury in 1721 and, in effect, the nation's first 'prime minister'. He was attacked by his many opponents for his excessive power and always denied that he was 'sole and prime minister', seeing the term as one of criticism. His long tenure of power was characterised by highly skilled parliamentary management and financial policies which revealed his great shrewdness and business acumen. He was brought down in 1742 during the early stages of a war which he had striven for many years to avoid.

◪ see George I

BOLINGBROKE, HENRY ST JOHN, VISCOUNT (1678–1751)

British politician. Bolingbroke served as foreign secretary and secretary of war, during which time he helped to negotiate the Treaty of Utrecht. He was a Jacobite sympathiser and his involvement in the plans to place James Edward Stuart on the throne led to his dismissal from government in 1714.

◪ see James Edward Stuart

EXCLUSION BILLS (1679, 1680, 1681)

Three seventeenth-century parliamentary bills introduced to stop James, Duke of York, from succeeding to the throne. The first bill was in 1679; the second in 1680 and the final bill was laid in 1681. The bills were introduced by the Country Party. This was made up of landed MPs who were anti-Catholic and did not have to depend on royal patronage. Its members were prominent anti-Royalists who provided the parliamentary opposition to the Crown. Parliament was dissolved after the second reading of the first bill and the House of Lords rejected the second bill. Charles II dissolved Parliament when the third bill was introduced. James II became king in 1685.

 see Charles I, Charles II, Roman Catholicism

MONMOUTH'S REBELLION (1685)

Short-lived rebellion against the rule of James II. The illegitimate son of Charles II, Monmouth believed the throne was rightfully his. After being forced into exile he returned with 150 supporters and landed at Lyme Regis to denounce the king as a usurper of the throne. Supporters from across the West Country joined him but his luck ran out at Bridgewater where he was cornered by the king's troops and captured. His troops were slaughtered and Monmouth was tried and executed. Over 300 rebels were hung, drawn and quartered at the trials that became known as the Bloody Assizes, presided over by the bloodthirsty Judge Jeffreys.

 see James II

GRAND ALLIANCE (1689)

Name given to a political and strategic alliance formed amongst major European powers, Austria, England, the Netherlands, Spain and a number of German states, aimed at checking French expansionism under Louis XIV. The alliance ultimately proved ineffective as war

◀ *LEFT: William of Orange united much of Europe*

raged in Europe throughout this period until almost the year 1700. A further 'grand alliance' was formed in 1701, this time between Austria, England and the Netherlands, aimed at preventing the all-powerful union of the French and Spanish Crowns. This was organised by William III of England. Portugal and Prussia eventually joined the alliance. This all ultimately led to the War of the Spanish Succession between 1701 and 1714, provoked by the childless death of Charles II of Spain.

◆ *see* William III

NEWCASTLE, THOMAS PELHAM-HOLMES, DUKE OF (1693–1768)

British prime minister (1754–56 and 1757–62). As a Whig politician Newcastle was secretary of state for over 30 years before succeeding his brother, Henry, as prime minister. He resigned after his first term in office after criticism of his policies in the Seven Years' War, but later returned.

◆ *see* Henry Pelham, Seven Years' War

PELHAM, HENRY (1696–1754)

British prime minister (1743–54). Pelham was from a well-to-do family and was first elected as an MP from 1717. He gained his reputation for his expert management of Parliament, although he was considered to be a dull character. He led the 'Broad-Bottom Administration', so called because of the broad political factions within it. His brother, the Duke of Newcastle, was also a leading figure in this administration.

CIVIL LIST (1697)

Money paid each year by Parliament to meet the expenses of the Royal Household. The first Civil List Act was passed in 1697. Initially it covered government expenses, but this stopped in 1831. It was substantially amended by George III in 1761, who gave up revenues from Crown land in return for an annual payment. In recent years the list has been amended after growing criticism of the behaviour of several members of the royal family.

GIBRALTAR

British colony in the Mediterranean. 'The Rock of Gibraltar', as it is commonly known, first passed into British control in 1704. Three separate treaties in the eighteenth century gave approval to British rule. However, the Spanish government still maintains that Gibraltar, which borders the southern coast of Spain, is part of its sovereign territory. The countries, although allies and both members of the European Union, are still in dispute over Gibraltar.

ACT OF UNION (1707)

Act that saw England and Scotland unite politically. The Act reflected English dominance and the loss of Scottish political independence. It created one Parliament covering the two countries, with the Scottish Parliament disappearing. Scotland was represented by 45 MPs and 16 peers in the new Parliament. It retained its own laws and religious

identity. The Act had its seeds in the seventeenth century when the two countries' Parliaments claimed precedent over each other. Queen Anne was the first monarch of the Union.

◆ see Act of Settlement, Queen Anne

◀ LEFT: Queen Anne receiving the Act of Union

PITT, WILLIAM THE ELDER (1708–78)

British prime minister (1766–68). Known as a great orator, Pitt was first elected to Parliament in 1735. He was denied the chance of top office until the 1750s. As secretary of state he directed the war effort in North America and India with great success. When he achieved the office of prime minister, he was dogged by ill health. Pitt suffered from depression and gout, and for a year between 1767 and 1768 he was incapacitated by the former. He resigned in October 1768. In his last speech in the House of Lords he collapsed before he had finished and died within a month.

BUTE, JOHN STUART, 3RD EARL OF (1713–92)

British prime minister (1762–63). Before becoming prime minister, Bute was the future George III's tutor and friend. His first experience of high office was when he was invited into the Cabinet in 1760. Two years later he succeeded Thomas Pelham-Holmes, Duke of Newcastle, as prime minister. His term of office was short and rancorous. Bute ended British involvement in the Seven Years' War in which Britain joined forces with Prussia and Hanover against Austria, France, Russia, Saxony and Sweden. The war established Britain as a major colonial power but Bute attracted criticism and resigned as prime minister in April 1763.

◆ *see* George III

ROCKINGHAM, 2ND MARQUESS OF (1730–82)

British prime minister (1755–66 and 1782). Rockingham is remembered mainly for his stand in support of American independence during the Revolution and as initiator of peace negotiations at the end of the war. He died in office.

◆ *see* American Revolution

HASTINGS, WARREN (1732–1818)

British colonial administrator who worked for the East India Company and who prepared the way for British rule in India. Hastings arrived in India aged just 18. By 1771 he had become governor of Bengal and the first governor general just three years later. His time there was turbulent. Although he was admired for his administrative reforms and his courting of some Indian leaders, he was also accused of high-handedness. He sentenced Maharaja Nandakumar to death by hanging after he had accused Hastings of corruption. On his return to England he was acquitted on charges of corruption following a seven-year trial in the House of Lords.

◆ *see* East India Company

NORTH, LORD FREDERICK (1732–92)

British prime minister (1770–82). Most notably this was the time of the American Revolution. His rule was marked by loyalty to the king, George III, even though he had reservations about the policy the king was taking. He introduced the Intolerable Acts in 1774 that led to the closure of Boston Harbour as retaliation for the Boston Tea Party in 1773.

◆ *see* American Revolution, George III

GRAFTON, AUGUSTUS HENRY, 3 RD DUKE OF (1735–1811)

British prime minister (1767–70). Descended from Charles II and his mistress Barbara Villiers, Grafton came to notice as first lord of the treasury in 1766. He was neither popular nor successful as prime minister and his attitude towards the American Revolution forced his resignation.

SHELBURNE, WILLIAM FITZMAURICE, 2ND EARL OF (1737–1805)

British prime minister (1783). Shelburne was an outspoken oppponent of George III's policies regarding the American colonies and he was instrumental in concluding peace with the new United States during his time as prime minister.

◆ *see* American Revolution, George III

PORTLAND, WILLIAM BENTINCK, 3RD DUKE OF (1738–1809)

British prime minister (1807–09). Portland took on the nominal role of prime minister during the coalition government of Frederick, Lord North, but assumed the role in full in 1807.

◆ *see* Lord Frederick North

PITT, WILLIAM THE YOUNGER (1759–1806)

British prime minister (1783–1801, 1804–06). Pitt, son of William Pitt the Elder, became the youngest ever prime minister of Britain in 1781 at the age of just 24. Initially he embarked upon a programme of parliamentary reform but the French revolution of 1792 made him halt this for fear of civil unrest in Britain. He paved the way for British control of India by placing the East India Company under governmental control and oversaw the division of Canada into different spheres of influence between France and England. He also introduced income tax in 1799. The

◀ *LEFT: William Pitt the Younger*

first rate was two shillings in the pound. Like his father
he suffered from poor health and died in his 40s.

PERCEVAL, SPENCER (1762–1812)

British prime minister (1809–12). Initially Chancellor of the Exchequer,
Perceval rose to become prime minister in 1809. He was assassinated
three years later.

GREY, CHARLES, 2ND EARL (1764–1845)

British prime minister (1830–34). Grey entered Parliament in 1786 and
was created lord of the admiralty 20 years later and then foreign
secretary. In his time as prime minister he pushed through the Great
Reform Bill and the Abolition Act.

CASTLEREAGH, ROBERT STEWART, VISCOUNT (1769–1822)

British statesman who twice served as war secretary and for 10 years as
foreign secretary in the early 1800s. Born in Ulster, Castlereagh was a
leading figure in Ireland's union with Great Britain when he served as
chief secretary for Ireland at the turn of the nineteenth century. His
greatest triumph was his work as foreign secretary when, at the
Congress of Vienna between October 1814 and June 1815 following the
Napoleonic Wars, Castlereagh secured British security and trading
interests. At home his image was less popular. A dispute over a failed
expedition to gain British control of Antwerp led to a duel with his
Cabinet colleague, George Canning. He was an unpopular spokesman for
the repressive government of Earl Liverpool. He was one of the Cabinet
members targeted by the Cato Street Conspiracy in 1820. Castlereagh
committed suicide two years later.

◆ *see* George Canning, Cato Street Conspiracy

CANNING, GEORGE (1770–1827)

British prime minister (1827). Seen as a progressive Tory, Canning's short term in office was marked by attacks from colleagues that undermined his power. Canning had been an MP since 1794. As foreign secretary 1807–09, Canning quarrelled with a Cabinet colleague war secretary Robert Stewart, Viscount Castlereagh. The feud was so bitter it ended up as a duel one morning on Putney Heath. Both men survived, but the loathing between them continued as Canning was kept out of office until 1816 because of his jealousy of the Viscount. He only re-entered the Cabinet after Castlereagh's suicide in 1822.

 see Viscount Castlereagh

LIVERPOOL, ROBERT BANKS JENKINSON, 2ND EARL OF (1770–1825)

British prime minister (1812–27). Liverpool became a member of the Tory Party in 1790 and served a number of roles there, including home secretary and war minister, before becoming prime minister in 1812. His government saw the country through the Napoleonic Wars, but his policies were not always popular.

 see Napoleonic Wars

O'CONNELL, DANIEL (1775–1847)

Irish nationalist and barrister. A central figure in Catholic Ireland's struggle for liberation from the British. O'Connell sought to improve the rights of the Catholics by non-violent means. He is revered in Irish history as the 'Liberator'.

▶ *RIGHT: Daniel O'Connell*

O'Connell established the Catholic Association in 1823 that sought to gain Irish emancipation from Britain. It survived on duties paid by members from the Catholic community. This became known as the Catholic tax. O'Connell also successfully achieved his goal of getting Catholics the right to sit in Parliament. He was one of the first to benefit from this. In 1830, a year after the right was granted, O'Connell was elected as MP for County Clare. His popularity waned due to his commitment to a peaceful solution. Many at the time thought the only way to secure a political solution was through violent means if necessary.

see George IV

MELBOURNE, VISCOUNT (1779–1848)

British prime minister (1834, 1835–41). First elected as a Whig MP in 1806, Melbourne was viewed as a moderate though he supported suppression of radical and working-class anger. His first government was brief, falling through disunity of its members. But he was asked to form another government in 1835. It was a period of turbulence, economic depression and Chartist opposition as well as the accession of the new monarch, Queen Victoria. His wife, Lady Caroline Ponsonby, had a love affair with Lord Byron.

GODERICH, FREDERICK JOHN ROBINSON, VISCOUNT (1782–1859)

British prime minister (1827–28). Goderich became Chancellor of the Exchequer in 1823. In 1927 the serving prime minister, George Canning, granted him his peerage; Goderich succeeded him the same year, but he was unable to control the warring Tories and Whigs and resigned the following year.

see George Canning

ABERDEEN GEORGE HAMILTON GORDON, LORD (1784–1860)

British prime minister (1852–55). Aberdeen held the positions of foreign secretary under the Duke of Wellington and Robert Peel. He became Tory prime minister in 1852, but criticism of his management of the crisis in the Crimea forced his resignation three years later.

◖ *see* Robert Peel, Duke of Wellington

PALMERSTON, HENRY JOHN TEMPLE, 3RD VISCOUNT (1784–1865)

British prime minister (1855–58, 1859–65). Originally a Tory, Palmerston broke with the party in 1830 and became foreign secretary for the Whigs. In his time he saw through a number of conflicts, including the Indian Mutiny and the Second Opium War.

PEEL, SIR ROBERT (1788–1850)

British prime minister. Peel first entered parliament in 1809 and was a minister a year later. He served as Chief Secretary for Ireland from 1812 to 1818 and became Home Secretary in 1822. In this position, he became famous for a number of administrative and judicial reforms. He instituted the Metropolitan Police (or 'Peelers') in 1829. His career became steeped in controversy from 1829 when, against both his previous reputation as a hardline Protestant and also the strong views of a majority in the Tory party, he persuaded Wellington to grant Roman Catholic Emancipation. He became leader of the party in 1834 and thereafter briefly prime minister in 1834–35. As prime minister from 1841–46, he instituted radical changes to the financial structure of the state, introducing income tax for the first time in peacetime, reducing or removing many protective tariffs and helping to pave the way for the long period of prosperity known as the 'mid-Victorian boom'. Repealing the Corn Laws in 1846, however, split his party and led to the end of his government. The Conservatives would not win another election for almost thirty years and Peel's career ended in controversy. He died as the result of a riding accident in 1850.

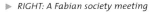 *see* Metropolitan Police

RUSSELL, JOHN, 1ST EARL (1792–1878)

British prime minister (1846–52, 1865–66). Russell came to Parliament in 1813 and became a cabinet minister. He was a supporter of Catholic Emancipation and was instrumental in drawing up the Reform Bill.

see Catholic Emancipation

DERBY, EDWARD STANLEY, 14TH EARL OF (1799–1869)

British prime minister (1852, 1858–59, 1866–68). First a Whig and then a Tory, Derby was responsible for introducing the bill for abolishing slavery.

FABIAN SOCIETY (19TH CENTURY)

Moderate left-wing organisation committed to achieving a socialist society through gradual, evolutionary rather than revolutionary means. Its influence on the Labour Party has been vast. It helped to establish the party in 1900 and has influenced its policies in the past. Labour prime minister Clement Attlee was a member of the Fabian Society. It is steeped in the cautious, centrist tradition of the British Labour Party.

see Labour Party

▶ *RIGHT: A Fabian society meeting*

HOME RULE (19TH AND 20TH CENTURIES)

Attempt to give Ireland a domestic Parliament during the latter stages of the nineteenth century and the earlier twentieth century. Britain's political dominance of Ireland had been formalised through the Act of Union in 1801.

In the 1870s the Home Rule Association was formed and 59 Irish MPs who supported the movement were elected in the 1874 General Election. The big push for home rule came after the 1886 election. Led by the Irish nationalist Charles Parnell, the Home Rule Association held the balance of power after the election. The party supported the Liberals who, under Gladstone, had by then converted to the cause of Home Rule. The cause was eventually undermined by unionists within the Liberal Party defecting and failing to support the demands of its own leaders or those of the Home Rule Association. By the 1890s, Gladstone had returned to power and set about pushing another Home Rule bill through Parliament. This got through the House of Commons but was defeated in the Lords.

The scenario whereby the Irish party again held the balance of power was repeated in 1910. This time there was more success. The bill once again proceeded through the Commons, only to be delayed by the Lords. However, parliamentary rules had changed by then and it means that the Lords could only delay bills for up to two years. Passed in 1912, the Home Rule Bill went onto the statute books in 1914, though it was suspended throughout the period of World War II. By 1920 a modified bill was passed which provided for separate Parliaments for southern and Northern Ireland. Throughout the period, pressure to give autonomy/independence to Ireland grew through such events as the Easter Uprising of 1916. The leaders of this uprising wanted full independence for Ireland.

see Easter Rising

LAND LEAGUE (19TH CENTURY)

Organisation, also known as the Irish Land League, that tried to achieve land reform in Ireland in the nineteenth century by boycotting unpopular landlords. It was established by Michael Davitt, an Irish nationalist, and proved successful in achieving its aims. In 1881 Gladstone introduced the Irish Land Act that gave in to the group on many of its demands for land reform. It was disbanded shortly after.

see Michael Davitt, William Gladstone, Charles Parnell

LIBERAL PARTY (19TH CENTURY)

British political party. The Liberals grew out of the former Whig party, whose emphasis had been on liberalism, in the nineteenth century. With the rise of the Labour Party to the far left of the Conservatives, the Liberals found themselves taking the middle road, and their momentum was lost. In 1988 they merged with the Social Democratic Party to become the Liberal Democrats.

see Labour Party, Whigs

▲ ABOVE: Dr David Owen and David Steele, after the SDP–Liberal alliance

DISRAELI, BENJAMIN (1804–81)

British prime minister (1868–74, 1874–80), statesman and novelist. Disraeli also served as Chancellor of the Exchequer and was made Earl of Beaconsfield by Queen Victoria, with whom he enjoyed good relations. Born to a Spanish Jew, but baptised a Christian, Disraeli was a Conservative. His career was marked by the introduction of social reforms including the Reform Act of 1867, which doubled the number of people eligible to vote and, when prime minister, he introduced the Public Health Act. On the international stage he made Queen Victoria Empress of India in 1876 and paved the way for British occupation of Cyprus. Disraeli was concerned with controlling Russian expansionism by asserting British power. His great political rival was William Gladstone. He was seen as a great parliamentary orator. His career as a novelist was also distinguished. His most famous works included Coningsby and Sybil. He once remarked that if he wanted to read a good novel then he would write one. In 1880 he lost his last election and decided to retire from politics. He died just one year later.

◆ *see* Queen Victoria

GLADSTONE, WILLIAM (1809–98)

British prime minister (1868–74, 1880–85 and 1892–94). In total Gladstone was an MP for 62 years, from 1832 until 1895 with only year in between when he did not serve in Parliament. Prior to becoming prime minister, he held junior office and was Chancellor of the Exchequer in the 1850s and 1860s. As leader of the Liberal party, Gladstone tried unsuccessfully to forge a political solution in Ireland. He also introduced an education act that provided schooling for all children in England and Wales aged between five and 13. During his second term in office he introduced the third Reform Act which gave the power of vote to farm workers. In his final term in office he again concentrated on the issue of Ireland and tried to force through, unsuccessfully, Home Rule for Ireland. Although a bill got through the House of Commons, it was defeated in the House of Lords, prompting Gladstone's resignation. He died of cancer in 1898.

◆ *see* Queen Victoria

▶ *RIGHT: Margaret Thatcher, prime minster from 1979 to 1990*

SIX ACTS (1819)

Series of six repressive parliamentary statutes passed in an attempt to halt the spread of radicalism following the Peterloo Massacre of August 1819. A peaceful rally of up to 80,000 people in Manchester, campaigning for more rights for industrial workers, ended with 11 people dead, killed by troopers' sabres. This became a symbol of repression. The Six Acts stopped any future meetings of more than 50 people.

◆ *see* Peterloo Massacre

CONSERVATIVE PARTY (1830S)

British political party. It first emerged in the 1830s, and in the twentieth century established itself as one of the two major parties in British politics. The party emerged from the Tory group, which began in the 1860s. The term, Irish for 'outlaw', is still used today to describe the Conservatives.

In the 1830s the Conservatives allied themselves to the reactionary and repressive government of Lord Liverpool. Under Robert Peel, the party adopted the Tamworth manifesto, which accepted reform where necessary, still a tenet of modern-day Conservatism. The party split during the mid-nineteenth century but was united over attempts at

giving Ireland Home Rule in the 1880s. In 1912 the Conservatives merged with the Liberal Unionists and became the Conservative and Unionist Party, still its official name.

◆ *see* Stanley Baldwin, Neville Chamberlain, Winston Churchill, Alec Douglas-Home, Anthony Eden, Edward Heath, Andrew Bonar Law, John Major, Margaret Thatcher

SALISBURY, ROBERT GASCOYNE CECIL, 3RD MARQUESS OF (1830–1903)

British prime minister (1885–86, 1886–92, 1895–1902). Salisbury entered Parliament in 1853 and soon became foreign minister. His interest in foreign affairs extended into his office as prime minister, where he concentrated on British expansionist policies in South Africa.

GREAT REFORM ACT (1832)

Three separate parliamentary acts throughout the 1800s which gave the vote to millions more within Britain. The first act in 1832 was initially defeated, sparking riots throughout the country. Only on the intervention of William IV did the act become law. It got rid of the 'Rotten Boroughs' and gave more areas the chance of electing their own MP to Parliament. Although the act increased the number of those who could vote by 50%, this still only extended the franchise to the middle class. The second Reform Act of 1867, under Disraeli, gave almost a million more people the vote, doubling the country's electorate overnight. The final act, in 1884, further increased the number of people who could vote to five million. The final act, introduced by Gladstone, came at a time of political unrest and increasingly loud demands from radical groups for Parliament to extend the power of franchise.

◆ *see* Benjamin Disraeli, William IV

DEVONSHIRE, SPENCER HARTINGTON, 8TH DUKE OF (1833–1908)

British politician. Devonshire was leader of the Liberal Unionists from 1886 to 1903. He was primarily responsible for the defeat of Gladstone's 1886 Home Rule Bill.

◆ *see* Home Rule

TOLPUDDLE MARTYRS (1834)

Group of six trade unionists from the village of Tolpuddle in Dorset who were deported to Australia for forming a trade union in 1834. The six were farm labourers and were sentenced to seven years' transportation. They were pardoned in 1836 following a long public campaign to clear their name.

▶ RIGHT: *Contemporary illustration of four matyrs*

CAMPBELL-BANNERMAN, HENRY (1836–1908)

British prime minister (1905–08). Campbell-Bannerman served as chief secretary for Ireland (1884–85) and war minister (1886, 1892–95). He was strongly opposed to the wars in South Africa and during his time as prime minister the colonies there were granted self-government.

DAVITT, MICHAEL (1846–1906)

Irish nationalist, instrumental in founding the Irish Land League in 1879, which sought land reform in Ireland. Davitt supported the notion of armed struggle against the English and spent several years in prison. During one jail sentence (1882), he was elected as an MP but was unable to take up his seat.

▶ see Land League, Charles Parnell

PARNELL, CHARLES (1846–91)

Irish nationalist. Parnell seemed an unlikely nationalist. He was a Protestant Anglo-Irish landowner but he proved a strong supporter of Irish rights. He was elected as an MP in 1875 and used the tactic of filibustering to try and draw awareness to the plight of the Irish. He was the first president of the Irish Land League and was arrested for inciting agrarian violence in 1881. He was a member of the Irish Home Rule Association and sided with Gladstone's Liberals when the Irish held the balance of power in Parliament.

see Michael Davitt, Land League

ROSEBERY, ARCHIBALD, EARL OF (1847–1929)

British prime minister (1894). Rosebery's term lasted less than a year. His leanings were Liberal, but he was forced to stand down after his imperialist views caused dissension in the Liberal ranks.

BALFOUR, ARTHUR JAMES, 1ST EARL (1848–1930)

British prime minister (1902–05). Balfour was elected as a Conservative MP in 1874 and became Secretary for Ireland and later First Lord of the Treasury. He is best known for his pioneering Education Acts. In 1915 he joined the coalition government as First Lord of the Admiralty and in 1917 issued the Balfour Declaration, which demanded a national home for the Jews in Palestine.

ASQUITH, HERBERT HENRY (1852–1928)

British prime minister (1908–16). Asquith was leader of the Liberal Party in its last period of dominance in British politics. He first became an MP in 1886 and prime minister in 1908. It was a time of great turbulence. He curbed the powers of the House of Lords, was challenged by the suffragette movement, and granted Home Rule for Ireland in 1914, though this was delayed. Asquith was ousted by David Lloyd George in December 1916, as his wartime coalition government was considered weak.

see Home Rule, House of Lords, David Lloyd George

HARDIE, KEIR (1856–1915)

First Labour politician. Working in a coal mine as a child, Scotsman, Keir James Hardie grew up developing socialist sympathies, having seen a need to improve the lot of his fellow miners at the pit face. At the age of 32, in 1886, he became the secretary for the Scottish Miners' Federation. He then became the first Labour candidate to run for Parliament in 1888, becoming a member of Parliament from 1892–95 and 1900–15.

LAW, ANDREW BONAR (1858–1923)

British Conservative politician. Bonar Law was elected leader of the Conservatives in 1911 and played a major role in the coalition government led by Herbert Asquith in the immediate post-war years, holding the positions of Chancellor of the Exchequer and Lord Privy Seal.

◆ see Herbert Henry Asquith

LLOYD GEORGE, DAVID (1863–1945)

British prime minister (1916–22). Although associated with the Welsh, Lloyd George was actually born in Manchester to Welsh parents. A Liberal, Lloyd-George was Chancellor of the Exchequer between 1908 and 1915 under Herbert Asquith. There he made his mark as a social reformer, unveiling a Budget in 1909 aimed to help those at the bottom of the social scale, and imposed a high tax on those who earned over £3,000 a year. During World War I he became minister of munitions, a task he excelled in. By the end of the war he had taken over as prime minister. At the Paris Peace Conference he resisted calls to impose retributive terms on Germany. At home his government was destabilised by the situation in Ireland and the revelations about Lloyd George selling honours for contributions towards party campaign expenses. He was ousted as prime minister in 1922 after losing the support of Conservatives in his government.

◆ see World War I

MACDONALD, RAMSAY (1866–1937)

British prime minister (1924, 1929–31). MacDonald was elected to Parliament in 1906 and became leader of the new Labour Party. He lost this position when he took a stand against World War I, but was re-elected in 1922. He became prime minister in January 1924 but was forced to resign again in October the same year. After his second term in 1931 MacDonald left the Labour Party and formed a coalition government with the Conservatives and Liberals.

BALDWIN, STANLEY (1867–1947)

Three times British prime minister (1923–24, 1924–29,1935–37). Baldwin was a Conservative who became an MP in 1908. He first became prime minister in 1923, succeeding Bonar Law. The Conservatives had lost their majority by the beginning of 1924 but were returned to power by the end of the year. Baldwin was prime minister at the time of the 1926 General Strike, introducing retaliatory legislation against the unions a year later. He was defeated in the next election in 1929, but returned to power in 1935. Baldwin was prime minister during the abdication crisis, when he forbade Edward VIII from marrying Mrs Simpson.

◆ see General Strike

CHAMBERLAIN, NEVILLE (1869–1940)

British prime minister (1937–40). Chamberlain is most associated with the policy of appeasement, which used diplomacy and concession rather than force to confront the expansionist policies of Nazi Germany. The most notable example of this was the Munich Agreement (September 1938), which ultimately surrendered Czechoslovakia to Nazi control. Chamberlain committed Britain to war if Hitler's forces invaded Poland, which happened in September 1939. The policy of appeasement was popular at the time, although it had critics – including Winston Churchill. Following disasters early on in the war, Chamberlain resigned amid much criticism. Churchill became prime minister and Chamberlain joined his Cabinet, but he later resigned and died in October 1940.

GANDHI, MAHATMA (1869–1948)

Indian spiritual and nationalist leader. Mahatma Gandhi's real name was Mohandas Karamchand Gandhi. Mahatma means 'great soul' in Hindi. Throughout his life, Gandhi was a champion of the poor and disenfranchised through non-violence. He moved to South Africa in 1893 where he developed his policy of peaceful non-co-operation, or 'satyagraha', with the authorities in the struggle against racial discrimination. A lawyer, he moved back to India in 1914 and became leader of the Indian National Congress. Frequently imprisoned by the British, Gandhi visited London in 1931 for the Round Table Conferences to determine India's political future. His message to the British was for them to leave India. Gandhi's simple style of dress won him many friends but his lack of formality apparently annoyed Winston Churchill. After World War II he was a central figure in negotiations for Indian independence. He was assassinated by a Hindu extremist who opposed Gandhi's support between Hindus and Muslims.

▶ RIGHT: Mahatma Gandhi

CRAIG, JAMES (1871–1940)

First prime minister of Northern Ireland (1921–40). During his time as leader Craig was a particularly strong defender of Protestants' rights in and domination of Northern Ireland. Craig was an MP from 1906 until 1921. Between 1913 and 1920 he also organised the Ulster Volunteer Force, preparing it for armed confrontation amid Loyalist fears of Home Rule being granted to Northern Ireland.

◆ *see* Home Rule

CHURCHILL, WINSTON (1874–1965)

British prime minister (1940–45, 1951–55). Possibly the most famous of all Britain's modern political leaders. He trained at Sandhurst and fought in India and Sudan at the end of the nineteenth century. Churchill was first elected as an MP in 1901 for the Conservatives but joined the Liberals in 1904. He was First Lord of the Admiralty between 1911–15, but was demoted after a failed expedition to the Dardenelles. During the 1930s he was an implacable opponent of appeasement. By the outbreak of World War II he was again First Lord of the Admiralty, but took over as prime minister in May 1940. Over the next five years he established his reputation as leader, statesman and orator. He popularised the phrase 'Iron Curtain' to describe Soviet expansion in Eastern Europe and was re-elected as prime minister in 1951. He was also the author of several historical works, was given a full state funeral and is the only British leader to have an American warship named after him.

◆ *see* World War II

DE VALERA, EAMON (1882–1975)

Irish prime minister and president (1937–48, 1951–54, 1957–59). De Valera was also president from 1959–73. American-born to a Spanish father and

Irish mother, De Valera was an early leader of the Sinn Fein movement. He headed the party's provisional government from 1919 to 1922 but De Valera opposed the terms of the 1921 Anglo-Irish Treaty. In 1926, he created the Fianna Fail party. It won the 1932 election and he was president of the Executive Council of the Irish Free State. He also served in a senior position during the 1916 Easter Rising. He revived the Irish language.

♦ *see* Easter Rising, Irish Free State, Sinn Fein

▶ *RIGHT: Eamon De Valera*

ATLEE, CLEMENT (1883–1967)

British prime minister (1945–51). Atlee was the first Labour prime minister to hold a majority in the House of Commons. Much of the work of his government set the tone for British social and economic policy up until the election of Margaret Thatcher. Labour introduced the National Health Service, and a heavy policy of nationalisation of the major industries. He granted independence to India. But Britain was a country exhausted and impoverished by war, forcing the government to introduce austerity measures. Many within the Labour Party, especially on the left of the party, criticised Atlee for being too cautious in his policies.

♦ *see* Labour Party

COLLINS, MICHAEL (1890–1922)

Irish nationalist leader. Collins first became a member of the Irish republican brotherhood and took an active part in the 1916 Easter Rising. Collins was a founder of the IRA and intelligence director. He died in 1922 at the hands of fundamentalists.

♦ *see* Easter Rising, Home Rule, Sinn Fein

MACMILLAN, HAROLD (1894–1986)

British prime minister (1957–63). An MP from 1924, Macmillan was a critic of appeasement in the years before World War II. Under the Churchill government of the early 1950s he was minister of housing, defence and Chancellor of the Exchequer. Following Eden's resignation after the Suez Crisis, Macmillan became prime minister in 1957, winning an election in 1959 where he was closely associated with the famous phrase: 'You've never had it so good'. He encouraged the independence of many of Britain's overseas colonies with his 'Winds of Change' speech. Macmillan tried to get Britain into the European Economic Community but was vetoed by the French. He retired in October 1963 through ill health. His last year in office was marked by the turmoil of the Profumo affair.

MOSLEY, OSWALD (1896–1980)

British fascist. Mosley was an MP from 1918 until 1931, in turn serving the Conservative Party, standing as an Independent and the Labour Party. Following the trend of right-wing policies in Europe, Mosley created the British Union of Fascists in 1932. The party was anti-Jewish, condemned free speech but was a supporter of the Commonwealth. An admirer of Mussolini, Mosley's attempts to create disorder largely failed though there were clashes with left-wing extremists in East London in the 1930s. Mosley was imprisoned during World War II.

EDEN, ANTHONY (1897–1977)

British prime minister (1955–57). Eden took over at Number 10 from Winston Churchill. His term in office was brief, though, dominated by the Suez Crisis of 1956. Egypt had nationalised the canal, prompting an Anglo-French military response. International condemnation was so high they were forced to withdraw. Eden resigned soon after.

see Suez Crisis

LABOUR PARTY (1900)

British political party. The party was formed in 1900 and first held office in 1924. Its socialist principles were evident during its first government (1945–51), when it introduced the National Health Service and social security. The Labour Party won its most overwhelming victory in 1997 under the leadership of Tony Blair and the banner of New Labour, ousting 18 years of Conservative government. The roots of the Labour Party lie with Keir Hardie and John Burns, who entered Parliament as independent Labour members in 1892, but it took nearly a decade for an official party to be set up. By 1922, however, the party was established enough to be seen as the official opposition party to the Conservatives – a position it has maintained since.

see Tony Blair, Conservative Party

DOUGLAS-HOME, ALEC (1903–95)

British prime minister (1963–64). From an aristocratic background, Douglas-Home renounced his title as Earl of Home to become prime minister. He succeeded Harold Macmillan as Conservative party leader. The party was in a weak state when he took over and was still feeling the effects of the Profumo Affair. His government was defeated at the polls by Harold Wilson's Labour Party in 1964. Home also served as Foreign Secretary in Edward Heath's government between 1970 and 1974.

see Conservative Party, Harold Macmillan

ENTENTE CORDIALE (1904)

British–French diplomatic rapprochement before and during World War I. Both countries used the alliance to draft military plans for use against Germany, whose power both countries feared. The alliance began in 1904 and continued throughout the next decade. They saw the alliance as a way of containing the threat of Germany. The joint plans formed the basis of the Allied strategy when war broke out in 1914.

see World War I

SINN FEIN (1905)

Irish nationalist political party founded in 1905. In Gaelic, the term means 'We Ourselves'. The founder was Arthur Griffith, a journalist from Dublin. The party's popularity grew through the failure of the Irish Home Rule Association to get any substantial reforms from London. Under Eamon De Valera's leadership it won, in 1918, a majority of votes in southern Ireland. Its victorious MPs decided not to go to Westminster, seeking to set up an alternative government in Ireland. The party split after the Easter Rising, as some members wanted a full republic. Towards the end of the century, its fortunes were revived, as it became the political wing of the republican movement. It currently holds 18 seats in the Northern Ireland Assembly and is headed by Gerry Adams.

see Irish Free State

▲ *ABOVE: Gerry Adams at a Sinn Fein press conference*

CALLAGHAN, JAMES (B. 1912)

British prime minister (1976–79). Callaghan's leadership came during a turbulent period in British political history. He led a government that went to the International Monetary Fund for a loan and oversaw the 'Winter of Discontent' in 1979, where wholesale worker dissatisfaction led to widespread strikes. Given a vote of no confidence by the House of Commons, Callaghan went to the polls and was defeated by Margaret Thatcher, heralding an 18-year period of domination for the Conservative Party.

see Margaret Thatcher

EASTER RISING (1916)

Uprising in Dublin, Ireland, protesting against British rule. The fighting involved about 3,000 men from organisations opposed to the British, including the Irish Republican Brotherhood and the Citizen Army. Fighting commenced on 24 April when the rebels took up positions in the centre of Dublin. The leaders hoped others would pick up their armed opposition in the country but their hopes proved unfounded. Within a weeks the fighting was over. However, although the uprising proved unsuccessful, the British authorities' repressive response fostered widespread resentment. Fifteen of the leaders were executed. Thousands of others were imprisoned. Politically, the uprising increased support for Sinn Fein.

see Home Rule, Sinn Fein

▶ RIGHT: Easter Rising in Dublin

HEATH, EDWARD (B.1916)

British prime minister (1970–74). An MP from 1950 until 2001, Heath has served British politics for over half a century. He was elected as prime minister in 1970 but his time in government was marked by deep industrial unrest that eventually saw him ousted by the electorate. A pro-European, his biggest achievement was to sign Britain up as a member of the European Economic Community. He was the last of the 'One Nation' Tory leaders before the more abrasive Margaret Thatcher took control.

◄ *see* Margaret Thatcher

WILSON, HAROLD (1916–95)

British prime minister (1964–70, 1974–76). Wilson helped to shape British politics in the 1960s and 1970s. He was first elected as an MP in 1945 and succeeded Hugh Gaitskell as leader of the Labour Party in 1963 while it was still in opposition. He first became prime minister in October 1964. Famous for smoking a pipe, Wilson was again elected in 1974, ousting his great Tory rival, Ted Heath. But he resigned only two years into his second term as prime minister for reasons that have never been properly explained. Later in life he suffered from Parkinson's disease.

COOPERATIVE PARTY (1917)

Political party. Formed in 1917, it was closely associated with the Labour Party. It emerged from the cooperative movement that sought to protect consumers by forming societies that made and sold produce without profit. Socialist Robert Owen pioneered the movement in the nineteenth century with the building of his model community in New Lanark.

◄ *see* New Lanark, Robert Owen

AMRITSAR MASSACRE (1919)

The killing of 379 Indians on 13 April 1919 by British troops in Amritsar, Punjab. A further 1,200 were injured. During World War I, over a million Indian soldiers served in the British armed forces. Half of these came from the Punjab. Once the war was over, Britain introduced the Rowlatt

Acts, which extended wartime emergency measures into peacetime. Those killed at Amritsar were protesting against these Acts. General Reginald Dyer led a force of 50 soldiers who fired 1,650 rounds of ammunition into a crowd of 10,000 unarmed people. The issue resurfaced in October 1997, when on a state visit to India, the queen resisted calls to apologise to India for the massacre.

IRA (1919)

Militant organisation campaigning for an independent Irish state. The Irish Republican Army was formed in 1919, helping to establish the Irish Free State in 1921. The movement split and was mostly unheard of between the 1920s and the advent of the Troubles in the late 1960s. The modern-day movement divided into the Officials and the Provisionals, the latter concerned with ejecting the British from Ireland. The Provisionals used terror to try and achieve their aims and were behind attacks such as the pub bombings in Guildford and Birmingham and the death of Earl Mountbatten. Following the limited success of the peace process, the organisation has split further with a faction known as the Real IRA continuing the violent struggle.

◆ *see* Northern Ireland

NORTHERN IRELAND

Country formed by six counties in the north-east of Ireland. The counties are Antrim, Armagh, Down, Fermanagh, Londonderry (Derry) and Tyrone. The Government of Ireland Act 1920 established the country. Following the peace progress in the 1990s and the Good Friday Agreement, Northern Ireland has once again become an autonomous region within the United Kingdom with its own Assembly and limited powers to make law. This followed almost 30 years of direct rule from Westminster, initiated during the height of the troubles. Prior to that, from 1921 to 1972, there was a Parliament at Stormont. The government was always composed of a majority of Ulster Unionists, a party that reflected the wishes of the majority Protestant community. The history of Northern Ireland has been shaped by British

rule there over the centuries. During the 1960s a civil rights movement was vociferous in trying to eradicate the discrimination among the Catholic minority. This discrimination was felt most keenly in jobs and housing. Protestant reaction to the movement led to the intervention of the British Army and Stormont was suspended in 1972, foreshadowing a rise in sectarian attacks.

 *see* Good Friday Agreement

IRISH FREE STATE (1922)

The state created by the Irish Free State Agreement Act 1922. Ireland was divided as a consequence of the Act, with the north, a largely protestant area, ruled from Belfast, and the south ruled from Dublin. The partition and other consequences of the act were extremely contentious. Michael Collins, one of the signatories of the Act, was murdered. It gave the new state limited autonomy and still meant the Irish had to accept the British monarchy. Republicans rejected the treaty and a civil war lasting until 1923 was launched. The Free State forces eventually overcame the Republicans. The first president of the republic was William Cosgrave. Eamon De Valera replaced him in 1932. In 1937 the state changed its name to Eire, the Gaelic name for Ireland. It remained a member of the

◄ LEFT: John Hume and Seamus Mallon following the announcement of the verdict of the referendum on the Good Friday Stormont peace agreement

Commonwealth until 1949 when it changed its name to the Republic of Ireland. It became a member of the European Economic Community in 1973 and has enthusiastically embraced European government. It had the fastest growing European economy at the end of the 1990s and the beginning of the new century.

◆ *see* Eamon De Valera

THATCHER, MARGARET (B. 1925)

First female British prime minister who won three general elections and ruled from 1979 to 1990. Her rule caused deep splits in the country between those who supported her and those who opposed her. It was marked by the Falklands conflict of 1982, the miners' strike in 1985 and a programme of privatisation. She first served in government in the 1960s. She was elected as Tory leader in 1975 and took the party to the right of the political spectrum. Elected in 1979, her government's policies were deeply unpopular at first, provoking many inner-city riots. However, the success of the Falklands resurrected her fortunes and she was returned in 1983 and 1987, continuing policies of low taxation, inflation and public spending. Her economic policies transformed Britain but at a high social cost. Her image abroad was of a tough leader, the 'Iron Lady'. She was eventually relinquished of her leadership in 1990 when Tory MPs saw her as an electoral liability. She described this as a 'betrayal of the highest order'. She was succeeded by John Major.

◆ *see* Conservative Party, John Major

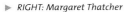

► RIGHT: Margaret Thatcher

COMMONWEALTH, THE (1931)

Group of independent sovereign states, formerly part of the British Empire. Some countries remain dependencies of the United Kingdom, but all are voluntary members of the Commonwealth. There is no charter of constitution for the Commonwealth because it does not operate officially on political or economic grounds. Instead it is run according to traditional and sentimental rules. Members of the Commonwealth benefit from a nepotistic relationship with one another so there are diplomatic advantages to be had from membership.

see British Empire

MAJOR, JOHN (B. 1943)

British prime minister (1990–97). Major took over as prime minister in 1990 when Margaret Thatcher resigned and led the Conservatives to a somewhat surprising victory at the 1992 general election. He was first elected as an MP in 1979 and Thatcher made him Chancellor of the Exchequer in October 1989. Wide divisions within his own party on the issue of Europe marked his time as prime minister. His party never recovered from the

◄ LEFT: John Major

collapse of the British entry in the European Exchange Rate Mechanism in 1993, an event that became known as 'Black Wednesday'. His party was elected out of office in a stunning defeat by Tony Blair's Labour in May 1997.

◆ *see* Conservative Party, Margaret Thatcher

NORTH ATLANTIC TREATY ORGANISATION (NATO) (1949)

Military alliance. Formed in 1949 and originally composed of 12 countries from Europe and North America including Britain, France, Canada and the United States. Greece, Turkey and Germany later became members. Originally it was a Cold War organisation and thus was composed of countries from the west. However, since the collapse of the Soviet Union, it has remodelled itself as a 'peacekeeping' body. NATO sanctioned and led the air raids over Kosovo in 1999.

◆ *see* World War II

ROME, TREATY OF (1952)

International agreement that saw the formation of the EEC. On 25 March 1952 six European countries signed two international agreements. Belgium, France, West Germany, Italy, Luxembourg and the Netherlands established themselves as the European Economic Community (EEC) and became members of the Atomic Energy Commission (Euratom). Both of these agreements were signed in the capital of Italy and were seen as a bond of friendship between nations, so they became known as the Treaties of Rome. The EEC has since become the European Union (EU) in 1993. The EU membership now comprises many more of the European nations. The collapse of communism has resulted in further applications being submitted.

◆ *see* European Union

BLAIR, TONY (B. 1953)

British prime minister (1997–). Blair, a former barrister, led Labour in May 1997 to its most comprehensive election victory, ending 18 years of Conservative rule. It won 418 seats, the highest ever recorded by Labour, and took its largest share of votes since the 1960s. At 44, Blair was the youngest prime minister since Lord Liverpool in 1812. His style is often described as 'presidential' and he is accused of relying too heavily on 'spin' to get across Labour's political message. Blair has committed British troops to action in Afghanistan, Iraq, Kosovo and Sierra Leone. He has introduced a Scottish Parliament, a Welsh Assembly, maintained the peace process in Northern Ireland and partially reformed the House of Lords.

◆ see Labour Party

SUEZ CRISIS (1956)

Attack by British and French forces on Egypt after it had decided to nationalise the Suez Canal Company in which Britain had a controlling stake. Stung by enormous international condemnation of the attack, British forces were forced to withdraw and it eventually led to the resignation of prime minister Anthony Eden. The British had controlled the canal, which connects the Red Sea with the Mediterranean, since 1875. In 1888 Britain became the guarantor of the canal's neutral status.

◆ see Anthony Eden

▶ RIGHT: British troops search local people during the Suez crisis

BLOODY SUNDAY (1972)

Name given to the day in which 13 unarmed protestors were killed in the Bogside, Derry (30 January 1972) after British soldiers opened fire on civilians protesting against internment, brought in the previous year. The killings exacerbated the tense situation in Northern Ireland.

see Northern Ireland

ANGLO-IRISH AGREEMENT (1985)

Agreement signed in 1985 by the British and Irish governments to increase the level of co-operation between the two countries. It was signed by prime minister Margaret Thatcher and the taoiseach Garret Fitzgerald. The agreement sought to limit terrorism and was a sign of the greater trust developing between London and Dublin. Contentiously, it gave Dublin a greater say in affairs in Northern Ireland. The agreement proved deeply unpopular with unionists who accused the British government of paving the way for control of the North by the Republic and the 'No Surrender' which reasserted the loyalists' position was launched.

see Margaret Thatcher

DEVOLUTION (1998)

Tony Blair's Labour government established an elected Scottish Assembly and smaller Welsh Assembly in 1998 after both countries voted for their own Parliaments. The Scottish Parliament, based at Holyrood, controls a budget of around £17 billion and has tax-raising powers. The budget in Wales is £7 billion, but with no tax-raising powers.

◆ see Scottish Assembly, Welsh Assembly

▲ ABOVE: As a member of the House of Lords Baron Elder of Kirkcaldy represents the continuation of the strong line of Scottish interests in the United Kingdom, enhanced now by devolution and the Scottish Parliament.

GOOD FRIDAY AGREEMENT (1998)

Political agreement that paved the way for a directly elected Northern Irish assembly. The agreement formed part of the peace process that had made faltering progress from the beginning of the 1990s. Although this process had been challenged intermittently, especially through the Omagh bombing in the summer of 1998, the Assembly was still elected with Ulster Unionist David Trimble becoming First Minister.

◆ see Northern Ireland

SCOTTISH ASSEMBLY (1998)

Autonomous government for Scotland created in 1998 with 129 members. The First Minister was Donald Dewar but, following his death, Henry McLeish replaced him. It has minor tax-raising powers but has already shown that it can pursue an independent path from Westminster, particularly over issues such as health provision and education

◆ *see* Devolution, Welsh Assembly

WELSH ASSEMBLY (1998)

Political body created in 1998 which allows a limited form of self-rule in Wales. It comprises 60 members and has the highest number of women members of Parliament outside Sweden and Norway. It controls a Budget of £7bn but it has no tax-raising powers. The current first secretary is Rhodri Morgan and the assembly is housed in Cardiff. Labour are the majority party with 30 of the 60 seats.

◆ *see* Devolution, Scottish Assembly

▲ ABOVE: Constitutionally the Queen remains sovereign of Wales as part of Great Britain

RELIGION

JEWS

Providers of commercial services and victims of persecution in an era of Christian dogmatism in Britain. Jews first traded in England in the sixth century, but it was at William the Conqueror's invitation that they first became significant in England's economy, being money-lenders at a time when Christianity forbade usury. The Norman and Angevin kings continued to use Jews, but public opinion often showed resentment. In 1189 the Third Crusade encouraged massacres back in England and in 1190 the Jews of York committed mass suicide rather than be murdered by their baronial debtors. Mistrust increased: the Statute of the Jewry, 1275, appointed Christians as wardens of their record chests and stigmatised them with compulsory yellow badges. Some Jews were even hung for coin-clipping. In 1290 Edward I expelled the Jews and in the following century Christian attitudes towards usury relaxed: Italian bankers arrived in England. By the Enlightenment the 20,000 Jews in London were tolerated, but largely poor.

◙ *see* Crusades, Edward I, Enlightenment, William I

ARCHBISHOP OF CANTERBURY

Primate of the Church of England. An archbishop has episcopal authority over his diocese, as does a bishop, but he also has jurisdiction over the other bishops in a province. The title of Archbishop of Canterbury first emerged in the

▶ *RIGHT: A Roman Catholic Service*

seventh century. It is primarily due to St Augustine's landing in Kent that Canterbury, rather than London, developed as the principal see in England. Significant archbishops have included martyrs and dictators, notably Thomas Becket and William Laud.

see St Augustine, Thomas Becket, William Laud

CHRISTIANITY

Exists in Britain in several denominations, predominantly Protestant, Roman Catholic and Nonconformist. Consistently the dominant religion of Britain since the end of the Dark Ages, though, it has an extraordinarily low rate of church attendance today.

In AD 313 Constantine was converted yet the spread of Christianity throughout Roman Britain remained slow. Christianity in Dark-Age Britain developed along two main strands: the Roman Christianity of Augustine and the Celtic Christianity of Aidan. The Protestant Reformation of the sixteenth century caused the next major religious divide, namely between Protestants and Roman Catholics.

The commercial and religious success of the Middle Ages led to incredible architectural feats in praise of God, namely cathedrals such as Salisbury. Equally, eras of trauma produced unusual sects of Christianity, for example, the Black Death and the Flagellants, or the Commonwealth and the Diggers and the Fifth Monarchy Men. The emergence of modern science with the Renaissance encouraged the secularisation of western Europe and the Industrial Revolution, with its social ills and the consequent rise of social conscience, all encouraged a philanthropic manifestation of Christianity in Britain.

see St Aidan, St Augustine, Black Death, Flagellants, Industrial Revolution, Roman Catholicism, Protestantism, Reformation, Salisbury Cathedral

ANDREW, ST (D. c. AD 60)

One of the 12 Apostles and patron saint of Scotland. A fisherman follower of John the Baptist until Jesus called him and Peter to become 'fishers of men'. The earliest record of his crucifixion is the fourth century, and it was not until the Middle Ages that it is recorded as an X-shape cross, as in the Scots flag. His relics travelled the Mediterranean, but Pope Paul VI finally returned his head to Patras, the place of his death, in 1964. His feast day is 30 November.

ROMAN CATHOLICISM

Major branch of Christianity, headed by the pope. Roman Catholics believe in Transubstantiation. Rome was established as headquarters of the western Church in the third century and during the Dark Ages papal authority developed. In 1054 the Church split and so the distinct Roman Catholic branch emerged. By the sixteenth century the demand for reform of this long-established faith covered most of northern Europe.

After the Dissolution of the Monasteries, the Roman Catholic Church in England not only lost much of its influence, but also its wealth. Initially tolerant regarding religion, even Elizabeth executed some recusants. Roman Catholicism attempted to regain pre-eminence, firstly by the persecutions of the Inquisition, then by the reforms of the Council of Trent. Foxe's Book of Martyrs, the Armada and the Gunpowder Plot, 1605, contributed to Roman Catholicism being associated with treason and xenophobia (particularly fear of Spain), thus anti-Catholic restrictions were implemented. Catholics fared little better in Britain during the High Anglican era of Laud and the Puritan extremism of the Commonwealth. Then fear of Catholics re-emerged, this time due to the Treaty of Dover and Charles II's alleged promise to re-establish Catholicism in England. This resulted in the anti-Catholic Test Act, 1673.

The accession of a Roman Catholic king, James II, and the birth of his Catholic heir, were the catalysts for Protestant reaction, namely the Glorious Revolution: Roman Catholicism was consigned to the sidelines of power in England. Today the principal Roman Catholic place of worship in England is Westminster Cathedral.

◆ *see* Counter-Reformation, Reformation, Test Acts

ALBAN, ST (AD 3RD CENTURY)

First British Christian martyr. Bede records that Alban was a Roman soldier who, on sheltering a fugitive priest, subsequently converted to Christianity. They exchanged clothes and Alban was martyred in his place sometime between AD 209 and AD 304. By AD 429 a church had been established on the site of his martyrdom and later the abbey of St Albans was built there. His martyrdom was typical of the periodic Roman persecution of Christians.

GEORGE, ST (c. AD 3RD CENTURY)

Christian martyr and patron saint of England. Legends about him date from the sixth century. Most famous is his slaying of a dragon in order to rescue a maiden. By the eighth century he was revered in England, then Edward III appointed him patron saint of the Order of the Garter. Finally he became England's patron saint.

CHURCH OF SCOTLAND

National Church of Scotland, but not the established Church. The first church in Scotland was probably established by St Ninian c. AD 400. With the settling of Iona, c. AD 563, by Columba, religious scholarship in Scotland gained worldwide respect. In 1192 the Church in Scotland became subject only and directly to the pope by a special decree.

Interestingly because of this allegiance Scotland initially rejected the Protestant Reformation more vehemently than England had, but by August 1560 the Protestants in Scotland had banned papal authority and adopted John Knox's Scots Confession.

For the next century Episcopalians and Presbyterians competed, until William and Mary's backing of Presbyterianism. In 1921 the State and the Church of Scotland became disassociated and attempts to affiliate the churches of Scotland and England in 1959 and 1971 have failed. Its archiepiscopal sees remain St Andrews (established 1472) and Glasgow (established 1492).

⬥ *see* Saint Columba, Episcopacy, Henry VIII, Iona, John Knox, Presbyterianism, William and Mary

DIVINE RIGHT OF KINGS

Doctrine of monarchical authority. The divine right was the belief that monarchs received their authority directly from God and were therefore unanswerable to anyone else. Originally a medieval idea, it came to England from Scotland via James I.

⬥ *see* Charles I, James I

PATRICK, ST (AD 5TH CENTURY)

Patron saint of Ireland. Patrick, a Romanized Briton, lived near the Severn until the Irish enslaved him. During these six years as a herdsman Patrick was converted, escaped back to England, then felt compelled to return to Ireland. He was at least partly responsible for the conversion of the Picts and Anglo-Saxons, but his English ecclesiastical superiors disliked him. By the seventh century the legends, that Patrick drove the snakes out of Ireland and used the shamrock (subsequently the national flower of Ireland) to explain the Trinity, were prevalent. His humble diary, Confessio, contributed to his long-lasting popularity. His feast day is 17 March.

◆ *see* Anglo-Saxons

CANTERBURY CATHEDRAL (AD 6TH CENTURY)

Cathedral of the primal see of England. Established by St Augustine at the end of the sixth century, Canterbury has remained the Christian headquarters of England ever since. The existing cathedral dates from 1070–89, although it has been added to several times. The site of Becket's murder, the cathedral houses his shrine and consequently receives many pilgrims. In the sixteenth century the large crypt was granted to the Huguenots and a weekly service is still held in French.

◆ *see* Archbishop of Canterbury, St Augustine, Thomas Becket, Huguenots

CHURCH OF WALES

Largely ruled over by the Church of England. The origins of the Church of Wales are usually ascribed to the legendary sixth-century Age of Saints. In the twelfth and thirteenth centuries failure to establish an archbishopric in Wales led to Canterbury's domination. The Church in Wales was consistently poorer than the Church in England, not having the same political power, and during the Reformation it received the Bible and Prayer Book in the vernacular only thanks to private initiative. Nonconformism undermined

▶ RIGHT: Henry VIII brought the churches of England and Wales under his control in the 1530s.

the established Church of Wales in the eighteenth century and finally, in 1920, the Church of Wales became disestablished and therefore distanced from the Church of England.

■ *see* Church of England

DAVID, ST (c. AD 520–600)

Patron saint of Wales. David's mother was St Non and he was born in St Bride's Bay, Pembrokeshire, and educated in Cardigan. He moved the headquarters of Church government from Caeleon to Mynyw, present-day St David's and the cathedral city in western Wales. Pope Calixtus II is said to have canonised David in about 1120, but as with many details relating to his life there is a degree of uncertainty. His feast day is 1 March.

COLUMBA, ST (c. AD 522–97)

Statesman, hermit and missionary to Scotland. Born in County Donegal, Columba carried Christianity from Ireland to Iona. Here he established the most prestigious monastery of the time, from which Aidan was to convert western Scotland. Columba also participated in the council of Druim Cetta, which decided issues of monarchical status within Ireland. He lived his last years on Iona, writing hymns and already being regarded as a saint. His feast day is 9 June.

■ *see* Saint Aidan,

AIDAN, ST (c. AD 600–51)

Saint and founder of Lindisfarne monastery. Aidan was born in Ireland and then became a monk on the isle of Iona. He went on to establish the monastery on Lindisfarne (Holy Island), convert the vast and prestigious kingdom of Northumbria and become its bishop. He and his missionaries worked under the monarchs Oswald and Oswy. Bede records Aidan's piety and preaching skills. He died on 31 August, subsequently his feast day.

◆ *see* Celtic Christianity, Lindisfarne Gospels

LINDISFARNE GOSPELS, THE (AD 7TH/8TH CENTURY)

Hiberno-Saxon illuminated manuscripts. They were illuminated in a style that amalgamated Irish, classical, Byzantine and Saxon influences and are renowned for their rich colour, detail and beauty. Probably produced for a bishop of Lindisfarne, Eadrith, they were made by the monastic community on Lindisfarne, established by Aidan in AD 635 and abandoned in AD 875 because of Danish attacks. The monks fled with St Cuthbert's body and presumably also the manuscripts, so explaining their remarkable survival. They are now kept in the British Museum.

◆ *see* Saint Aidan, Book of Kells

AUGUSTINE, ST (D. c. AD 604)

First Archbishop of Canterbury. Pope Gregory I chose Augustine to convert the predominantly pagan population of southern England. In AD 597 they landed on the Isle of Thanet, Kent. King Ethelbert welcomed them and on Christmas Day 1,000 of his subjects were converted. Gregory ordered that 12 suffragan bishops be appointed and Augustine effectively assigned himself first Archbishop of Canterbury. Augustine's feast day is 26 May in England and Wales.

◆ *see* Archbishop of Canterbury, Celtic Christianity, Ethelbert

HILDA, ST (AD 614–80)

Founder of Whitby Abbey and key player in the Synod of Whitby. Hilda was baptised c. AD 627. In AD 657 she founded her unisex abbey (Whitby or Streaneshalch Abbey) of which Caedmon was a significant member.

Being now a prime Anglo-Saxon abbess, Hilda led the Celtic party in the Synod of Whitby, unfortunately unsuccessfully.

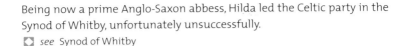 *see* Synod of Whitby

WHITBY, SYNOD OF (AD 663–64)

Council of the Anglo-Saxon church to discuss Roman or Celtic usage in Britain. Northumbria was originally converted by the Celts, but by AD 662 the Roman church had influence there. Hilda hosted the synod at her abbey of Whitby and with bishops Colman and Cedd she led the Celtic church; Bishop Wilfrid led the Roman church. A key issue was the date of Easter and Wilfrid won the argument. Due to the outcome of the synod the English church became more closely linked with Rome.

see Celtic Christianity, Hilda, Oswy, Roman Christianity

ALCUIN (c. AD 732–804)

Innovator, educator and cleric, but not a saint. Alcuin lived in York for 50 years before becoming the pre-eminent scholar at Charlemagne's court at Aachen in AD 781. His formative influence in western Europe was his development of the Frankish liturgy and his introduction of Humanist thought. Despite being only a deacon he retains his place in history: his legacy of approximately 300 Latin letters remain a valuable contemporary source.

BENEDICTINE ORDER

Educational monastic order, influential in northern and western Europe, from Charlemagne's reign until the twelfth century. Whilst the Benedictine, Lanfranc, was Archbishop of Canterbury extensive church reform was carried out in England.

see Archbishop Lanfranc

KELLS, BOOK OF (AD 8TH–9TH CENTURY)

Pre-eminent Celtic illuminated manuscripts. Produced on Iona, the highly coloured and detailed illustrations show Irish and Northumbrian influences. Their name probably originates from the migration of the Ionan community to Kells in Ireland in the face of Norse invasion. They are now kept in Trinity College, Dublin.

see Columba, Vikings

DUNSTAN, ST (AD 924–88)

Hermit, noble and Archbishop of Canterbury. A chief adviser to Edmund and Eadred of Wessex, Dunstan's career was marked by his conflict with Edwy, AD 955, regarding Edwy's monarchical laxity. On Edgar's succession Dunstan became Archbishop of Canterbury and an era of major monastic reform and intellectual blossoming occurred.

see Archbishop of Canterbury, Edwy

WINCHESTER CATHEDRAL

Longest cathedral in Britain, at 169 m (556 ft). In the seventh century the West Saxon episcopal see moved to Winchester and the cathedral consequently houses Alfred the Great's bones. Building began in the latter part of the eleventh century and during William of Wykeham's lifetime the fourteenth-century perpendicular nave was built. Winchester not only had a religious role: Alfred the Great encouraged education there and it developed as a seat of royal government.

see Alfred the Great

LANFRANC, ARCHBISHOP (c. 1005–89)

William the Conqueror's Archbishop of Canterbury (1070–79). The Italian Benedictine, Lanfranc, began his career teaching in Normandy. In 1070, however, Stigand was deposed and Lanfranc became the first Norman primate. He initiated reorganisation of the English Church and Norman bishops replaced Anglo-Saxons. He also secured the younger brother William II's succession, rather than Robert Curthose's.

◆ *see* William I

ANSELM, ST (c. 1033–1109)

Archbishop of Canterbury and player in the investiture controversy. Born in Lombardy, Anselm's intellectual, pious career continued on the continent until William II appointed him Archbishop of Canterbury in 1093. Then arose the investiture controversy. The Council of Rockingham was called to decide whether it was a monarchical or papal right to grant an ecclesiastical position: the bishops backed the king. Anselm left for Europe and wrote his key work, Cur Deus Homo? ('Why Did God Become Man?'). Henry I recalled Anselm but in 1103–06 the controversy re-emerged and Anselm again went into exile. In 1163 Becket submitted Anselm's life for canonisation.

◆ *see* Thomas Becket, Henry I, William II

CRUSADES (1095–1270)

Military and religious expeditions to the Holy Land initiated by the popes. During this time pilgrimages and relics were in vogue, commercial ventures were undergoing expansion and the Turks were threatening the Byzantine Church. Thus the popes' crusading calls were welcomed initially. In the First Crusade Jerusalem fell to the Christians in 1099. The Second Crusade was a failure and in 1187 Saladin recaptured Jerusalem. It was in the Third Crusade (1189–92), under the leadership of Richard I, that England played a more prominent role. Despite Richard's victory at Arsuf, which allowed the crusaders to gain Joppa, the

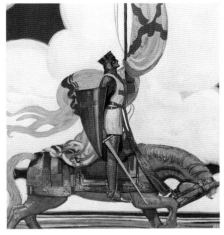

◀ *LEFT: A Crusader Knight*

Christians failed to recapture Jerusalem and infighting emerged, culminating in Richard's kidnap. By the Fourth Crusade (1198), the crusaders sidetracked and aided Venice's trading ventures, sacking Constantinople in 1204. Consequently the Byzantine and Latin churches were deeply divided.

▶ *see* Richard I, Jews

ROCKINGHAM, COUNCIL OF (1095)

Synod to resolve William II's and Anselm's conflict over investiture. The bishops agreed with William that he should choose his own pope. Anselm, however, supported the pope and wanted his own religious appointment to be out of the king's jurisdiction. After his defeat at Rockingham Anselm left for Rome until Henry I's reign.

▶ *see* Saint Anselm, William II

CISTERCIAN ORDER (1098)

Ascetic monastic order founded in 1098. Dissatisfaction with the Benedictine Order's laxity led to the emergence of the Cistercians. Manual labour and uniformity between houses were their tenets. In 1120 the first sister house was established and that century was their apogee.

▶ *see* Benedictine Order, Dissolution of the Monasteries, Roman Catholicism

BREAKSPEAR, NICHOLAS (1100–59)

Also known as Adrian IV: the only English pope to date. Born in Abbots
Langley, in 1152 Breakspear successfully reorganised the Church hierarchy
in Scandinavia, before being elected pope in 1154. He argued with the
Sicilian Frederick Barbarossa and introduced the bill, Laudabiliter, that
allegedly granted Ireland to Henry II.

BECKET, THOMAS (c. 1118–70)

Archbishop of Canterbury, martyr and English saint. Becket's rise was
meteoric, becoming firstly archdeacon of Canterbury, then chancellor,
then Archbishop of Canterbury (1162). On being appointed archbishop
he now miraculously cast off his flashy clothes and adopted the
austerity of the Gregorian reforms, thus sowing the seed of conflict
between himself and Henry II. The reforms concerned jurisdiction over
clerical trials and Henry opposed Becket, who fled to France (1164–70).
Henry then confiscated Becket's diocesan lands, but in 1170 agreed
to the restoration of his lands and position, much to the general
population's approval and consequently Henry's aggravation.
Apparently four knights took Henry's request to be rid of the
'meddlesome priest' literally: on 29 December, his feast day since 1173,
he was slain in Canterbury Cathedral, and remains a heroic martyr to
his ideals.

◻ *see* Canterbury Cathedral, Henry II

EDMUND, ST (1175–1240)

Outspoken Archbishop of Canterbury and scholar. Edmund introduced
the teaching of Aristotelian philosophy to western Europe and his
seminal work, Speculum Ecclesiae, was a major contribution to medieval
theology. Edmund excommunicated Henry III after clashing with him

over Church rights. Henry therefore delayed the referral for his canonisation until 1247. Patron saint of the weather.

⬥ *see* Henry III

DOMINICAN ORDER (1215)

Mendicant Roman Catholic order, also known as the Black Friars. Established by St Dominic in France, there are also Dominican sisters. From 1278 the order was based on Thomas Aquinas's ideas. The Dominicans' extensive membership aided the implementation of the Inquisition.

⬥ *see* Roman Catholicism

BACON, ROGER (c. 1220–92)

English Franciscan polymath. Initially Bacon was influenced by Aristotle. Among many inventions, Bacon proposed flying machines with flapping wings, and studied the rainbow using lenses. In 1257, whilst very ill, Bacon entered the Franciscan order. They disapproved of his teeming ideas so Bacon produced his great work, Opus Maius, in secret. Bacon was imprisoned by the Franciscans between 1277 and 1279.

⬥ *see* Franciscan Order

SALISBURY CATHEDRAL (1220)

Highest spire in Britain at 123 m (404 ft). Its location at New Sarum was allegedly determined by an arrow being shot from Old Sarum. Purbeck marble was used for the slender columns and the architecture is unique, being almost completely early English.

▶ *RIGHT: Salisbury Cathedral*

FLAGELLANTS (14TH CENTURY)

Fourteenth-century sadomaschistic religious sect. Many people regarded the Black Death as punishment from God. In the aftermath minority sects grew up. Possibly the most disturbed were the Flagellants, who would walk the streets each whipping the back of the person in front in an attempt to purge them of their sins.

◆ *see* Black Death

LOLLARDS (14TH CENTURY)

Fourteenth-century religious reformers. As Christianity began to develop in the Middle Ages people evolved different opinions on how it should be practised. The Roman Catholic division celebrated their faith with a flamboyant style which grated with followers of the Orthodox Church. In the fourteenth century a religious reformer, John Wycliffe, asserted that the Bible, and not the Church, was the supreme authority. His followers, the Lollards, believed the church should help people to live lives of evangelical poverty, thereby imitating Christ. They abhorred showy ritual, particularly the transubstantiation of the bread and wine of the Eucharist.

◆ *see* John Wycliffe

WYCLIFFE, JOHN (c. 1330–84)

Forebear of the Protestant Reformation. Ordained a clergyman, Wycliffe was a controversial yet popular figure. He advocated preaching and the rejection of worldly goods and corruption: views that became the backbone of the Lollards. Arrested in 1377 for the political slant of his religious views, Wycliffe nevertheless supported the Peasants' Revolt in 1381, and consequently much of his work was condemned. Less conscientiously, he practised absenteeism, a corruption he opposed, from his parish of Westbury-on-Trym.

◆ *see* Peasants' Revolt, Protestant Reformation

JULIAN OF NORWICH (1342– c. 1416)

Medieval mystic and writer. On 13 May 1373, now her remembrance day, Julian was healed after experiencing visions of Christ's suffering and of the Virgin Mary. She then wrote up her visions in Revelations of Divine Love, which also included discussions of predestination and evil. She ended her days as a recluse in Norwich.

BEATON, DAVID (c. 1494–1546)

Scottish cardinal. Beaton had a tumultuous career. In 1539 he became Archbishop of St Andrews, then in 1544 papal legate and consequently quasi-ruler of Scotland. He encouraged the persecution of Protestants: George Wisheart, for example, was burnt at the stake under Beaton's orders. In turn, avenging Scottish nobles murdered him.

🔹 *see* Church of Scotland

▶ *RIGHT: The Cardinal sentenced many protestants to the stake*

HUGUENOTS

French Protestant minority in the sixteenth and seventeenth centuries. In 1523 the first French Protestant was burned at the stake and executions such as this soon escalated into nationwide massacres and mass imprisonment, such as the St Bartholomew's Day Massacre, 1572. With the Protestant King Henri IV's accession to the throne the Edict of Nantes, 1598, gave Huguenots religious freedom. This improved situation continued until Louis XIV's Revocation of the Edict of Nantes in 1685 when 250,000 French Protestants fled abroad. In England they became eminent craftsmen, such as silversmiths.

🔹 *see* Canterbury Cathedral

POLE, REGINALD (1500–58)

Cardinal of Mary Tudor. After Henry's Break with Rome, Pole sided with the pope and left for Padua. Returning to England in 1554, as the papal legate, he encouraged a return to Catholicism. In 1556 he became Archbishop of Canterbury, but died demoralised in 1558 after papal accusations of heresy due to Anglo-Spanish alliances.

🔁 *see* Break with Rome, Counter-Reformation, Henry VIII, Mary Tudor

PRESBYTERIANISM

Doctrine supporting Church government by presbytery. Presbyterianism sees Christ as the head of the Church and the members as equals, from which the ministers are elected for a term of office, although ordination is for life. Several presbyteries combined make a synod, and the central authority is the General Assembly. Presbyterianism developed out of the Protestant Reformation and became very popular in Scotland, where it was propagated by Calvin. However, the Calvinism of James I was less extreme: when he declared, 'no bishop, no king', at the Hampton Court Conference he was denying the implementation of Presbyterianism. Religious intolerance led to some Presbyterians fleeing to America. Presbyterianism's only era of significant power in England was during the English Civil War and its conflict with Episcopalianism led to the National Covenant and the Bishops' Wars in Scotland. In 1972 Presbyterianism in England and Wales took the form of the United Reformed Church.

🔁 *see* Covenant Martyrs, English Civil War, Episcopacy National Covenant, Protestantism

PURITANISM (LATE 16TH AND 17TH CENTURIES)

Doctrine aimed at purifying the Church of England. Puritans developed Calvinism: combining strict Bible reading and his theory of predestination they concluded that they alone were the 'elect'. Dissatisfaction emerged with Elizabeth I's religious settlement of 1559 as some regarded it as having too many remants of Roman Catholicism. Also separatist Puritans emerged who wanted the Church and State to be separate. Under Charles I and Laud intolerance towards Puritans increased. In contrast the Commonwealth was tolerant to Puritan sects such as Levellers, Diggers, Fifth Monarchy Men and Quakers. In Wales and Scotland Puritanism consistently had proportionally more dominance than in England. Although a disparate group, Puritans were recognisable by their black and white dress and rigid morality.

◆ *see* Calvinism, William Laud

KNOX, JOHN (c. 1514–72)

Leader of the Reformation in Scotland. Details of Knox's early life are few, but it is known that by 1540 he had been ordained and in 1547 he unwillingly became leader of the Scottish Reformation. After a 19-month capture by the French in 1547–48, Knox helped Edward VI with his Protestant reforms. In 1559 Roman Catholicism ceased to be the official religion in Scotland and Knox returned from Geneva full of Calvinist ideas. Knox publicised his view that the body and blood were not literally

present at Communion and his idea that ministers should be elected by the people was a key to the Presbyterianism of the future. His quote, in Predestination (1556–58)

◀ *LEFT: John Knox admonishing Mary, Queen of Scotts*

'against the monstrous regiment of women', and his attitude regarding women and religion led to Elizabeth I banning him from England and continual confrontation with Mary, Queen of Scots. Despite his austere language Knox's ideas were moderate when compared with the extremism to come.

◆ *see* Church of Scotland, Elizabeth I, Mary, Queen of Scots, Protestantism, Reformation

PROTESTANTISM

Christian belief that emerged out of the Protestant Reformation. Protestantism was marked by the belief in justification by faith alone and the authority of the Bible. It emerged in England, then the rest of Britain, with Henry VIII's rejection of papal authority and it was furthered by the religious reforms that simultaneously came over from the Continent.

Under Edward VI Protestantism was applied more fanatically, namely via the Prayer Book and the Act of Uniformity, both 1549. The next monarch, Mary Tudor, nicknamed Bloody Mary, burnt several hundred Protestants at the stake, including the bishops, Latimer and Ridley, at Oxford in 1555, and the archbishop, Cranmer, 1556. When faced with the flames Latimer presciently declared: 'We shall this day light such a candle, by God's grace, in England, as I trust shall never be put out.' Elizabeth's accession and the Acts of Uniformity and Supremacy, 1559, re-established Protestantism as the religion of England, although her self-professed intent was 'not to make windows into men's souls'.

During the English Civil War and the Commonwealth, mainstream Anglicanism was usurped by minority Puritan sects. With the Restoration Charles II's reign supported Protestantism, but in the form of Anglicanism. Nevertheless wider Protestant dominance and political power led to the Glorious Revolution. From then on Protestantism, manifest in all its denominations and breakaways, remained the main religion of England, Scotland and Wales. The Catholic-Protestant conflict in Ireland continues to this day.

see Break with Rome, Dissolution of the Monasteries, Edward VI, Elizabeth I, Glorious Revolution, Henry VIII, Mary I, Reformation

REFORMATION (16TH CENTURY)

Sixteenth-century reform movement in the western Christian Church. Wycliffe and Erasmus wrote attacks on the corruption within the Church, namely absenteesim and the sale of indulgences and relics. Then Luther acted, famously pinning his 95 theses on the door of Wittenberg Cathedral in October 1517. Luther was not actually anti-pope, just anti-

▲ ABOVE: *Leaders of the Reformation in Europe including Luther (centre)*

corruption; nevertheless Calvin, Zwingli and Knox developed the original Reformation ideas and an independent Protestant church emerged in northern Europe. Henry VIII took advantage of the era of religious change, appointing himself Supreme Head of the Church of England. Religious reform continued to be a key political, and religious, issue in Britain for the next 150 years.

◖ *see* John Calvin, Henry VIII, John Knox, Protestantism, John Wyclif

ANGLICANISM

Pre-eminent branch of Protestantism in England, being the doctrine of the established Church of England. The seeds of Anglicanism were sown with the break with Rome and the Reformation. Charles I and William Laud implemented High Anglicanism, which was intolerant and particularly unacceptable in Scotland. After the Restoration, Charles II made the Church of England the established Church and the whole spectrum of Anglicanism, from Anglo-Catholicism to Evangelical Puritanism, developed. This variety continues to this day.

◖ *see* Break with Rome, Charles I, Elizabeth I, William Laud, Protestantism, Reformation

CHURCH OF ENGLAND

England's national Church since Henry VIII. After his break with Rome an independent Church developed in England. This – subsequently Anglican – Church became the established Church of England, rather than simply the Church in England that it had been previously.

In 1549 Edward VI introduced the Book of Common Prayer. After a temporary, yet violent, Catholic interlude under Mary Tudor, Protestantism and the Church of England resumed under Elizabeth I with the Acts of Supremacy and Uniformity and the Thirty-Nine Articles.

She, however, modestly desired to be only 'governor', rather than 'head' of the Church.

During Charles I's controversial reign the Church of England became High Anglican, abetted by William Laud, Archbishop of Canterbury. After an 11-year respite, due to the Commonwealth and extreme Puritanism, Anglicanism revived with Charles II. The Church of England remains the established Church.

🔹 *see* St Aidan, St Augustine, Catherine of Aragon, Edward VI, Elizabeth I, Henry VIII, William Laud, Mary I, Puritanism, John Wycliffe

BREAK WITH ROME (1532)

Henry VIII's self-appointment as Supreme Head of the Church of England. His request for the annulment of his marriage denied, Henry decided to remove himself from papal authority. His break with Rome provided an opener for the emergent Protestant ideas to take hold in England.

🔹 *see* Dissolution of the Monasteries, Henry VIII, Reformation

JESUITS (1534)

Roman Catholic monastic order, also known as the Society of Jesus. Founded by St Ignatius of Loyola, who wrote Spiritual Exercises, the order's innovations included: lengthy probation, strict obedience, central authority and no female members. The Jesuits largely ignored Wales and their ministry in England was unwelcomed as it encouraged recusancy. English xenophobic fear of Jesuits was realised when the Catholic revival culminated in the Gunpowder Plot. A very significant English Jesuit, Edmund Campion, was hanged and other Jesuits during Elizabeth I's and James I's reigns resorted to hiding in priest holes.

🔹 *see* Recusancy, Roman Catholicism

CALVINISM

Theology developed by John Calvin. Calvinism was a specific branch of Puritanism that linked theology with church organisation: its key idea was Presbyterianism. Calvin studied in Geneva and came to believe in predestination and its relation to the works of the individual. After Calvin's death Calvinism became increasingly intolerant: his successors upheld that Jesus died only for certain souls (the elect).

  ◗ *see* Presbyterianism, Puritanism

DISSOLUTION OF THE MONASTERIES (1536)

Policy of Henry VIII and Thomas Cromwell during the Protestant Reformation. Having appointed himself Supreme Head of the Church, Henry set about destroying the monasteries in England and Ireland. The dissolution was organised by Thomas Cromwell and provided Henry with about £100,000 per annum, but left between 7,000 and 10,000 monks homeless. The traditional north of England especially resented the dissolution, as demonstrated by the Pilgrimage of Grace. Nevertheless Henry pressed on and chantries were also dissolved. Although his motives were not religious, the dissolution did ensure the long-term survival of the Reformation in England: the nobility and gentry were unwilling to return their newly acquired land to the re-Catholicised Church of Mary Tudor.

  ◗ *see* Thomas Cromwell, Henry VIII, Pilgrimage of Grace

PILGRIMAGE OF GRACE (1536)

Anti-Reformation uprising in northern England. Henry VIII and Thomas Cromwell's policies of increased central government and taxes and the dissolution of the monasteries led to uprisings. In October 1536 Aske took York and soon had 30,000 supporters. Thomas Howard delayed the rebels by false negotiations. On 2 December the rebels named their demands at Pontefract, namely that the papacy be restored and royal influence be limited. Howard vaguely agreed and the rebels consequently dispersed. In January and February 1537 the riots re-emerged, this time under government control: 220-250 rioters were executed, including Aske.

◆ *see* Robert Aske, Henry VIII

RECUSANTS

Those who refused to attend Church of England services. Persecution for recusancy began under Edward VI, came to a head under Elizabeth, due to the activity of the Counter-Reformation, and continued under James I. Punishments included fines, confiscation of property, imprisonment and even death. Covert priest holes were used to secrete Jesuits and other Roman Catholic priests to prevent their capture and persecution.

◆ *see* Counter-Reformation, Elizabeth, James I, Roman Catholics

CHURCH OF IRELAND

Independent Anglican Church in the Republic and Northern Ireland, administered by archbishops in Armagh and Dublin. Centuries of conflict with England, on account of the power and interference of Canterbury and Anglicanism, ended with the disestablishment of the Church of Ireland and its detachment from England.

After Norse raids easily destroyed the church infrastructure of St Patrick's monastic Church, Canterbury gained a hold. Henry VIII's Irish Supremacy Act of 1537 increased English domination. However, the dissolution of the monasteries was only partial in Ireland and the language of the new prayer book – English – was largely unspoken. Despite Ireland remaining predominantly Roman Catholic English

▶ *RIGHT: Papists torture Protestants*

Anglican priests were appointed to Church posts there and the 1801 Act of Union bolstered the Anglicanism of the Church of Ireland. According to the 1861 census less than one-sixth of the population of Ireland belonged to the established Church and therefore by 1869 the Disestablishment of the Irish Church was passed.

🔄 *see* Church of England, Henry VIII, St Patrick

TRENT, COUNCIL OF (1545–63)

Nineteenth ecumenical council of the Roman Catholic Church. The council opened under Pope Paul III. An interval occurred, 1555–59, due to Pope IV's opposition, then it continued under Pius IV. It implemented some self-reform and so helped the Catholic revitalisation, namely the Counter-Reformation.

🔄 *see* Counter-Reformation, Jesuits, Martin Luther, Recusants

LAUD, WILLIAM (1573–1645)

Anti-Puritan bigot and Archbishop of Canterbury (1633–45). Charles I's religious adviser, Laud, regarded the Church and the State as inseparable and therefore hated Nonconformism. His imposition of Anglicanism, his English Prayer Book and his policy called 'thorough' were ultimately unsuccessful.

🔄 *see* Bishops' Wars, Charles I, Nonconformism, Puritanism

COUNTER-REFORMATION (17TH CENTURY)

Roman Catholic retaliation against sixteenth- and seventeenth-century Protestantism. Also called the Catholic Reformation, its origins were in the Roman Inquisition, particularly the Spanish Inquisition, established in 1542 to fight heresy. The Council of Trent (1545–63), was a more self-contemplative attempt to regain religious ground in western Europe and proposed some internal reforms within the Catholic Church.

◖ see Jesuits, Mary I, Catholicism, Council of Trent, Recusants

COVENANT MARTYRS (17TH CENTURY)

Signatories of seventeenth-century Scottish Presbyterian covenants, persecuted under Charles II. With the Restoration in 1660, Episcopacy was re-established, the oaths of the covenants were deemed unlawful and Archbishop Sharp initiated the use of troops to collect intimidatory fines. The covenanters' rebellions (1666, 1679 and 1685) were fiercely suppressed and 210 covananters were transported.

◖ see National Covenant, Restoration

▲ ABOVE: The signing of the covenant in Grey Friars' churchyard, Edinburgh

MILLENARIANISM (1603)

Beliefs behind the Millenary Petition, 1603. The petition, signed by 1,000 Puritan ministers, was presented to James I requesting ceremonial changes to the Church of England; for example, the abolition of wedding rings and surplices. James, fancying himself a theologian, called the Hampton Court Conference to consider these demands.

◆ *see* Hampton Court

KING JAMES BIBLE (1611)

Also known as the Authorised Version of the Bible. In 1604 James I called the Hampton Court Conference to decide religious issues between the Anglican party and the Puritan party. The only Puritan demand at the Hampton Court Conference that James I accepted was the request that the Bible be translated and used nationwide. James is credited with the idea for the eponymous Bible and it remained the official version for many centuries.

◆ *see* James I

NATIONAL COVENANT (1638)

Scottish anti-Laudian oath. The National Covenant of February 1638 aimed, via Presbyterian government, to assert the rights of Parliament rather than those of Charles I in the Scottish Church. As the agreement urged continued loyalty to Charles, most of the nobles and a third of the clergy in Scotland signed it. Charles's disapproval of the abolition of Episcopalianism led to the first Bishops' War. By the Solemn League and Covenant, 1643, the English Parliament was allied with the now more extreme Presbyterian covenanters; more moderate covenanters remained loyal to Charles and war resulted. With the restoration of Episcopalianism in 1662 the covenanters were persecuted. With the accession of William and Mary in 1689, the Covenanters' mission was complete and Presbyterianism in place.

◆ *see* Covenant Martyrs, Presbyterianism

QUAKERS

Also known as the Society of Friends. The Quakers were founded by George Fox in England in the middle of the seventeenth century. He renounced church buildings, liturgy and clergy and valued the inner voice and spirituality. At the monthly meetings the group would wait for God to choose a member to receive his word and 'quake'. Despite persecution (450 died in prison because of the Quaker Act, 1662) Quakerism spread rapidly from the north of England. Quakers earned respect for their dignified calm. They also advocated the abolition of slavery and supported women's rights and pacifism.

◆ *see* Abolitionists

CLARENDON CODE (1661–65)

Four anti-Nonconformist Acts passed by Edward Hyde, 1st Earl of Clarendon. Clarendon did not entirely agree with these intolerant, eponymous, pro-Anglican Acts. The Corporation Act (1661) forbade municipal office to non-communicants of a parish church. The Act of Conformity (1662) similarly provided exclusion from church offices. The Conventicle Act (1662, revised 1667) made public Nonconformist meetings illegal. Finally the Five Mile Act (1665) stipulated that Nonconformist ministers must live at least 5 miles (8 km) outside towns.

◆ *see* Charles II, Edward Hyde Clarendon

▲ *ABOVE: The Quakers were persecuted for the beliefs in the 1600s*

DECLARATIONS OF INDULGENCE (1662, 1672, 1687 AND 1688)

Series of Acts passed by Charles II and James II to alleviate religious intolerance. Their sympathies were Roman Catholic, but they were willing to attempt to grant religious freedom to Nonconformists and other Puritans. Charles's first declaration (1662) failed: he capitulated to Parliament in return for extra taxes. His second declaration (1672) also had limited success due to his financial dependency on an unwilling Parliament and his association with the Treaty of Dover and Catholic France. James's declaration of 1687 was motivated by his desire to gain Nonconformist supporters to create a new Parliament. His reissued declaration (1688) and its stipulated reading in every parish church was refused by many bishops.

see Charles II, Clarendon Code, Treaty of Dover, James II

EPISCOPACY

Church government by bishops. The Episcopalian Church in Scotland is an independent branch within the Anglican Church and has seven dioceses.
Episcopalianism developed out of Protestantism, but was nevertheless opposed to Presbyterianism. The Episcopalians became involved in the Jacobite Rebellions of 1715 and 1745 and therefore their old enemies,

the Presbyterians, almost totally banned them. In 1792 these laws were repealed and in 1929 the Episcopalian prayer book was published.

see Jacobites, Presbyterianism

ACT OF TOLERATION (1689)

Legislation passed immediately after the Glorious Revolution which allowed religious dissenters to worship in their own meeting houses under licence from the bishop. Ministers were nevertheless intended to subscribe to most of the Thirty-Nine Articles which defined the faith of the Church of England. Thus, although this Act has been seen as a turning point in the history of religious toleration, and although it encouraged the growth of a large number of dissenting places of worship, its impact can easily be exaggerated. Catholics and Unitarians were excluded from its provisions.

see Church of England, Church of Scotland, Church of Wales, Enlightenment, Glorious Revolution, Mary II, William III

METHODISM

John Wesley's attempt to revive the Anglican Church. Wesley, an Anglican priest, began to preach, motivated by his personal salvation. His brother, Charles, wrote hymns and George Whitefield joined them. Methodists believe in the power of the Holy Spirit and value simplicity and spirituality. Although Wesley intended only to create a society within the Church of England, in 1795, four years after his death, Methodism and Anglicanism split. In the nineteenth century harsh economic conditions increased the appeal of Methodism's thriftiness and concern for social improvement.

see Church of England, John and Charles Wesley

◄ *LEFT: Scottish Presbyterians worship*

WESLEY, JOHN AND CHARLES (1729)

Founders of Methodism. John, an Anglican priest, returned to Oxford and joined his brother Charles's Holy Club, pejoratively called the 'Methodists', due to their methodical approach to the Bible and worship. John preached widely and in 1743 he published rules for the Methodist society. Charles published 4,500 hymns, some of which Handel put to music, but at heart he remained an Anglican, uncomfortable with John's radical ordination of preachers.

▶ *see* Anglicanism, George Frederick Handel, Methodism

GORDON RIOTS (1780)

Anti-Catholic riots in London, led by Lord George Gordon. Gordon made himself head of the Protestant Association, which aimed to abolish the Catholic Relief Act of 1778. He and his supporters marched on Parliament, carrying their petition against the tyranny of Catholicism. That June rioting was quashed by 12,000 troops, resulting in 700 fatalites and 25 executions.

▶ *see* Catholic Emancipation

MILL, JOHN STUART (1806–73)

Philosopher and social reformer. His friend, Thomas Carlyle, encouraged Mill's idealism. Mill wrote extensively, including A System of Logic, Principles of Political Economy and Subjection of Women, which showed an interest in women's rights. Intellectual followers of Mills' utilitarian philosophy made moves towards the implementation of religious equality in the 1860s and 1870s. Consequently the Church of Ireland was disestablished and the Second Reform Bill opened universities to people of any religion.

▶ *see* Church of Ireland

OXFORD MOVEMENT (1833)

Catholic revival. In 1833 Anglican divine and poet John Keble (1792–1866) gave a sermon at Oxford, attempting to revive Catholic religion in the Church of England. From then, on the Catholic Revival or Tractarian Movement became popularly known as the Oxford Movement. The Oxford Movement had a transforming effect on Anglican communion, and emerged as Anglo-Catholicism, as opposed to Roman Catholicism which is far more conservative in its doctrines, rituals and traditions.

FREE CHURCH OF SCOTLAND (1843)

Organised by the First General Assembly of the Free Church of Scotland. These evangelical dissenters from the Church of Scotland were led by Thomas Chalmers. They raised funds for ministers, schools and charitable work in the age of Victorian philanthropy. In 1929 the Free Church and the Church of Scotland reunited.

▷ see Church of Scotland

CATHOLIC EMANCIPATION (1871)

Movement to gain toleration for Roman Catholics in Britain. After the Reformation, Roman Catholics suffered from persecution then restrictive legislation. Daniel O'Connell ('the Liberator') fought to end this. By the 1770s the Catholic threat was seen to be diminished and various Acts were passed. In 1791 Roman Catholics were granted freedom of worship. O'Connell formed the Catholic Association in 1823 and was elected to Parliament in 1828. He refused to take his seat, however, due to the prerequisite anti-Catholic oath. Finally with Robert Peel's Emancipation Act (1829), English and Irish Catholics were readmitted to Parliament. With the universities' Test Acts of 1871 emancipation was all but complete.

▷ see Daniel O'Connell, Reformation, Roman Catholicism

ROYALTY

CROWN JEWELS

Jewellery or regalia for royal ceremonial. The Crown Jewels include jewellery used at coronations, comprising St Edward's Crown, the Imperial State Crown, the jewelled Sword of State and the ampulla, containing the oil for anointing the monarch. Other crown jewels consist of swords of state, the orb and the sceptre.

see Tower of London

BOUDICCA, QUEEN (D. c. AD 61)

Queen consort of Iceni tribe. Wife of Prastagus. Also known as Boadicea. She raised a rebellion against the Romans in AD 60, after they had tried

to incorporate her late husband's kingdom into their province of Britannia. Boudicca, who resisted the takeover, was flogged and her two daughters were raped. Personally led by Boudicca, the Iceni captured and destroyed the Roman colonies at Colchester and London before their defeat. Boudicca died soon afterwards; it is likely that she committed suicide.

see Roman Invasion

▲ *ABOVE: Boudicca, Queen of the Iceni*

ARTHUR, KING (c. AD 6TH CENTURY)

Legendary British king, first made famous by Geoffrey of Monmouth in his Historia Regum Brittaniae (History of the Kings of Britain,1136). The real-life 'King Arthur' was possibly a Romano-British chieftain called Artorius or Ambrosius Aurelianus, who used Roman military methods to fight Anglo-Saxon invaders.

◼ *see* Glastonbury Tor

ETHELBERT (c. AD 833–65)

King of Kent and Wessex. Ethelbert, already sub-king of Kent, from AD 855, succeeded his brother Ethelbald to the throne of Wessex in AD 860. Soon afterwards, England was invaded by the Vikings, followed by a larger force under Ragnar Lodbrok in AD 865. The Vikings raided along the east coast and despite an agreement with the Saxons, they ravaged east Kent. At the height of this crisis, Ethelbert suddenly died, aged about 32, and was buried at Sherborne Abbey. He was succeeded by his brother Ethelred I.

◼ *see* Ethelred I, Kingdom of Wessex

ETHELRED I (c. AD 837–71)

King of Wessex. On succeeding his brother Ethelbert, Ethelred I had to deal immediately with the Danish raids and invasions of England. In AD 866, Vikings from Dublin attacked and captured York. Mercia sought help from Wessex, but their two armies failed to dislodge the Danes, who now prepared to march south and

▶ *RIGHT: Ethelred I*

attack Wessex, plundering the countryside as they went. In AD 871, Ethelred and his younger brother Alfred narrowly escaped being killed in a battle at Ashdown, Wiltshire. Ethelred, however, was seriously wounded in a subsequent battle, at Martin, Hampshire and died some weeks later at Witchampton, near Wimbourne.

▶ *see* Alfred the Great, Ethelbert

ALFRED THE GREAT (c. AD 847–99)

King of Wessex (AD 871–99). The youngest son of Athelwolf, king of Kent and Wessex, Alfred was the last of four brothers to rule Wessex in succession. His reign was marked by successful struggles against the Danish invaders. He is also remembered for his encouragement of learning.

▶ *see* Anglo-Saxon Chronicle, Athelstan, Edward the Elder

▶ *RIGHT : Alfred fighting off the Vikings*

DUNKELD DYNASTY

Scottish royal dynasty. The Scots Dunkeld dynasty was descended from Duncan I, whose two sons, Malcolm III and Donald III, ruled after him. Malcolm's son Duncan II ruled briefly after his father. Three other Dunkeld monarchs – Donald MacWilliam, grandson of Duncan II, and MacWilliam's sons, Gothred and Donald, were killed in attempts to regain the throne. Subsequent Scots kings were descended from Donald III.

▶ *see* Donald III, Duncan I, Malcolm III

EDWARD THE ELDER (c. AD 871–924)

King of Wessex (AD 899–924). Son of Alfred the Great. A worthy successor to his famous father. After AD 910, Edward retrieved much of the Danelaw from Danish rule. Edward was recognised as overlord by the Welsh princes, the Scots kings, and by rulers in the north of England.

▶ *see* Alfred the Great, Danelaw

MALCOLM I (c. AD 886–954)

King of Scotland (AD 942–44). Malcolm's reign was troubled by recalcitrant Scots nobles and invasions and attacks on his Viking allies by King Edmund of Wessex. Edmund gave Malcolm Cumbria in exchange for his alliegance but his wars with his nobles continued. Malcolm died in battle against them in AD 954.

▶ *see* Eric Bloodaxe, Edmund of Wessex

ATHELSTAN (c. AD 895–939)

King of the English. A grandson of Alfred the Great, Athelstan exercised authority over the Viking monarchs of the north, the king of Scotland and the Welsh princes. Athelstan was best known for his victory at Branunburgh (AD 937) against the combined army of the kings of Dublin, Strathclyde and Scotland.

▶ *see* Alfred the Great, Edward the Elder

EDMUND I (c. AD 922–46)

King of England (AD 939–46). Edmund succeeded his brother Athelstan. At this time, the Vikings were active in the north of England and Olaf Guthfrithsson, king of Dublin, forced Edmund to give up control of the area. In AD 942, however, Edmund retrieved the 'Five Boroughs' – Lincoln, Nottingham, Derby, Stamford and Leicester – after the local Anglo-

Danish people expressed a preference for a Christian Saxon ruler rather than their Irish-Scandinavian overlords. Edmund also regained Viking York and Northumbria by AD 946, but he was murdered at Pucklechurch in Gloucestershire soon afterwards.

see Erik Bloodaxe

EDWY (c. AD 941–59)

King of the English (AD 955–59). Son of Edmund I. Edwy was headstrong and intransigent and soon clashed with Abbot Dunstan of Glastonbury, whose character was similar. Dunstan was enraged when Edwy disappeared during his coronation and was eventually found romancing a young lady. Edwy banished Dunstan from England in AD 957, but he continued to clash with other members of his council. Edwy died suddenly aged 18; it is possible that he was murdered.

see Saint Dunstan, Edmund I

BLOODAXE, ERIK (D. AD 954)

King of Jorvik (Viking York). Erik, last Scandinavian king of Jorvik, was the son of King Harold Hairfair of Norway. Expelled from Norway in AD 947, Erik dominated Jorvik, where he offered protection against Saxon attacks. Erik was driven from Jorvik by Eadred, king of the English, but he regained his power there in AD 952. He was probably thrown out again in AD 954 and was killed at Stainmore while fleeing to the Viking kingdom of Dublin.

see Eadred

FORKBEARD, SWEYN (c. AD 960–1014)

King of Denmark and England (1013–14). Sweyn first raided England in AD 993 and returned each year on fresh raiding expeditions. In 1013, having obtained the submission of Wessex, Sweyn marched to London and was recognised as king of England. Sweyn Forkbeard died six weeks later after a fall from his horse.

see Canute, Kingdom of Wessex

EDWARD THE MARTYR (c. AD 962–78)

King of the English (AD 975–78). Son of Edgar the Peaceable. Edward was arrogant and soon alienated his council. In AD 978 Edward was visiting his stepmother Elfrida at Corfe Castle when her retainers stabbed him to death. Elfrida was blamed for the murder.

ETHELRED II (c. 968–1016)

King of the English (AD 978–1016). Known as 'the Unready' ('noble counsel'). Son of King Edgar. His government was controlled by his mother Elfrida and the powerful Alfthere. Ethelred took over after AD 983 and reversed their policy of reducing the power of the monasteries. Ethelred updated the laws in the Wantage Code of AD 977, which included acceptance of Danish customs. After AD 991, Ethelred faced fresh Danish raids and had to pay the Danegeld several times to keep the invaders at bay.

see Danegeld, Edgar

EDMUND II (c. 990–1016)

King of England (1013–16). Known as Edmund Ironside. Son of King Ethelred

▶ RIGHT: Edmund II

the Unready, Edmund resisted the invasion of England by Canute in 1016. Canute was prevented from capturing London, but Edmund was defeated at Ashingdon in Essex in the autumn of 1016. Canute agreed to share England with Edmund, who would have possession of Wessex. However, Edmund died on 30 November, possibly murdered. Subsequently, Canute was able to take over the whole of England as its king and Edmund's children fled abroad. Edmund's grandson was Edgar the Atheling.

◆ see Canute, Edgar the Atheling, Kingdom of Wessex

DUNCAN I (1001–40)

King of Scotland (1034–40). The 'King Duncan' of Shakespeare's play Macbeth. Duncan was possibly appointed as successor by Malcolm II. In 1039 Duncan unsuccessfully attacked Northumbria. Macbeth, king of Moray, challenged him for the throne and Duncan was killed at the Battle of Pitvageny. Subsequently, Macbeth became king of Scotland.

◆ see Malcolm II, William Shakespeare

EDWARD THE CONFESSOR (c. 1005–66)

King of England (1042–66). Known as the 'Confessor' because of his saintliness. After a long exile in France, Edward succeeded the throne in 1042. Often portrayed as a pious weakling, Edward was in fact an astute ruler who reconciled his Anglo-Saxon and Danish nobles and kept his kingdom intact. Edward was childless and the king apparently promised the throne to both his brother-in-law Harold and William of Normandy, thus causing the dispute that would lead to the Norman Conquest. Edward spent much time on the rebuilding of Westminster Abbey, where he was buried in 1066.

◆ see Harold II, Norman Conquest, Westminster Abbey, William I

HAROLD I (c. 1016–40)

King of the English (1035–40). Known as Harold Harefoot. Son of King Canute. Harold I was crowned in 1037, in the absence in Denmark of his younger half-brother Harthacanute. Harold's legitimacy was dubious. He died in 1040 and after Harthacanute returned from Denmark in 1042, he had the body exhumed and beheaded.

see Canute, Harthacanute

HARTHACANUTE (c. 1018–42)

King of England (1035–42). Son of King Canute. Harthacanute was in Denmark, fighting to maintain his power there, when his father died in 1035. He returned to claim his English throne in 1040. Brutish, cruel and vengeful, Harthacanute died suddenly while drinking at a wedding. He may have been poisoned.

see Canute, Harold I

HAROLD II (c. 1022–66)

King of the English (1066). Eldest surviving son of Godwin, Earl of Wessex, Harold was ostensibly promised the throne when Edward the Confessor made him 'Duke of the English' in 1064. In 1065, however, King Edward also, apparently, named Duke William of Normandy as his successor. King Edward died in January 1066 and Harold was crowned. William of Normandy regarded this as treachery and invaded the south of England in October 1066 and Harold's army fought

RIGHT: The burial of Harold II

him at the Battle of Hastings, where Harold was killed.

🔹 *see* Edward the Confessor, Battle of Hastings, Norman Dynasty, Battle of Stamford Bridge, William I

WILLIAM I (1028–87)

King of England (1066–87). Known as William the Conqueror or William the Bastard because of his illegitimate birth. William, first king of the Norman dynasty, seized power in England in 1066. Not all of England accepted him as king and in 1067, he began a systematic conquest to control the population. He built 78 castles including the Tower of London and appointed Normans to powerful positions, giving them large estates taken from the Anglo-Saxon aristocracy. William faced several rebellions, but suppressed them with considerable force. The traditionally restless north of England was virtually laid waste by William's armies and its inhabitants were ruthlessly killed or terrorised. By 1074, when the Saxon claimant to the throne Edgar the Atheling submitted to William, Norman power in England was complete.

🔹 *see* Feudal System, Harold II, Battle of Hastings, Norman Dynasty, Tower of London

MALCOLM III (c. 1031–93)

King of Scotland (1058–93). Known as Canmore, meaning 'Bighead'. Son of Duncan I. Malcolm supported the invasion of England in 1066 by Haardrada of Norway and Tostig, rebellious brother of King Harold II. Malcolm, however, was a Saxon sympathiser and his sister Margaret married Edgar the Atheling, Saxon claimant to the English throne. He aided Edgar in his unsuccessful bid to unseat the Norman, William I. Subsequently, Malcolm raided the north of England, prompting William to invade Scotland and force Malcolm to recognise him as his overlord.

After William's death in 1087, Malcolm prepared to invade England, but was defeated by William II in 1090. In 1093 Malcolm was ambushed and killed by Robert Mowbray, Earl of Northumberland.

◆ *see* Donald III, Duncan I, William I, William II

DONALD III (c. 1033–99)

King of Scotland (1093–99). Also known as Donald Bane. Donald seized the Scots throne on the death of his brother Malcolm III. Donald was opposed by Duncan II, Malcolm's eldest son and, helped by William II of England, he forced Donald out in 1094. Duncan was himself dislodged soon afterwards, and was killed in battle. Donald retrieved his throne, but not for long. Edgar, another of Malcolm's sons, won the backing of William II in 1097. He defeated and imprisoned Donald, who was blinded on his orders two years later. Donald died sometime around 1099.

◆ *see* Duncan II, Edgar, Malcolm III, William II

CANUTE, KING (D. 1035)

King of England (1016–35), Denmark (1019–35) and Norway (1028–35). Also known as Cnut or Knut. A Dane by birth, Canute came to England with his father, Sweyn Forkbeard, in 1013. In 1016 Canute defeated Edmund Ironside and conquered England. The Witangemot elected him as king in April 1016. At first Canute behaved like a conqueror, giving English earldoms and estates to his Danish followers. He was, however, careful not to isolate the English nobles and after 1021, two of Canute's three advisers were English. Canute's reign was remarkably peaceful for an age in which rivalry and warfare were common. Canute's sons, Harold and Harthacanute, succeeded him.

◆ *see* Edmund II, Edward the Confessor, Sweyn Forkbeard, Harold Harefoot, Harthacanute

EDGAR THE ATHELING (c. 1052–1125)

Edgar, great-grandson of Ethelred II (the Unready) was proclaimed king of England by the defeated English after William's victory at Hastings in 1066. Edgar took part in the revolts against Norman rule in 1069–70. He was reconciled with William in 1074, becoming one of his courtiers.

◖ *see* Edmund II, Norman Dynasty, William I

WILLIAM II (c. 1057-1100)

King of England (1087–1100). Third son of William I. Nicknamed 'Rufus' because of his red hair, William II was a strong, capable king, who tamed the Welsh princes and controlled the Scots in the north. He was, however, detested by churchmen for his avarice and godlessness. After Lanfranc, Archbishop of Canterbury, died in 1089, William failed to appoint a successor and meanwhile appropriated the Canterbury revenues. William made Anselm archbishop in 1092, when he thought he was dying, but he so mistreated the archbishop that he left England in 1097. William died while out hunting in the New Forest, mysteriously shot by an arrow.

◖ *see* Saint Anselm, Henry I, William I

DUNCAN II (c. 1060–94)

King of Scotland (1094). Eldest son of Malcolm III, Duncan was handed over as a hostage after his father submitted to William I of England in 1072. Duncan spent 15 years as a captive, but was freed and made a knight by William in 1087. In 1094 William supported Duncan in his bid to unseat his uncle, the usurper Donald III. Duncan was successful at first, but his uncle hit back and he was forced to dismiss his Norman supporters. Afterwards, Duncan was killed at Mondynes, near Aberdeen, and Donald III was restored to the Scots throne

◖ *see* Donald III, William II

NORMAN DYNASTY

French royal dynasty that conquered England under William of Normandy. The Norman dynasty originated in the Duchy of Normandy in northern France where a Viking, i.e. 'Northman', chieftain called Rollo was granted lands in the early tenth century. Although the dynasty lasted less than 90 years, the Normans transformed England. They introduced the feudal system and eliminated the existing Anglo-Saxon aristocracy, replacing them with Normans in all the richest and most powerful offices of state.

see Domesday Book, Harold II, Henry I, Henry II, William I, Empress Matilda, William II

HENRY I (1068–1135)

King of England (1100–35). Youngest son of William I. In 1100, Henry succeeded his brother William II and was crowned within three days. Henry was challenged by his eldest brother, Robert, Duke of Normandy, whom he defeated in battle and imprisoned for life. Henry quarrelled with – and exiled – Anselm, his Archbishop of Canterbury, over papal authority in England but when threatened with excommunication, he gave in. After the tragic death of his only son, William, in 1020, Henry made his nobles swear alliegance to his daughter, Matilda, as their future queen, but after the king's death, they reneged.

see Saint Anselm, Matilda, William I, William II

▲ *ABOVE: From a Manuscript dated 1130-1140, Henry I Sales for England*

ALEXANDER I (c. 1080–1124)

King of Scotland (1107–24). A younger son of Malcolm III. Alexander succeeded his brother Edgar as king of Scotland in 1107. Alexander built several castles in Scotland, including Stirling Castle. Among many important reforms, Alexander introduced the first sheriffs into Scotland as Guardians of the King's Peace. Alexander died at Stirling Castle and was buried in Dunfermline Abbey.

◆ see Malcolm III

▲ ABOVE: Philotas being threatened by pikes before Alexander

DAVID I (c. 1085–1153)

King of Scotland (1124–53). An exemplary ruler, who established his independence as sovereign ruler of Scotland, David married Matilda, great-niece of William I of England and drew on his Norman connections to modernise his realm. He brought Norman knights to Scotland, where they established strong lordships, manned castles for the defence of the country and knights for the king's army. David also 'normanised' Scots law and government, and developed the religious and economic life of his kingdom. The Normans were not allowed to be dominant in Scotland: David also promoted the Celtic nobility and included them in the governing élite.

◆ see Feudal System, William I

MATILDA, EMPRESS (c. 1102–67)

Daughter of Henry I. The title 'Empress' came from her first marriage to Emperor Heinrich V of Germany. When the English barons reneged on their promise to Henry to support Matilda as Queen Regnant, she and her second husband, Geoffrey of Anjou, invaded England in 1139. This precipitated a civil war with the usurper King Stephen. The arrogant Matilda alienated the English and she abandoned her efforts to acquire the crown in 1148.

◖ *see* Henry I, Henry II, Geoffrey Plantagenet, Stephen

PLANTAGENET, GEOFFREY (1113–51)

Husband of Empress Matilda. Father of Henry II. Geoffrey was Count of Anjou and Duke of Normandy. Though he supported her, Geoffrey did not personally participate in Empress Matilda's civil war against the usurper Stephen. Geoffrey's own ambitions centred around the conquest of the dukedom of Normandy which he began to attack in 1135. Geoffrey achieved his objective in 1144, so laying one of the most important foundations for the Angevin Empire in France later created by his son, King Henry II.

◖ *see* Henry I, Henry III, Empress Matilda, Plantagenet Dynasty

ELEANOR OF AQUITAINE (c. 1122–1204)

Wife of Henry II. Eleanor married Henry in 1152 and added the duchy of Aquitaine to his possessions. Eleanor resented Henry's infidelities and backed her sons when they rebelled against him. The rebellion failed and Eleanor was imprisoned in 1173. She was not released until after Henry's death in 1189. While his successor, her son Richard I, was abroad on Crusade and in France, Eleanor helped rule England on his behalf.

◖ *see* Henry II, King John, Richard I

STEPHEN, KING

King of England (1135–54). Originally Stephen of Blois, son of Adela, daughter of William I. In 1135, when the succession of Henry I's daughter the Empress Matilda as Queen Regnant of England was in dispute, Stephen made a pre-emptive strike and usurped the throne for himself. In 1139 Matilda and her supporters invaded England and civil war ensued. King Stephen was defeated in the only major battle, at Lincoln in 1141. Subsequently, he was imprisoned at Bristol. Stephen nevertheless clung on to his throne and in 114, Matilda gave up the struggle and returned to France. Stephen planned that his son Eustace should succeed him, but Eustace died in 1153. His heartbroken father agreed to accept Matilda's son Henry as his heir. When Stephen died in 1154, Henry succeeded him as King Henry II.

◆ see Henry I, Henry II, Empress Matilda, Geoffrey Plantagenet

HENRY II (1133–89)

King of England (1154–89). First monarch of the Plantagenet (Angevin) dynasty. Henry was the son of Empress Matilda, who agreed with the usurper King Stephen in 1153 that he should succeed him. Henry II established strong royal rule over his empire and reformed the operation of the law with the new jury system, among other important legal procedures. In an attempt to establish royal, as opposed to papal, control over the English church, Henry appointed his friend, Thomas Becket, as Archbishop of Canterbury in 1162. Becket, however, unexpectedly upheld papal rights in England and this led to his exile and, in 1170, his murder at Canterbury Cathedral. Afterwards, Henry was forced to do penance for the killing. Henry was also opposed by his own sons, who had been given important titles and positions but were denied power. They rebelled against him, with the support of their mother Eleanor, and finally drove the king to his death in 1189.

⬧ *see* Thomas Becket, Eleanor of Aquitaine, King John, Matilda, Richard I, Stephen

MALCOLM IV (1141–65)

King of Scotland (1153–65). Malcolm became king at the age of 11, but was treated as a vassal by Henry II of England. This roused fears of anglicisation among the Scots nobles. They rebelled in 1160 and 1164. With the aid of his Anglo-Norman barons, Malcolm suppressed both rebellions. He died suddenly when he was just 23 years old.

⬧ *see* Henry II

ANGEVIN DYNASTY (1154–1485)

Alternative name for the more commonly called Plantagenet dynasty, which ruled England from the accession of Henry II in 1154 to the death of Richard III in 1485. Both the names Angevin, the more correct, and Plantagenet derived from Count Geoffrey of Anjou, father of Henry II. Geoffrey is said to have acquired the nickname of Plantagenet from the *planta genista*, a stick of broom he habitually wore in his hat.

⬧ *see* Plantagenet dynasty

PLANTAGENET DYNASTY

Alternative name for the Angevin Dynasty. The Angevin kings of England did not use 'Plantagenet' as their surname, but they are most commonly called by this name. The Plantagenets were the longest-lasting dynasty to rule in

▶ *RIGHT: Geoffery Plantaginet, father of Henry II*

England, over a period of 331 years. There were 14 Plantagenet kings in all. The first was Henry II, followed by Richard I the Lionheart, King John, Henry III, Edward I, Edward II, Edward III, Richard II, Henry IV, Henry V, Henry VI, Edward IV, Edward V and Richard III.

RICHARD I (THE LIONHEART) (1157–99)

King of England (1189–99). Third son of Henry II. Richard, who succeeded his father in 1189, has a glorious reputation as a warrior king, and as the crusader saviour of Christendom. He cared little for England, where he spent only around six months of his 10-year reign. He preferred his duchy of Aquitaine and the task of guarding it against French incursions.

Richard financed his crusade by selling offices, lands, estates or rights. He even contemplated selling London, but could not find anyone rich enough to buy it. In 1192, on his way home from the Third Crusade, he was imprisoned by a rival. In 1194, after an enormous ransom had been paid, he was back in England, but soon left for France and never returned. He died during a siege in 1199 when an arrow wound turned poisonous.

see Eleanor of Aquitaine, Crusades, Henry II, King John

▲ *ABOVE: Richard I The Lion Heart*

JOHN, KING (1167–1216)

King of England (1199–1216). Youngest and favourite son of Henry II. Contrary to popular belief, John was a responsible king, with a particular interest in justice for his subjects in the law courts. However, he made some serious errors. First, he angered the English Church by refusing the pope's choice for Archbishop of

Canterbury. The pope then laid England under interdict (1208) and excommunicated the king (1209). These punishments were lifted after John's submission in 1213 . Secondly, John infuriated his barons by refusing their rights as royal advisers. In addition, by losing Angevin possessions in France, John failed to display the military prowess expected of a medieval king. The result of these failings was that John's barons forced him to sign the famous Magna Carta in 1215, which set out their rights and privileges. Subsequently, John renounced the document. The barons again rebelled, but John died of a fever in 1216 during the subsequent civil war.

◆ *see* Eleanor of Aquitaine, Henry II, Magna Carta, Richard I

▲ *ABOVE: King John and his barons at the signing of the Magna Carta*

ALEXANDER II (1198–1249)

King of Scotland (1214–49). Although known as 'The Peaceful', Alexander ruled with an iron fist. When the English barons rose up against King John, Alexander supported them and was one of the signatories of the Magna Carta (1215). The lords of Argyll rebelled against Alexander in 1249, but he died of a fever while preparing for battle against them.

◆ *see* King John, Magna Carta

HENRY III (1207–72)

King of England (1216–72). Son of King John. Henry III came to the throne in 1216. He assumed his powers as king in 1227. Henry immediately quarrelled with his nobles over his refusal to accept their right to act as his advisers. In 1258 the nobles lost patience and, led by Simon de Montfort, Henry's brother-in-law, forced Henry to sign the Provisions of Oxford, which limited his powers. When Henry reneged, civil war followed in 1264–65. Henry was captured and imprisoned by Simon de Montfort, who directed his actions as king. In 1265 Simon was killed in battle by Prince Edward, Henry's son. Subsequently, Henry became senile and spent the rest of his life in artistic pursuits, including the rebuilding of Westminster Abbey.

◆ *see* Edward I, Simon de Montfort

▲ *ABOVE: Henry III*

EDWARD I (1239–1307)

King of England (1272–1307). Son of Henry III. Known as 'Longshanks' because of his height. Edward was the first strong king in England after over 80 years of weak or ineffectual royal rule. During his father's reign, he acquired valuable experience of government and was a notable military leader. He frequently took part in tournaments and went on crusade to the Holy Land in 1270. He defeated the rebellious barons in battle during his father's reign and, as king, he had conquered Wales by 1283 and put down a rebellion by the Welsh princes (1294–95). On his orders, castles were built in Wales to control the population. After 1296 he established English influence in Scotland, whose king became his vassal. The Scots under Robert Bruce rebelled in 1306. The following year Edward marched north with an army to suppress the rebellion, but died on the way, near Carlisle. Edward I recognised Parliament as a necessary adjunct to his rule, and worked with its members, including the barons, in his tax and legislative reforms. Edward's famous Model Parliament of 1295 included knights of the shire and burgesses for the first time.

◄ *see* Henry III, Model Parliament, Simon de Montfort

ALEXANDER III (1241–86)

King of Scotland (1249–86), son of Alexander II. Alexander III was seven years old when he succeeded his father. Scotland was peaceful and prosperous during his reign, hence Alexander's nickname 'The Glorious'. Alexander set the boundaries of Scotland after purchasing the Western Isles from Norway in 1266. His personal life was tragic: his wife Margaret died young, in 1275, followed by three of their four children. Alexander himself died in 1286, when his horse stumbled over a cliff.

BALLIOL, JOHN (c. 1250–1313)

King of Scotland. John Balliol was crowned king in 1292 and recognised Edward I of England as his overlord a month later. Balliol rebelled against Edward's control in 1296 and joined the English king's enemy, King Philippe IV of France. Balliol was defeated by the English, stripped of his royal authority and imprisoned in the Tower of London. Released in 1299, John Balliol spent the years until his death on his estates in France.

◄ *see* Edward I, Edward Balliol

BRUCE, ROBERT (1274–1329)

King of Scotland as Robert I. Bruce was a claimant to the Scottish throne in 1291, but his rival John Balliol was chosen instead by Edward I of England. Robert Bruce was involved in the uprising headed by William Wallace in 1297–98, but despite this he maintained good relations with Edward. He was, however, simply biding his time until the right moment came to seize the Scots throne, which he did in 1306. However, Edward II of England and the pope refused to recognise Robert as king. Recognition came only after Edward's murder in 1327. Robert's greatest achievement was to gain formal recognition for Scotland as a separate and independent kingdom from England (1328). He died in 1329, probably from leprosy.

◆ *see* John Balliol, Edward I, Edward II, William Wallace

▲ *ABOVE: Robert the Bruce on his deathbed*

GRUFFYD, LLEWELLYN AP (D. 1282)

Welsh prince. The last native Welsh prince to be recognised by the English as Prince of Wales. In 1255 Llewellyn seized power in Gwynned. He attempted to make Gwynned all-powerful in Wales and received the homage of other Welsh princes in 1258. In 1276–77 Edward I of England conquered Wales and defeated Llewellyn. Llewellyn and his brother David raised a rebellion in 1282, but after Llewellyn was killed in a skirmish near Builth, the rebellion collapsed.

◆ *see* Edward I, David ap Gruffyd

GRUFFYD, DAVID AP (D. 1283)

Welsh prince. David opposed his brother, Llewellyn ap Gruffyd, when he became sole Prince of Gwynned (1255) but like Llewellyn fought against the encroachments of the English kings in Wales. David became Prince of Gwynned on Llewelyn's death (1282) but was captured and hung, drawn and quartered as a traitor in 1283.

see Edward I, Edward II, Llewellyn ap Gruffyd

EDWARD II (1284–1327)

King of England (1307–27). Son of Edward I. In 1301, he became the first English Prince of Wales. As king, Edward II was a total contrast to his father. Weak, impressionable and petulant, he was uninterested in matters of government. An incompetent military leader, his army was crushed by Robert Bruce at the battle of Bannockburn in 1314. Edward enraged his barons by ruling through favourites. Edward refused to discard them and the barons took their revenge. Edward's first favourite, Piers Gaveston, was murdered in 1312. The other two, Hugh Despenser and his son (also Hugh), were executed in 1326. Edward neglected and insulted his French wife, Isabella. Together with her lover, Roger Mortimer, Earl of March, Isabella invaded England from France late in 1326. Edward was forced to abdicate in favour of his son, who became Edward III. Edward II was imprisoned in Berkeley Castle, Gloucestershire, where he was murdered on 27 September 1327.

see Battle of Bannockburn, Edward I, Roger Mortimer, Princes of Wales, Robert I

MORTIMER, ROGER, EARL OF MARCH (c. 1287–1330)

Roger Mortimer took part in a rebellion against Edward II in the Welsh marches, but escaped from the Tower of London to Paris in 1324. There, he became the lover of Queen Isabella, the king's estranged wife, and later aided her in the overthrow of her husband in 1327. The subsequent rule of Mortimer and Isabella in England was corrupt and incompetent. Isabella's son, Edward III, had Mortimer seized in 1330 and executed.

▷ *see* Edward II, Edward III

▲ *ABOVE: Roger Mortimer is arrested and taken to the Tower*

WALES, (ENGLISH) PRINCES OF

Title held since 1301 by the heir apparent to the throne of England. The first Prince of Wales was the future King Edward II, who was said to have been presented to the Welsh after the last of their own, native princes was killed. Since 1301, there have been twenty further Princes of Wales. The Princes' estate, the Duchy of Cornwall, was created in 1337 for Edward, the Black Prince, heir to King Edward III.

▷ *see* Edward I, Edward II, Edward, the Black Prince, Heir to the Throne

EDWARD III (1312–77)

King of England (1327–77). Son of Edward II. Succeeded on his father's abdication. Edward spent much of his youth in France with his mother Isabella and was largely influenced by Isabella and her lover, Roger Mortimer, until he took control in 1330. Mortimer was executed and

Isabella entered a convent. Edward III took positive steps to include the barons in the processes of government, through Parliament. The strong and well-organised royal systems were able to retain control in England despite the catastrophe of the Black Death (1348–50). Edward organised his court along lines taken from the recently written tales of King Arthur and the Knights of the Round Table and held frequent tournaments which were attended by the greatest knights in Europe. In 1346 he claimed the French throne and precipitated the Hundred Years' War.

◆ *see* Edward II, Edward, the Black Prince, Hundred Years' War, Roger Mortimer

▲ *ABOVE: Coronation of Edward III*

DAVID II (1324–71)

King of Scotland (1329–71). Only son of Robert Bruce, David II became king in 1329 but fled to France when Scotland was invaded in 1332 by Edward Balliol and Edward III of England. While the English king was engaged in war in France, David invaded Scotland, but was defeated and captured by an English army at Neville's Cross in 1346. He was ransomed in 1357. King at last after almost 30 years, David proved a strong ruler. He crushed several revolts by his nobles. However, on his death he had no heir and the Bruce dynasty ended with him.

◆ *see* Edward III, Hundred Years' War, Robert I

EDWARD, THE BLACK PRINCE (1330–76)

Prince of Wales (1343). Son of Edward III.
The Black Prince – so called because of the
black armour he wore – earned his
military reputation at the Battle of Crécy
(1336) and added to it at Poitiers (1356)
and Najerá in Spain (1367). He was
afterwards regarded as a great chivalric hero. In 1362 his father made
him Prince of Aquitaine, but he was a careless ruler, incompetent with
finances, and returned Aquitaine to the king's control in 1372. The Black
Prince died before his father in 1376.

▷ *see* Edward III, Hundred Years' War, Richard II

▲ *ABOVE: Gilt copper effigy of Edward, the Black Prince*

JOHN OF GAUNT, DUKE OF LANCASTER (1340–99)

Third surviving son of Edward III. The name 'Gaunt' came from his
birthplace, Ghent (Belgium). John of Gaunt was the richest and most
powerful magnate in England. As a military commander, he took part in
the Hundred Years' War with France after 1355 and his forces represented
one quarter of the army raised for a campaign against Scotland in 1385.
John of Gaunt called himself King of Castile (Spain) by right of his second
wife, but renounced the title in 1387. During the senility of his father,
John of Gaunt was virtual ruler of England. John of Gaunt married three
times. His first wife, Blanche, was the mother of the future Henry IV. By
his third wife, Catherine Swynford, he fathered the Beaufort family, from
which Henry VII was descended.

▷ *see* Margaret Beaufort, Edward III, Henry IV, Henry VII, Hundred Years' War,
Richard II, John Wycliffe

BALLIOL, EDWARD (D. 1364)

Intermittent king of Scotland (1332, 1333–34, 1335–36). Son of John Balliol. A rival of Robert Bruce's family, Edward was crowned on 24 September 1332 but was deposed the following December by rebellious Scots nobles. Balliol's hold on his crown was always precarious. He resigned all his lands to his overlord, Edward III of England, in 1336. Balliol never married and the claims of his family to the Scottish throne ended with his death.

  see Edward III, John Balliol, Robert Bruce

PERCY, HENRY (1364–1403)

Known as 'Hotspur'. Son of Sir Henry Percy, 1st Earl of Northumberland. An active military commander, he fought against the Scots in 1388. He supported Henry IV in his usurpation of the English throne in 1399, and joined his father to defeat a Scots invasion in 1402. Henry IV ordered the ransom of the Percys' prisoners, at which they rebelled against him. Hotspur marched to Wales to join the rebel Welsh prince, Owain Glendower, but was intercepted and killed in battle by Henry's forces at Shrewsbury.

  see Owen Glendower, Henry IV

RICHARD II (1367–1400)

King of England (1377–99). Son of Edward, the Black Prince. Richard succeeded his grandfather, Edward III. He acquired a hero's reputation in 1381 when he confronted Wat Tyler, leader of the Peasants' Revolt. Heroics, however, were not typical of Richard. He was despotic and relied on favourites, ignoring the rights of his nobles and his Parliament. In 1386 five disgruntled nobles, the Lords Appellant, imposed their own advisers on the king. One of the Lords Appellant was Richard's cousin, Henry Bolingbroke, son of John of Gaunt, whom the king exiled in 1398. Richard

afterwards appropriated Henry's duchy of Lancaster. In 1399 Henry returned to retrieve his duchy, forced Richard to abdicate and afterwards took his throne as King Henry IV. Richard was imprisoned in Pontefract Castle where he died, probably from starvation, in February 1400.

◆ *see* Edward III, Edward, the Black Prince, Henry IV, Peasants' Revolt, Wars of the Roses

◀ *LEFT: The burial of Richard II*

LANCASTER, HOUSE OF (1399–1461)

Branch of the Plantagenet (Angevin) dynasty, descended from John of Gaunt, Duke of Lancaster, third surviving son of Edward III. The first Lancastrian king, Henry IV, usurped the throne from his cousin, Richard II, in 1399. Henry IV was succeeded by his son Henry V, one of the most popular romantic warrior kings in history. His early death meant the throne passed to his son Henry, who was less than a year old at the time. Henry VI could not live up to his father's reputation and the Wars of the Roses ensued between the Lancastrian line and the House of York. Henry VI was to be the last Lancastrian king.

◆ *see* Henry IV, Henry V, Henry VI, Richard II, Wars of the Roses

▶ *RIGHT: The Battle of Barnet during the Wars of the Roses between the Houses of Lancaster and York*

▶ RIGHT: Edward IV

HENRY IV (1367–1413)

King of England (1399–1413). Grandson of Edward III. Before becoming king, Henry – known as Henry Bolingbroke – was a much-admired chivalric figure. As one of the Lords Appellant in the 1380s, Henry had strongly opposed his cousin, King Richard, and his reliance on court favourites. In 1399 he usurped Richard's throne after the king had exiled him and illegally confiscated the lands of his dukedom of Lancaster. Despite the support Henry had received from Parliament, the usurpation and Richard's subsequent murder troubled his conscience and bedevilled his reign. Henry suppressed numerous revolts and plots with considerable force and cruelty. By 1408, Henry was reasonably safe from revolts, but by then he was a sick man, suffering from a disease thought to be leprosy. He died aged 45 in 1413.

◊ see Edward III, Henry V, Richard II

HENRY V (1387–1422)

King of England (1413–22). Henry V, who succeeded his father Henry IV, was one of England's great warrior monarchs. When he came to the throne, Henry V revived the claim of his great-grandfather, Edward III, to the throne of France. He invaded France in 1415, captured Harfleur after a punishing siege and, on 25 October, he confronted the French at the

Battle of Agincourt. Henry's victory, where his army was outnumbered by the French, made him one of England's great hero kings. However, Agincourt did not give Henry the French throne. Despite support from the Burgundian faction, he got no further than recognition – at the Treaty of Troyes – as heir to the French king, Charles VI. To seal the bargain Henry married Catherine, Charles's daughter, in 1421. Henry was strongly opposed by the dauphin, Charles's son. War followed. In 1422 Henry was in France where he captured the dauphin's stronghold, Meaux. However, Henry fell ill with dysentery and died, aged 34, on 31 August.

⬙ see Battle of Agincourt, Henry IV, Henry VI, Treaty of Troyes

JAMES I OF SCOTLAND (1394–1437)

King of Scotland (1406–37). In 1424 James I inherited a poverty-stricken, lawless kingdom, controlled by the warlike Murdoch family, who were James's cousins. James imprisoned several of its members, then ruthlessly attempted to curb the power of the Scots clans and nobles. James made many enemies, and he was assassinated in 1437.

⬙ see Stuart Dynasty

▶ RIGHT: James I of Scotland

VALOIS, CATHERINE DE (1401–37)

Queen Consort of Henry V. Catherine, daughter of Charles VI of France, married Henry in 1420, coinciding with the signing of the Treaty of Troyes making him her father's heir. The only child of Henry and Catherine de Valois became Henry VI on his father's death in 1422. In 1428 Catherine secretly married her Welsh servant, Owen Tudor. Their grandson became Henry VII, the first king of the Tudor dynasty in 1485.

◆ see Henry V, Henry VI, Tudor Dynasty

HENRY VI (1422–71)

King of England (1422–71). Son of Henry V. Henry VI was only nine months old when he became king. He was crowned in both London (1429) and Paris (1431), but never ruled in France. In England, his hold on power was very tenuous, not only because of his extreme youth but because of his mild, unwarlike, susceptible nature and his complete lack of interest in government. Henry's gentle character, coupled with his bouts of madness after 1453, was a crucial factor in giving rise to rival claims to the English throne. Henry was exiled, twice deposed and twice imprisoned in the Tower of London. He was eventually murdered there by Yorkist agents in 1471.

◆ see Battle of Bosworth, Henry IV, Henry V, Henry VII, Wars of the Roses

YORK, HOUSE OF

Branch of the Plantagenet (Angevin) dynasty which challenged the right to the throne of the House of Lancaster, another branch of the same dynasty. The basis of the Yorkist claim was that their ancestor, Lionel, Duke of Clarence had been an older son of King Edward III than John of Gaunt, Duke of Lancaster, from whom the Lancastrians were descended. Richard, Duke of York, great-grandson of Lionel claimed the throne from the Lancastrian King Henry VI, great-grandson of John of Gaunt. The challenge precipitated the civil Wars of the Roses.

🔘 *see* Battle of Bosworth, Edward IV, Edward V, Henry VI, John of Gaunt, House of Lancaster, Richard III, Wars of the Roses

EDWARD IV (1442–83)

King of England (1461–70, 1471–83). Son of Richard, Duke of York. First king of the Plantagenet House of York. After his father's death at the battle of Wakefield in 1460, during the Wars of the Roses, Edward IV inherited the Yorkist claim to the throne and was proclaimed king on 4 March 1461. His reign was troubled by threats from the deposed Lancastrian king, Henry VI. In 1470 Queen Margaret, wife of Henry VI, in her efforts to regain her husband's crown, invaded England and Edward was forced to flee to Burgundy. Henry was restored to his throne, but Edward returned in 1471 and Queen Margaret was beaten at the battle of Tewkesbury and her only son, Edward, was killed. Henry VI was subsequently murdered. Edward remained secure on his throne until his sudden death in 1483.

🔘 *see* Edward V, Henry VI, Queen Margaret, Richard III Richard Neville,

BEAUFORT, LADY MARGARET (1443–1509)

Mother of Henry VII, her only child. Margaret was descended from Edward III of England through Edward's third surviving son, John of Gaunt, Duke of Lancaster. She was married to Edmund Tudor, Earl of Richmond, who died three months before she gave birth to Henry in 1457.

🔘 *see* Henry VII, John of Gaunt, Wars of the Roses

▲ *ABOVE: Edward IV*

RICHARD III (1452–85)

King of England (1483–85). Youngest son of Richard, Duke of York. Richard fought bravely and loyally for the Yorkist cause in the Wars of the Roses. His brother, the first Yorkist monarch, Edward IV, put Richard in charge of government in the traditionally unruly north of England. Despite his youth, Richard proved a just and much-admired administrator. In 1483 he usurped the crown from his young nephew, Edward V, and afterwards, reputedly, murdered both him and his brother. Other suggested victims of Richard's ambition were Henry VI, murdered in 1471, and Richard's brother George, Duke of Clarence, killed in 1478. However, it is likely that Richard was no more violent than his contemporaries. His life story was, however, worked over by Tudor propaganda to create the popular picture of Richard as an evil monster. There is no doubt, though, that by usurping the throne from his nephew, Richard made many powerful enemies. They combined with Henry Tudor to defeat and kill the usurper at the Battle of Bosworth in 1485.

🔄 *see* Edward IV, Henry VII, Thomas More, William Shakespeare, Wars of the Roses

EDWARD V (1470–83)

King of England (1483). Son of Edward IV. After his accession in 1483, Edward's uncle, Richard, Duke of Gloucester, removed him from the custody of his mother, Elizabeth Woodville. Together with his brother Richard, Duke of York, he was sent to the Tower of London to await his coronation. Meanwhile, Richard declared the child king to be illegitimate because his father had been betrothed to Lady Eleanor Butler when he married Elizabeth Woodville. Edward was deposed on 25 June 1483 and Richard became king in his place. Edward and his brother were probably murdered in the Tower about three months later.

🔄 *see* Richard III, Tower of London, Elizabeth Woodville

WOODVILLE, ELIZABETH

Queen Consort of Edward IV. Edward married the beautiful widow, Elizabeth Woodville, in 1464. The marriage was disliked by the Yorkist nobility because Elizabeth was a commoner and came from a Lancastrian family. After the sudden death of Edward IV in 1483, his brother, Richard of Gloucester, usurped the throne. Elizabeth fled for sanctuary with the younger of her seven children to Westminster Abbey. For reasons unknown, she gave them into Richard's care. Subsequently, after Richard's downfall in 1485, the former queen's daughter, Elizabeth, married King Henry VII. Elizabeth Woodville appears to have indulged in treasonable activities, for in 1487 she was disgraced and forced to enter a convent where she died five years later.

see Edward IV, Edward V, Princes in the Tower, Richard III, Tower of London

TUDOR DYNASTY

The Tudor dynasty, which reigned between 1485 and 1603, was descended from John of Gaunt, Duke of Lancaster, third surviving son of Edward III. Lady Margaret Beaufort, the mother of the first Tudor king, Henry VII, was the great-great-granddaughter of Edward III. The name of the dynasty derived from Lady Margaret's husband, Edmund Tudor, Earl of Richmond.

The Tudor claim to the crown was very distant and was complicated by the fact that the Beaufort family, the product of John of Gaunt's third marriage, was not considered legitimate: the Beauforts had to

▲ ABOVE: The Tudor dynasty was descended from John of Gaunt

be legitimised in 1397. Nevertheless, Henry VII's right to the crown was susceptible to challenge on the grounds that he was the descendant of a 'bastard' royal line. The second Tudor King, Henry VII's son, Henry VIII, also created problems for the legitimacy of his own dynasty. Henry VIII was succeeded in turns by his offspring Edward VI, Mary I and finally Elizabeth I. The last Tudor monarch, Elizabeth I, left no heir and her throne passed to the Stuart king, James of Scotland, a direct descendant of King Henry VII through his daughter, Margaret.

◆ Battle of Bosworth, James VI, Spanish Armada, Stuart Dynasty,

HENRY VII (1457–1509)

King of England (1485–1509). Henry's claim to the throne came through his descent from Edward III and the Beauforts, the children of Edward's son, John of Gaunt, by his third wife, Catherine Swynford. Henry was the only child of Lady Margaret Beaufort and her husband, Edmund Tudor, Earl of Richmond. Henry's army defeated the last Plantagenet (Angevin) king, Richard III, at the Battle of Bosworth in 1485. Subsequently, Henry became the first king of the Tudor dynasty.

Henry created a royal fortune which enabled him to do without Parliament for much of his reign. He avoided expensive wars, encouraged overseas trade and exploration and exploited Crown lands to the full. As a move to reconcile the opposing Houses of York and Lancaster, Henry, representative of Lancaster, had married Elizabeth, daughter of the Yorkist Edward IV in 1486. They had eight children. Henry used his children to cement alliances with other countries. When he died in 1509, Henry VII bequeathed a richer, more powerful throne than any England had known before to his successor, Henry VIII.

◆ *see* Margaret Beaufort, Battle of Bosworth, Catherine of Aragon, Edward IV, Henry VIII, Lambert Simnel, Perkin Warbeck, Wars of the Roses

HENRY VIII (1491–1547)

King of England (1509–47). Second son of Henry VII, Henry became heir to the throne on the premature death of his brother, Prince Arthur, in 1502, and succeeded in 1509. The same year, Henry VIII married Catherine of Aragon, Arthur's widow.

A successful monarch, the one blight on Henry's brilliant reign was his lack of a son to succeed him. All his children by Catherine, except for a daughter, Mary, had been stillborn or died in infancy. In around 1526, Henry resolved to divorce Catherine and marry one of her-ladies-in-waiting, Anne Boleyn, in hopes of having a son by her. The pope, to whom Henry applied for a divorce, refused to give it. Ultimately, Henry removed the Church in England from the pope's jurisdiction, pronounced his own

divorce and married Anne Boleyn in 1533. This fundamental change involved the dissolution of England's monasteries by 1540, which provoked a protest, the so-called Pilgrimage of Grace, in 1536. The Pilgrimage was put down with considerable force.

The only surviving child of Henry and Anne Boleyn was a daughter, the future Queen Elizabeth I. Anne Boleyn fell from favour and was executed in 1536. Henry married four more times. His third wife, Jane Seymour, was one of Anne's

◄ *LEFT: Henry VIII*

ladies-in-waiting. She married Henry in 1536. Their son, the future Edward VI, was born in 1537, but Jane died as a result. Henry then married Anne of Cleves, whom he divorced after only six months, Catherine Howard, who was executed for adultery in 1542, and finally Catherine Parr, in 1543.

As his reign progressed, Henry grew more and more tyrannical and became the terror of his ministers and his family. His health declined and he was tortured for many years by an ulcerous leg. Henry, 55, died at Whitehall Palace.

see Church of England, Dissolution of the Monasteries, Henry VII

▲ *ABOVE: Songs and music at the court of Henry VIII*

JAMES V OF SCOTLAND (1512–42)

King of Scotland (1513–42). James came to the throne of Scotland at the age of 17 months. In 1537 he married Madeleine, daughter of François I of France. James followed a policy of friendship with France and the pope and curbed the power of his nobles. They refused to support him against English invaders in 1542, as a result of which James was easily defeated. He went into a depression and died, leaving an infant daughter – Mary, Queen of Scots.

see Mary, Queen of Scots

▶ *RIGHT: James V of Scotland*

MARY I (1516–58)

Queen of England (1553–58). Daughter of Henry VIII and Catherine of Aragon. Mary was their only surviving child. On becoming queen, Mary set about re-establishing England as a Catholic country, and the persecution of the Protestants during her reign caused her to be dubbed 'Bloody Mary'. Mary became the first Queen regnant of England in 1553 on the death of her brother, Edward VI. John Dudley, Duke of Northumberland, tried, but failed, to deny her the throne by substituting his own candidate, his daughter-in-law, Lady Jane Grey. Mary's marriage to the Catholic Philip of Spain in 1554 was unpopular and caused violent public demonstrations. Greeted with joy and celebration on her accession, Mary died in 1558, deserted by Philip, and vilified by her subjects. The day of her death, 17 November, was kept as a public celebration for many years.

🔄 see Edward VI, Elizabeth I, Henry VIII

▶ RIGHT: Catherine of Aragon, mother of Mary I

PHILIP OF SPAIN (1527–98)

King of Spain. Philip was first involved with England in 1554, when he married Mary I. He was less interested in her than in an alliance with England and the use of her resources for Spain's wars in Europe. After Mary's death in 1558, he proposed marriage to her half-sister and successor, Elizabeth I, but was refused. Philip actively encouraged the Catholic plots to destroy Elizabeth and place Mary, Queen of Scots on the English throne. In 1588, the year after Mary's execution, Philip sent the Spanish Armada to England as part of a plan of invasion. It failed.

🔄 see Elizabeth I, Mary I, Mary, Queen of Scots, Spanish Armada

ELIZABETH I (1533–1603)

Queen of England (1558–1603). The last monarch of the Tudor dynasty. Daughter of Henry VIII and his second wife, Anne Boleyn. Elizabeth has become one of the most famous of English monarchs. She attempted to find a middle road in the question of religion, abhorring the extremes of the previous two reigns, and under her the country saw a new flourishing of art and literature. Her reign was marked by conflict with Catholic Spain, culminating in Sir Francis Drake's decisive defeat of the invading Spanish Armada in 1588. She never married and on her death she bequeathed the throne to the Scottish James VI.

see Anne Boleyn, Francis Drake, Henry VIII, Mary I, Spanish Armada

EDWARD VI (1537–53)

King of England (1547–53). Only son of Henry VIII. Edward became king at the age of just nine. He had been brought up and educated as a Protestant and during his brief reign steps were taken to reform the Church of England along Protestant lines: the reforms included the introduction of a new Prayer Book in 1552. Tragically, Edward contracted tuberculosis when he was only 15. Edward died at Greenwich Palace on 6 July 1553.

see Elizabeth I, Lady Jane Grey, Henry VIII, Mary I

GREY, LADY JANE (1537–54)

Eldest daughter of Henry Grey, Marquis of Dorset and cousin of Edward VI. Lady Jane was used as a pawn by her father-in-law, John Dudley, Duke of Northumberland, who wanted to perpetuate his own power by making her queen in place of the rightful heir, Edward's elder half-sister, Princess Mary. After Edward's death on 6 July 1553, Northumberland proclaimed Jane queen, and his son, Guildford Dudley, proclaimed himself king. However, there was a public outcry and, after nine days, he had to admit defeat. Lady Jane was imprisoned in the Tower of London and with her husband, Guildford Dudley, executed on 12 February 1554.

🡸 *see* Edward VI, Mary I, Tower of London

MARY, QUEEN OF SCOTS (1542–87)

Queen of Scotland (1542–67). Mary became queen of Scotland aged six days. She was married three times: to the young king of France (1559–60); to Henry, Lord Darnley (1565–67); and to James Hepburn, Earl of Bothwell (1567–78). Her Catholic marriage to Lord Darnley angered the Scots nobles and alienated the Protestant English queen, Elizabeth I. Mary was implicated in the killing of Darnley in 1567, which was believed to have been masterminded by James, Earl Bothwell. Bothwell was acquitted of the murder, but suspicions remained. Mary was totally discredited by these events, all the more so after she married Bothwell in May 1567. Mary and Bothwell fled but were soon captured. Bothwell afterwards escaped to Denmark, where he died mad in 1578. Mary was sent to Lochleven Castle, where she miscarried of twins in July 1567. The Scots nobles forced Mary to abdicate in favour of her son by Darnley, who became King James VI of Scotland and, after 1603, James I of England. Mary escaped and fled to England to seek protection from Queen Elizabeth. Mary was kept under house arrest, but she was executed in 1587 for her involvement in several Catholic plots aimed at murdering Elizabeth and restoring England to Catholicism.

Earl of Bothwell, Lord Darnley, Elizabeth I, James Hepburn, James VI

DARNLEY, HENRY STUART, LORD (1546–67)

Son of Malcolm Stuart, Earl of Lennox. Husband of Mary, Queen of Scots. Like Mary, whom he married in 1565, Darnley was descended from Henry

VII through Henry's daughter Margaret. The couple were soon estranged, over Mary's refusal to grant Darnley the Crown Matrimonial. He grew extremely jealous and was implicated in the plot by Scots nobles to murder Mary's Italian secretary, David Rizzio, in 1566. Rizzio enjoyed Mary's confidence and Darnley suspected him of being her lover. Darnley was himself murdered in 1567.

◆ *see* Mary, Queen of Scots

STUART DYNASTY

Originally a Scots dynasty that provided seven monarchs of England between 1603 and 1714. The first Stuart king of Scotland was David II who came to the throne in 1371. The first of the Stuart kings of England, James I, was already James VI of Scotland when he succeeded the last Tudor monarch, Queen Elizabeth I, in 1603. The royal Stuarts were an extremely unlucky family. Their history in Scotland was full of sudden deaths, deaths in battle, assassinations, depositions and rebellions against their rule. In England, the Stuarts' history was very troubled, due mainly to their adherence to the Divine Right of Kings. Both King James I and his son and successor King Charles I were devoted to the Divine Right.

The English Civil War of 1642–49 ended with the execution of King Charles. His son was restored to the throne in 1660 as Charles II. His Catholic brother, James, succeeded as King James II. James II was ousted and exiled in 1688, and his Protestant son-in-law and daughter replaced him as King William III and Queen Mary II. Their successor, Mary's sister, Queen Anne, the last of the Stuart monarchs, died in 1714.

◆ *see* Church of England, Constitutional Monarchy, Parliament

◀ *LEFT: James I of England and VI of Scotland*

JAMES I OF ENGLAND AND VI OF SCOTLAND (1567–1625)

King of Scotland (1567–1625) and England (1603–25). The only child of Mary, Queen of Scots. He had a claim to the throne of England based on his descent from Margaret, daughter of Henry VII, who married James IV of Scotland in 1503. James became king of Scotland as an infant, on his mother's abdication in 1567, and was controlled for several years by the Stuart family and his nobles. He took power personally in 1586 and followed a policy of friendship with England (even after the execution of his mother in 1587), moderate government in Scotland and royal authority over the Presbyterians. The Anglican Church in England welcomed James's Protestantism and his religious reforms, which included imposing moderation on the Puritans and introducing the Authorised Verison of the Bible, the King James Bible, in 1611.

see Charles I, Lord Darnley, Elizabeth I, Mary, Queen of Scots

CHARLES I (1600–49)

King of England and Scotland (1625–49). Second son of the Stuart king, James I. Charles's disagreements with Parliament led to his ruling for 11 years without it. Eventually Parliament fought back and the English Civil War broke out. In 1649 Charles was summarily tried for treason and executed, and the country became a commonwealth until Charles's son was restored to the throne in 1660.

see Oliver Cromwell, Eleven Years' Tyranny, English Civil War, Ship Money

RIGHT: Charles I

CHARLES II (1630–85)

King of England (1660–85). Son of Charles I. Charles II was restored to the throne in 1660. Charles was a great patron of the arts and his reign was marked by the new Renaissance architecture and a revival of theatre, art and literature. But this was also a time of great social disasters, the plague and the Great Fire of London among them. On his death the throne passed to his brother, James II.

◆ *see* Charles I, James II, Restoration, Test Acts

▲ *ABOVE: Charles II*

JAMES II OF ENGLAND AND VII OF SCOTLAND (1633–1701)

King of England and Scotland (1685–88). Second son of James I and VI. James's first wife, Anne Hyde, by whom he had two daughters, Mary and Anne, died in 1671. In 1673 James married the Catholic Mary of Modena, daughter of the Duke of Modena. By about 1668, James and Anne Hyde had converted to Roman Catholicism, but this was kept secret due to public and parliamentary antipathy to the faith. After Charles's death in 1685, James came to the throne as James II. From the first, he was determined to return his realm to Roman Catholicism and caused outrage. When a son was born to James and Mary of Modena, thus opening up the prospect of a line of Catholic monarchs, James was deposed and forced into exile with his wife and son. He attempted to retrieve his throne, but was defeated at the Battle of the Boyne in Ireland in 1690. James died in France in 1701.

◆ *see* Anglo-Dutch Wars, Battle of the Boyne, Charles II, Test Acts

INTERREGNUM (1649–60)

Meaning 'between the reigns', term used to describe the years of the English Republic created by Parliament, between the abolition of the monarchy in England in 1649 and the restoration to the throne of King Charles II in 1660. The Interregnum was divided into the Commonwealth (1649–53) and the Protectorate (1653–59). During the Commonwealth, power was exercised by the Rump Parliament, which angered the Puritans by failing to support their idea of a 'godly reformation' in the governance of England. Puritans regarded monarchy as tyranny, but to them the Rump, with its emphasis on materialism, was simply another form of tyranny. In 1652 the Rump was pressured by the army to introduce a bill calling for a new parliament. The army, however, did not trust the Rump Parliament and remained dissatisfied. So did Oliver Cromwell, who eventually expelled the Rump from Westminster. Subsequently, Cromwell became Lord Protector and head of state. His policy was to reconcile the opposing sides in the Civil War but divisions of opinion on policy within his Parliaments made this very difficult and it was never achieved. After Cromwell died in 1658, he was succeeded by his well-meaning but incompetent son, Richard. England began sinking into chaos as law and order broke down and this led to the move to restore the Stuart monarchy in 1660.

❖ *see* Charles I, Charles II, Oliver Cromwell, Rump Parliament

WILLIAM III (1650–1702)

Joint monarch of England with his wife Queen Mary II (1689-1702). Originally Prince of Orange in Holland. William married Mary, daughter and heir of the Catholic James II in 1677. In 1688, to prevent King James from re-Catholicising England, seven English peers invited William to invade England. James fled to France. Parliament considered that he had

▶ RIGHT: William III

abdicated, but MPs were worried that if his daughter, Mary, became reigning queen, she could have been considered a usurper. William, for his part, had no intention of becoming a King Consort. He had his own uses for England and its resources, as financial aid in his fight to keep Louis XIV of France from invading Holland. William, therefore, insisted on becoming king and in 1689 he was offered the throne jointly with Mary. They became England's only dual monarchy as William III and Mary II. Mary died of smallpox in 1694. However, with the agreement of Princess Anne, Mary's sister and the next direct heir to the throne, William remained king until his death in 1702.

◆ see Queen Anne, Battle of the Boyne, Constitutional Monarchy, James II, Mary II, Parliament

GEORGE I (1660–1727)

King of England (1714–27). The first monarch of the Hanoverian dynasty, George was not popular amongst his subjects. George succeeded to the throne after the death of Queen Anne, the last Stuart monarch, by right of his descent from James I. Unable to speak English, he communicated with his ministers in England in French, relying on his son, George Augustus, the future George II, to translate for him. George was divorced from his wife, Sophea Dorothea, 20 years before he became king. She was imprisoned for life for adultery in 1694. George endured a difficult relationship with his son, who had revered his mother, and spent much time abroad in his old electorate. He was succeeded by George II.

◆ see George II, Robert Walpole

MARY II (1662–94)

Joint queen of England (1689–94) with her husband, William III. Mary was the direct heir of her deposed father, James II. She was content to leave the government of England to her husband but, to his great grief, died of smallpox in 1694. The couple had no children.

↻ *see* Queen Anne, James II, William III

ANNE, QUEEN (1665–1714)

Queen of England (1702–14). Younger daughter of James II. Anne inherited the throne after the deaths of the joint monarchs Mary II and William of Orange. The most notable event of her reign was the Act of Union, which saw England and Scotland united politically. Anne married Prince George of Denmark in 1683. The premature death in 1701 of her last surviving child, William of Gloucester, prompted Parliament to pass the Act of Succession in which the throne passed to the Electors of Hanover.

↻ *see* Act of Succession, Act of Union, John Churchill, James II, Mary II, William III

▲ *ABOVE: Queen Anne of England*

GEORGE II (1683–1760)

King of England (1727–60). Essentially a soldier, George II became the last English king to lead his troops in battle during the War of the Spanish Succession. He had a loving relationship with his wife, Caroline, who was a beneficial influence, and worked well with his prime minister Robert

Walpole. Britain's importance vastly increased during George's long reign and, by the time he died in 1760, he was ruler of an appreciable overseas empire. He was succeeded by his son, George III.

◆ *see* George I, George III, Robert Walpole

▶ *RIGHT: George II*

GLORIOUS REVOLUTION (1688–89)

Name given to the deposition of the Catholic James II in 1688 and the accession in his place of his son-in-law and daughter as the joint monarchs William III and Mary II. Also known as the Bloodless Revolution because it took place without violence.

◆ *see* Queen Anne, Charles II, Mary II, William III

STUART, JAMES EDWARD (1688–1766)

Known as the 'Old Pretender'. Son of James II whose birth to his Catholic parents prompted the deposition of his father and lifelong exile. In 1708 James Edward attempted to invade Scotland and in 1715 he joined the Jacobite Rebellion which was aimed, unsuccessfully, at restoring him to his throne.

◆ *see* Bonnie Prince Charlie, Jacobite Rebellions, James II

HANOVERIAN DYNASTY

Royal dynasty of Electors of Hanover. The Hanoverians' right to the throne of England was based on their descent from Elizabeth, Queen of Bohemia, who was a daughter of the Stuart, James VI of Scotland and I of England. Elizabeth's daughter, Sophia, was Electress consort of Hanover, and the mother of George I. In 1701, after the death of the last child of the then Princess Anne, younger daughter of James II, Parliament passed the Act of Settlement: this named the Electress, Sophia, as Anne's heir. George I came to the throne in 1714; his son and successor, George II, became king in 1727. The other monarchs of the Hanoverian dynasty were King George III, who succeeded to the throne in 1760, George IV (1820), William IV (1830) and Queen Victoria (1837).

◆ George I, George II, George III, George IV, William IV, Victoria

ACT OF SETTLEMENT (1701)

Act of Parliament passed in 1701, decreeing that Queen Anne should be succeeded by Sophia, Electress of Hanover, a Protestant descendant of James I. Other provisions of the Act were that sovereigns must be members of the Church of England, could not dismiss judges except at Parliament's request or pardon ministers already impeached by Parliament.

◆ see Queen Anne, Hanoverian Dynasty, Test Act

FREDERICK, PRINCE OF WALES (1707–51)

Son of George II, with whom he quarrelled violently. At Leicester House, Frederick's court, separate from his father's, became a meeting place for opponents of Robert Walpole, the king's chief minister. The influence of the Leicester House group in Parliament faded quickly after Frederick suddenly died.

◆ see George II, George III, Robert Walpole

'BONNIE PRINCE CHARLIE' (1720–88)

Charles Edward Stuart, also known as the 'Young Pretender'. Charles was the grandson of the Catholic James II and son of James, the 'Old

Pretender'. In 1745 Charles raised the second Jacobite Rebellion in the Highlands of Scotland in a bid to regain the Stuart throne in England. The Jacobites were defeated at Culloden in 1746, and Charles became a fugitive. He returned to France, but was expelled by Louis XV. He died in Rome in 1788.

◆ *see* Battle of Culloden, Jacobite Rebellion, James II, James Edward Stuart

GEORGE III (1738–1820)

King of England (1760–1820). Son of Frederick, Prince of Wales, grandson and successor to George II. George III was the first Hanoverian monarch to be born and educated in England. His great interest in farming and botany earned him the nickname of 'Farmer George'. King George was stubborn and his political judgment was poor, but he was very religious and very moral. In 1788 George had his first attack of madness, which has since been ascribed to the blood disease porphyria. He recovered in 1789, the madness returned in 1810. George, now blind as well as mad, spent the rest of his life a prisoner in Windsor Castle while his son, the Prince of Wales, ruled in his place as Prince Regent. George III died in 1820.

◆ *see* Queen Charlotte, Frederick, Prince of Wales, George IV, William Pitt the Younger

▲ *ABOVE: George III*

CHARLOTTE, QUEEN (1744–1818)

Queen of England. Wife of George III. Born Charlotte of Mecklenburg-Strelitz. Although their marriage was arranged, the king and queen had a very happy relationship and he was devoted to her. She remained loyal to him throughout his bouts of illness. They had 15 children. Queen Charlotte set the pattern for moral royal domestic life that was followed by later royals.

◆ *see* George III

GEORGE IV (1762–1830)

King of England (1821–30). Son of George III. Both as Prince of Wales and king, George IV was uninterested in his royal duties and preferred the pleasures of high society social life. When his father went mad in 1810, George became Prince Regent, but his powers were limited by Parliament. The Prince Regent became George IV on the death of his father in 1820. His daughter and only child, Princess Charlotte, had died in childbirth in 1817. He was succeeded by his brother, William IV.

◆ *see* Brighton Pavilion, George III, Royal Marriages Act

WILLIAM IV (1765–1837)

King of England (1830–37). Son of George III. William IV was so delighted to become king, on the death of his brother, George IV, in 1830, that he drove round London personally greeting his new subjects. In his youth, William had served in the Royal Navy and commanded ships. William married Adelaide of Saxe-Meiningen in 1818 after the death of Princess Charlotte, George IV's daughter, had removed the last heir to the throne in her generation. Sadly, the two daughters of William and Adelaide, who were devoted to each other, died in infancy and William's heir was his niece, Victoria.

◆ *see* Abolitionists, Queen Adelaide, George IV, Great Reform Act, Queen Victoria, William Wilberforce

◀ *LEFT: William IV*

CAROLINE OF BRUNSWICK, PRINCESS (1768–1821)

Princess of Wales. Prince George (the future George IV) married Caroline in 1795 to 'repay' Parliament for discharging his debts. George took an instant dislike to Caroline, and the couple separated within nine months, after their daughter, Princess Charlotte, was born in 1796. Afterwards, Caroline became notorious for her outlandish conduct and adulterous relationships. She died a few weeks after a failed attempt to attend the coronation of her husband in 1821.

 *see* George IV

ROYAL MARRIAGES ACT (1772)

Act of Parliament designed to prevent princes from marrying unsuitable wives. It was prompted by the marriage of George III's brother, Henry, to a commoner. The Act made it illegal for princes under age 25 to marry without the king's permission. The Act is still in force today.

see George III, George IV

ADELAIDE, QUEEN (1792–1849)

Born Adelaide of Saxe-Meiningen. Wife of William IV. They married in 1818 in the 'rush to the altar' by George III's sons with the intention of providing heirs to the throne after the death of Princess Charlotte, the Prince Regent's daughter. Two daughters were born to William and Adelaide, but both died in infancy.

see William IV

▶ RIGHT: Queen Adelaide

ALBERT, PRINCE (1819–61)

Prince of Saxe-Coburg-Gotha, Germany. Husband of Queen Victoria, whom he married in 1840. Albert was made prince consort by the queen in 1857. Although not greatly liked in England, Albert performed sterling services to the British monarchy and to British cultural life. Victoria, by whom he had four sons and five daughters, adored Prince Albert and was shattered by his early death, probably from typhoid, at the age of 42.

🔹 *see* Edward VII, Great Exhibition, Queen Victoria

▲ *ABOVE: Prince Albert*

VICTORIA, QUEEN (1819–1901)

Queen of England (1837–1901). Victoria succeeded her uncle, William IV, in 1837. In 1840, she married Prince Albert of Saxe-Coburg-Gotha and they had nine children. When Albert died in 1861, Victoria was distraught and she mourned him extravagantly for the next forty years until her own death in 1901. None of Victoria's children married English spouses, which explains her nickname 'Grandmother of Europe'. During Victoria's 63-year reign, the longest yet in British history, Britain made substantial social progress, with acts of Parliament designed to control working hours and conditions in factories and mines, establish education for all

children, improve the position of women and emancipate Catholics and Jews. Britain became the dominant world power, with a vast, far-flung empire on which 'the sun never set'. India was considered the 'jewel in the crown' of the British Empire and in 1876 Victoria was granted the title Empress of India by Parliament.

see Prince Albert, Boer War, British Empire, Crimean War, Edward VII

▶ *RIGHT: Queen Victoria*

EDWARD VII (1841–1910)

King of England (1901–10). Son of Queen Victoria and Prince Albert. Edward was married to Princess Alexandra of Denmark in 1861, but he was an unfaithful husband. He had numerous mistresses and he came close to public scandal on more than one occasion. Edward became king on Victoria's death in 1901 and his years of socialising proved to be an asset as he became a royal ambassador for England, able to converse easily with other monarchs and their ministers. He died in 1910 after a series of heart attacks.

see Queen Victoria, Prince Albert

WINDSOR, HOUSE OF

The royal House of Windsor is not a dynasty in the true sense. The monarchs of the House of Windsor – George V, Edward VIII, George VI and Elizabeth II – were direct descendants of the Hanoverian dynasty which inherited the throne when the Elector of Hanover became King George I in 1714. The dynasty's name was changed in 1901, to 'Saxe-Coburg-Gotha', a German state where Queen Victoria's husband, Prince Albert, was born. Edward VII, son and heir of Queen Victoria and Prince Albert, was the first king of the House of Saxe-Coburg-Gotha. In 1910 his son, George V, came to the throne as the second king of this House, but in 1917, he altered its name to Windsor. He did so because of the British hatred of Germany and its Kaiser, Wilhelm II, that developed during World War I. Anti-German feeling was a severe embarrassment to George V, who not only ordered the change of name to Windsor but told his royal relatives to drop their German titles and take new ones.

◆ see Prince Albert, Edward VII, Edward VIII, Elizabeth II, George V, George VI, Hanoverian Dynasty, Queen Victoria, World War I

GEORGE V (1865–1936)

King of England (1911–36). Second son and successor of Edward VII. When his elder brother, Prince Albert Victor (Eddy) died in 1892, Prince George became his father's heir and was obliged to resign from the Royal Navy. He married Albert Victor's bereaved fianceé, Princess May of Teck, in 1893. They had six children. King George supported political moves, such as the Irish Home Rule Bill and he repeatedly warned his first cousin, Kaiser Wilhelm II of Germany, against his warlike policies. In public, the King and his wife, now Queen Mary, preferred their role as exemplars of royal social leadership, which placed them above political controversies. Their style was somewhat aloof and distant, but they became very popular and highly respected. George V was the first English monarch to be crowned Emperor of India in Delhi, in 1911. King George was a model royal leader of the nation during World War I, but the post-war years were saddened by his estrangement from his son and heir, who became King Edward VIII on his father's death in 1936.

◆ *see* Edward VII, Edward VIII, George VI, Victoria, World War I

▶ *RIGHT: George V*

INDIA, EMPRESS/EMPEROR OF

The title Empress of India was granted to Queen Victoria under the Royal Titles Act of 1876. Its main purpose was to emphasise British power as exemplified by its vast empire abroad. The title also put Victoria on a par with European royal families with imperial titles. Edward VII, George V, Edward VIII and George VI were called Emperors of India until the title was relinquished by George VI with the independence of India in 1947.

◆ *see* British Empire, George VI, Victoria

EDWARD VIII (1894–1972)

King of England (1936). Eldest son of George V and Queen Mary. As Prince of Wales, Edward rejected the elitist royal social life, preferring the hedonistic, night-clubbing company of the nouveaux riches and social climbers. It was in this company that he met Mrs Wallis Simpson and her husband Ernest in 1931. Edward fell in love with Wallis. He succeeded the throne after George V's death on 20 January 1936 and intended to marry Wallis and make her his queen. This move was strongly opposed by the British and Commonwealth governments, the Church and his family. Prime minister Stanley Baldwin told him that the now twice-divorced Wallis would not be acceptable as queen of England. Rather than give her up, Edward abdicated on 11 December 1936. His brother took his place as George VI. The Duke and Duchess of Windsor, as Edward and Wallis became, married in 1937 and spent most of their life together abroad. Edward died in Paris in 1972.

see Abdication Crisis, George V, George VI, Wallis Simpson

▶ *RIGHT: Edward VIII*

GEORGE VI (1895–1952)

King of England (1936–52). Albert, Duke of York, who succeeded his brother Edward VIII after the latter's abdication in 1936. In 1923 the duke married Lady Elizabeth Bowes-Lyon, who became his staunch helper and support as his queen. Despite his drawbacks, George VI became a highly respected king. The king and queen became the social leaders of Britain at war and remained in London, where Buckingham Palace was bombed several times in air raids. The royal couple toured England constantly, travelling by special train, and were there to comfort victims of air raids in London and other cities. In 1951 he underwent an operation for lung cancer. He appeared to recover, but died suddenly on 6 February 1952, and his daughter, Elizabeth II, succeeded him.

see Elizabeth Bowes-Lyon, Edward VIII, Elizabeth II, World War II

BOWES-LYON, ELIZABETH (1900–2002)

Queen consort of England. Ninth of 10 children and youngest daughter of the Earl and Countess of Strathmore. Elizabeth married Albert, Duke of York, second son of George V and the future George VI in 1923. She became queen unexpectedly, when her husband was obliged to accept the Crown after his brother, Edward VIII, abdicated in 1936. At that juncture, Elizabeth was considered too dull and provincial to be queen consort, but she rose magnificently to the challenge. Her finest hour came after 1939, when she and the king became the much-admired social leaders of the country during World War II. Widowed at 51, Elizabeth went on to become a greatly loved queen mother and lived to celebrate her 100th birthday in 2000.

see Edward VIII, Elizabeth II, George VI

ELIZABETH II (B. 1926)

Queen of England (1952–). Daughter of George VI. Elizabeth became heir presumptive to the throne after her uncle, Edward VIII, abdicated in 1936. She succeeded the throne after the untimely death of her father in 1952. The half-century in which she has ruled has been one of enormous change for the monarchy, but Elizabeth has remained a dutiful and well-informed queen. Elizabeth married Lieutenant Philip Mountbatten RN, a distant cousin, in 1947. He became Prince Philip, Duke of Edinburgh. They subsequently had four children.

see Elizabeth Bowes-Lyon; Charles, Prince of Wales; Edward VIII; George VI

ABDICATION CRISIS (1936)

Furore surrounding the relationship between King Edward VIII and the twice-divorced American Wallis Simpson. The king abdicated on 11 December 1936 after it had been made clear by prime minister Stanley Baldwin and others that Mrs Simpson would not be acceptable as queen. He resigned his throne rather than give her up.

▶ *see* Edward VIII, Wallis Simpson

▶ *RIGHT: Edward VIII*

CHARLES PHILIP ARTHUR GEORGE, PRINCE OF WALES (B. 1948)

21st Prince of Wales. Heir to Queen Elizabeth II. Married to Lady Diana Spencer in 1981, the couple separated acrimoniously in 1992. Diana's intense popularity with the British public led to criticism over the way the royal family and Prince Charles in particular treated the princess, but he maintained his dignity throughout a difficult time for the monarchy and recent years have seen a revival in his own popularity. Diana and Charles had two sons, Prince William, born in 1982, and Prince Henry (Harry), born in 1984.

▶ *see* Diana, Princess of Wales; Elizabeth II, Heir to the throne; Wales, Princes of

DIANA, PRINCESS OF WALES (1961–97)

Diana, daughter of Earl Spencer, married Prince Charles on 29 July 1981. She achieved phenomenal worldwide popularity as a fashion icon, for her charitable work and as devoted mother to her two sons, William and Harry. Diana became the most photographed woman in the world and attracted intense media interest. The marriage dissolved due to allegations that Charles was having an affair; Diana is also believed to have had an affair. In 1997 Diana was in Paris with her friend Dodi Fayed when their car crashed while being pursued by paparazzi. Dodi was killed and Diana, who was severely injured, died a few hours later. Her funeral in London attracted extraordinary public grief. Diana was afterwards buried at the Spencer family home, Althorp House, in Northamptonshire.

◆ see Prince Charles, Elizabeth II, House of Windsor

▶ *RIGHT: Diana, Princess of Wales*

WILLIAM, PRINCE (B. 1982)

Elder son of Charles, Prince of Wales. Second heir to the throne after his father. Prince William made his first official public appearance when he accompanied his parents on their tour of Australia in 1983. Despite intense public interest, the media granted Prince William an unusual degree of privacy for a member of the Royal Family, during his schooldays.

◆ see Charles, Prince of Wales, Diana, Princess of Wales, House of Windsor

▲ *ABOVE: Prince William*

SOCIETY

2700 BC	Beaker People settle in Britain
3rd century BC	Celts inhabit Britain
AD 43	Britain added to Roman Empire
AD 5th–11th centuries	Anglo-Saxons inhabit Britain
1086	Domesday Book
12th century	Cambridge University founded
12th century	Oxford University founded
1348	Black Death
1381	Peasants' Revolt
1596	Death of Sir Francis Drake, explorer
1601	Poor Laws passed
1618	Death of Walter Raleigh, explorer
1620	Pilgrim Fathers set sail for the New World
1665	Plague
1666	Great Fire of London
1694	Bank of England founded
18th century	Age of Enlightenment
18th century	Industrial Revolution
1715–46	Jacobite Rebellion
1720	South Sea Bubble financial crash
1173	Boston Tea Party
1811	Luddite movement
1819	Peterloo Massacre
1829	Metropolitan Police established
1870	First Education Act passed
1882	Death of Charles Darwin
1884	GMT established
Early 20th century	Suffragette movement founded
1910	Death of Florence Nightingale
1929	Start of Great Depression
1939–54	Rationing due to World War II
1945	Welfare State established
1948	NHS established
1988	Lockerbie bombing, Scotland
1993	EU formed

CLANS

Family groups, especially Scottish. The word 'clan' is derived from the Gaelic clann, meaning 'children', because Scottish clans are characterised by their own ancestry. The prefixes 'Mac' and 'Mc' both indicate that someone is descended from a particular ancestral line, so McCartney means 'son of Cartney'. Originally clan members kept strictly to themselves and there was intense rivalry between clans.

◀ LEFT: A gathering of the Clan John Gordon, in 1949

THAMES, RIVER

The artery of London. London began as a Roman settlement around the river. The river is 338 km (210 miles) long, making it the longest English river. It rises near Cirencester in the Cotswold Hills in the west of England and flows in a roughly easterly direction until it meets the North Sea at Southend. The Thames is tidal as far as Teddington just west of London. The Thames Barrier, completed 1982, was built downstream of London to prevent flooding.

BEAKER PEOPLE (c. 2700 BC)

Group of early settlers in the British Isles. At a time during the transition from the late Neolithic to the early Bronze Age – around 2700 to 1700 BC – a culture arose that swept across the greater part of Europe. Beaker people probably originated from the Iberian peninsula. They made distinctive waisted drinking vessels, called bell beakers, from earthenware clay.

CELTS

Early settlers in the British Isles. The Celts dominated large parts of Europe from the third century BC. In Britain the Celtic culture would be subsumed by the Romans, but their language, religion and art would have a lasting influence on subsequent cultures.

The Celts had begun their expansion from a stronghold in Alpine Europe, although they are thought to have been of Indo-European origin. In 390 BC they sacked Rome and overran a good deal of the Continent. They eventually occupied territory as far west as the Iberian peninsula, as far east as Greece and as far north as the British Isles. Despite their success at conquering new lands, the Celts lacked the communicational and organisational skills to unite their empire in the way that the Romans would. Instead emigrant bands would set off and establish permanent settlements. This meant that vast areas all over Europe were dominated by similar cultures and languages. In fact the Celtic culture left such an indelible mark on Europe that Celtic enclaves survived through the subsequent Roman occupation and into medieval times. Celtic languages even survive today as vestiges of a culture that profoundly influenced a Europe heading toward civilisation. Remarkably, Celtic styles of art and music are also still influencing modern cultures in Europe over 2,000 years later.

🔹 *see* Druids

▶ *RIGHT: A characteristic Celtic cross*

IRON AGE

Period of prehistory. Metallurgy in Britain
began with the Bronze Age. Bronze had been
put to all kinds of technological uses and was
a marked improvement on working stone
because it could be melted and poured into
shapes, and it could be reworked when cutting
edges were blunted. Then came the arrival of
iron. Iron was more difficult to work than

▲ *Iron Age Tools*

bronze because it required far higher temperatures to soften it.
Nevertheless, iron offered a material for tools and weapons that was far
more hard-wearing and tough than bronze. It eclipsed bronze and gave
rise to the Iron Age culture in Europe.

CAESAR, JULIUS (100–44 BC)

Roman emperor. Caesar first set foot in Britain in 55 BC, during his
conquest of Gaul, intending to prevent the Celts from sending aid to
the Gauls. He remained only a few weeks before bad weather forced
him to retreat. The following year he returned with greater forces and
engaged in successful battle against the tribes of ancient Britain.
Although neither of these expeditions were planned as invasions, he
gained promises from the tribes that they would not interefere in his
conquest of Gaul. It was left to the Emperor Claudius, nearly 100 years
later, to begin the Roman occupation of the British Isles.

◆ *see* Emperor Claudius

ATREBATES (c. 50 BC)

Celtic tribe. The Atrebates lived in south-central England from 50 BC
under the leadership of Commius, who followed an anti-Roman policy.

His son and successor Tincommius, however, was more amenable to Roman rule and was made a client king in around 15 BC.

BATH SPA (c. AD 43)
Roman settlement in the west of England. The city of Bath originated as a Roman spa town. Its Roman name was Aquae Sulis, meaning 'waters of Sul'. Sul was then the British goddess of wisdom. The settlement was established and largely built within 20 years of the Roman invasion in AD 43. The natural, hot springs were used for therapeutic bathing by the Romans.

see Roman Empire

CLAUDIUS, EMPEROR
Roman emperor. Leader of the Roman conquest of Britain. Although Julius Caesar had made forays into the British Isles in 55 BC, it was Claudius who conducted the first campaign of conquest in AD 43. He stayed only for the initial stages of the campaign against the tribes, leaving the remainder of the conquest to his generals.

see Julius Caesar, Roman Invasion

▲ *ABOVE: Minerva as seen on copper dupondius of Claudius*

ROMAN EMPIRE
In AD 43 Emperor Claudius I added England, Wales and lowland Scotland to the Roman Empire. He called the new territory Brittania. Brittania was the northernmost outpost of the Roman Empire. The Romans had seized territory reaching as far south as Egypt (Aegyptus), as far east as Iraq

(Mesopotamia) and as far West as the Iberian peninsula (Hispania) by the height of expansion in AD 117 under Emperor Trajan.

Hadrian who was emperor AD 117–38 is famed for having a defensive wall built at the boundary between Britannia and Scotland to fend off attacks from clansmen, such were hostilities between the Romans and the natives. Nevertheless, the Romans occupied Britannia until AD 410, when Rome fell to the Visgoths and the Roman legions were withdrawn.

◆ *see* Roman Invasion

ROMAN SETTLEMENTS

When the Romans arrived in ancient Britain they found a land full of heathen, warlike, Celtic tribes. Although they put up some resistance, the Celts were quickly conquered by the Roman army. The Romans set about building settlements for themselves, using the technologies they had mastered during the expansion of the empire since 753 BC.

Roman houses were masterfully constructed using blocks of stone and clay bricks held together with mortar. Roofs were made from tiles on wooden frames and floors were made from tiles. In essence they were the template for most building design ever since. Some Roman houses had the luxury of under-floor heating and were elaborately embellished with floor and wall mosaics.

Public buildings were even more impressively constructed. They featured pillars and arches which enabled the

▶ RIGHT: *Roman excavations*

Romans to build very large structures with out using enormous amounts of material. The same technology was used in building bridges, viaducts, aquaducts and defensive walls.

Roman roads were remarkable feats of engineering. They comprised various layers of building material and included cambers and gullies for drainage. Their roads are well known for being extremely straight. This is because they were designed to take the shortest route possible between locations.

Roman towns often included sewerage systems carefully planned and built before the streets and buildings, so that they ran beneath. The towns were paved to keep the streets clean and carefully laid out so that public facilities could be utilised to optimum effect.

ICENI

Tribe of ancient Britain. During the Roman occupation of Britain there were native populations who attempted revolts against the Romans. One such population was the Iceni from eastern England. The Iceni had been ruled by King Prasutagus, a Roman tributary. Upon his death in AD 60, the Romans annexed the Iceni territory. Prasutagus's widow Boudicca (Boadicea) and her daughters were cruelly treated along with the other native Britons. In response Boudicca raised an army and launched a bloody, but short-lived revolt.

◆ *see* Boudicca

DRUIDS

Celtic priests. When the Celts took control of Britain they brought with them their heathen religion, called Druidism, which involved belief in spirits of the Earth. Druids held that the oak tree was sacred and centred their rituals around great oak trees. They also believed in reincarnation, considering the soul to be immortal. They were responsible for the stone circles and related Neolithic features in the landscape. Druidism was largely stamped out eventually by the invading Romans.

◆ see Celts

ANGLO-SAXONS (5TH–11TH CENTURIES)

Name given to the descendants of the Jutes, Angles and Saxons, Germanic tribes who invaded the British Isles between the fifth and seventh centuries. Once they had settled into their respective kingdoms they were subject to further threats of invasion from overseas, mainly marauding Vikings, but it was the Normans who finally overthrew the Anglo-Saxons in 1066.

The Anglo-Saxons left behind some valuable contributions to British culture. Not least the Anglo-Saxon or Old English language, which was the foundation for modern English. They also bequeathed intricate and decorative manuscripts and pieces of early Christian religious artwork.

◆ see Alfred the Great, Anglo-Saxon Chronicle, Danelaw, Norman Dynasty, Vikings

EAST ANGLIA, KINGDOM OF

Province of Ancient Britain. During the era of Anglo-Saxon occupation in Britain the territory was divided into kingdoms. One kingdom was dominated by the Angles and so called East Anglia. It covered an area which roughly corresponds with the modern counties of Norfolk and Suffolk. It used to be geographically isolated by fen land.

◆ see Anglo-Saxons, Sutton Hoo

ESSEX, KINGDOM OF

Province of Anglo-Saxon Britain. During the height of Anglo-Saxon rule in Britain, England was divided into seven kingdoms, known as the heptarchy. The Saxons claimed rule over the three kingdoms of Essex, Sussex and Wessex. Essex was easily accessible to the Teutonic invaders from mainland Europe, forming part of the East Coast that looks out over the North Sea. It also comprised the north bank of the Thames estuary and had natural harbours at Harwich and Malden. In fact it was at Malden in the year AD 991 that the Saxons were defeated in a battle against the Vikings, who landed there having sailed from Scandinavia.

see Anglo-Saxons

KENT, KINGDOM OF

Province of ancient Britain. The south-eastern corner of England, Kent, had been ruled by a Briton who was having trouble with an enemy force called the Picts. He requested help from the Jutish chieftain brothers Hengist and Horsa. They obliged the Briton king by defeating the Picts but then overthrew him to seize control of Kent themselves. The Jute territory comprised the Kingdom of Kent and South Hampshire.

see Anglo-Saxons

KNIGHTS

Medieval Britain was a place where warrior skills were highly prized. The most honourable military rank was knight. A knight was usually raised by the sovereign, having served as a page and squire. Knights were mounted soldiers in armour. This meant having to acquire riding skills and be robust enough to do battle dressed in metal. Only a select few were up to the job and so were accorded considerable respect, social status and wealth.

see Order of the Garter

MERCIA, KINGDOM OF

Province of Ancient Britain. The Angles claimed three kingdoms: East Anglia, Northumbria and Mercia. Mercia lay in central England with its western perimeter bordered by Wales. It covered most of England between the Humber and the Thames, except East Anglia. In AD 633 the king of Mercia, Penda, defeated and killed Edwin, who had declared himself overlord of Britain. Penda was assisted by the king of Wales, Cadwallon. He also defeated the Christian King Oswald of Northumbria in AD 642.

🔹 *see* Anglo-Saxons

NORTHUMBRIA, KINGDOM OF

Province of ancient Britain. Northumbria was a kingdom which comprised the north-east of England and south-east Scotland and was governed by the Angles. In the sixth century Northumbria comprised the two lesser kingdoms of Bernicia and Deira, but by the seventh century they had been united. In AD 664 King Oswy of Northumbria asserted the supremacy of the Roman Church in Britain by calling the Synod of Whitby. In AD 827 Northumbria fell under the overlordship of Wessex and by AD 886 was subject to Danelaw following invasion by the Danes.

🔹 *see* Anglo-Saxons

WESSEX, KINGDOM OF

Province of ancient Britain. The kingdom of the West Saxons was known as Wessex. Legend has it that Cerdic founded Wessex in c. AD 500. Wessex corresponded with the modern counties of Hampshire, Dorset, Wiltshire, Berkshire, Somerset and Devon. In around AD 829 Wessex became the supreme Anglo-Saxon kingdom under Egbert as overlord or Bretwalda. The most famous king of Wessex was Alfred the Great (c. 847–c. 899). He became king in AD 871. Alfred created the first English navy to help fend off invasions from his archenemies the Danes.

🔲 *see* Anglo-Saxons

DANES

Invaders of Scandinavian origin who plundered and eventually settled in the British Isles. The Dark Ages in Britain were characterised by waves of invasion from foreign forces. The Anglo-Saxons came from the Germanic region of Europe, while Norsemen came from Scandinavia. Norsemen, known as Vikings or Danes, were skilled sailors and efficient warriors. Initially they paid Britain fleeting visits to raid villages, plundering and pillaging as they went. Eventually, though, the Danes secured a foothold in Britain and conquered the Danelaw region of northern and eastern England.

🔲 *see* Danelaw

◀ *LEFT: Eric the Red sets sail for Greenland*

BURHS (AD 9TH CENTURY)

Fortified towns in Anglo-Saxon Britain. The suffix 'borough' to a place name is a reference to the place originating as an Anglo-Saxon 'burh'. During the reign of Alfred the Great, a network of defended enclosures was constructed to safeguard people, goods and livestock from the marauding Danes, with whom the Britons were warring. The king decreed that no village should lie farther than 20 miles from one of these bolt holes.

🔲 *see* Alfred the Great

SCONE, STONE OF

A little farther north than Perth, Scotland, is a village called Scone in Tayside. Scone is the location where most of the kings of Scotland were crowned. The coronations occurred on the Stone of Destiny or Stone of Scone which is now incorporated into the Coronation Chair at Westminster, London.

DANELAW (AD 886)

Area of north-east England settled by the Danes in the eleventh century. By the late ninth century Norsemen had managed to secure a good deal of the British territory formerly occupied by the Anglo-Saxons. By the year AD 886 they held most of northern and eastern England, an area known as the Danelaw, and had introduced their own laws, customs and language.

◆ *see* Vikings

ANGLO-SAXON CHRONICLE (AD 891)

Record of life during the Anglo-Saxon period begun in the reign of Alfred the Great. The Anglo-Saxon Chronicle gave a year-by-year account of life in England from the Roman invasion and continued right through to the twelfth century. Although some parts are less detailed than others, the Chronicle remains the most valuable source of information about the early history of Britain to date.

◆ *see* Alfred the Great, Anglo-Saxons

▲ *ABOVE: A page from the Anglo-Saxon Chronicle*

TITHES

Taxes levied in the Middle Ages. Tax was paid by members of a parish community for the upkeep of the church and its incumbent priest. This tax was known as the tithe and typically amounted to 10 per cent of each parishioner's income. It was often produce, stored in the tithe barn.

FEUDAL SYSTEM

Social hierarchy in the Middle Ages. When the Normans took control of Britain under William I they introduced the feudal system as a means of structuring society. The feudal system was based on land ownership and extended over much of medieval Europe because it was a logical way of assessing power. The king owned large areas of Crown land across the country. This put him at the very top of a hierarchical triangle which extended downwards from him. Beneath the king were other members of royalty, then nobility, lesser gentry, free tenants, villeins and serfs. These groups were linked by legal duties and obligations.

◆ see Domesday Book, William I

▲ ABOVE: Peasants rebel against the feudal system

RETAINERSHIP

Medieval system by which all land ultimately belonged to the Crown, but effective ownership of land was retained by the payment of feudal dues. A hierarchy meant that land rent was paid upwards until it reached the monarch's purse.

◖ *see* Feudalism

DOMESDAY BOOK (1086)

Survey conducted by William I after the Norman Conquest to establish the extent of Crown lands in England. Following the Battle of Hastings (1066) William I commissioned a survey of England. The purpose of this was to assess the wealth of William's kingdom. Carried out in 1086, the survey covered land tax and other dues owed by the population. It also ascertained the value of lands belonging to the Crown and enabled William to estimate accurately the wealth and power of his vassal barons, who held their lands by feudal tenure on conditions of homage and allegiance to the king. The survey document is known as the Domesday Book.

◖ *see* William I, Normans, Anglo-Saxons

CAMBRIDGE UNIVERSITY (12TH CENTURY)

English university. As Europe emerged from the Dark Ages, knowledge began to be perceived as a form of power, giving rise to the first seats of learning that we now know as universities. One of the first European universities was established at Cambridge sometime in the 1100s. It now comprises many separate colleges; the oldest is Peterhouse, founded in 1284.

see Oxford University

OXFORD UNIVERSITY (1100S)

English university. The most ancient seat of learning in Britain is Oxford University, which was established through the 1100s. The founding of the oldest existing college is dated to 1249. The university suffered land confiscation during the Reformation, 1534, but Henry VIII's daughter, Elizabeth I, reorganised the situation in 1571.

▶ *RIGHT: Oxford University*

PALE, THE

English enclave in Ireland. During the fourteenth and fifteenth centuries Irish chieftains recovered much of the territory invaded by Anglo-Normans in 1167. The enclave of land still under English control, which ran 50 miles inland from Dublin, was known as the Pale. The Pale remained under English rule and subsequently proved the foothold needed for the Tudors to impose the Reformation and English law on Ireland. They adopted a policy of conquest, confiscation of land and settlement by Englishmen.

see Elizabeth I

◀ *LEFT: Cambridge University*

WALLACE, WILLIAM (1272–1329)

Scottish nationalist. Wallace led an uprising against English rule in Scotland in 1297. He shared the uprising with Robert Bruce but declared himself 'governor of Scotland' following the success of his campaign at Stirling. He was defeated, however, in 1298, by Edward I, and put to death in 1305. Robert the Bruce was eventually recognised as king of Scotland in 1328 at the Treaty of Northampton.

◆ see Robert Bruce, Edward I

GARTER, ORDER OF THE (1344)

Highest order of English knighthood. Edward III was responsible for creating the Order of the Garter in around 1344. Legend has it that whilst dancing with the Countess of Salisbury a garter dropped from her leg and the king placed it on his own leg in a moment of merriment. He then said 'shamed be he who thinks evil of it' in French, which became the motto of the order.

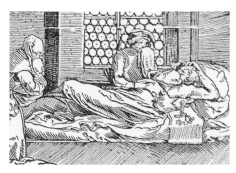

BLACK DEATH (1348)

Form of the Plague. Just as Europe was finding its feet after the Dark Ages it suffered a catastrophic setback in the form of disease. Originating in Asia the bubonic plague took hold rapidly in Europe, spread by fleas carried on

▲ *ABOVE: A victim of the Black Death*

rats that flourished in the overcrowded medieval towns. So called because it causes buboes or boils to erupt under the skin, bubonic plague reached Britain in 1348, killing almost half of the population in a few months. The epidemic had such a profound effect on the infrastructure of Europe that it became known as the Black Death. A second plague struck in 1665.

▷ *see* Plague

PEASANTS' REVOLT (1381)

Uprising against the new poll tax. In June 1381 Richard II introduced a new poll tax in an attempt to sort out the economy following the Black Death (1348–49) which had seen between a third and half of the British population die from bubonic plague. Two previous poll taxes, in 1377 and 1379, had already been introduced but the new one was a threefold increase. The peasants of Britain, who still laboured under the system of serfdom and feudalism, were prompted to revolt in protest. Riots broke out all over England.

Two men – Wat Tyler and John Ball – emerged as rebel leaders and marched on London where they plundered and ransacked parts of the city. Richard, still only a teenager, attempted to appease the mob by announcing concessions but order was not restored until Tyler had been murdered. The king's concessions were then revoked and the revolt suppressed.

▷ *see* Richard II, Wat Tyler

▲ *ABOVE: John Ball preaches to the peasants*

SLAVERY

When European traders first visited the coast of West Africa, there was already a flourishing slave trade going on. Rich Africans were capturing tribesmen from villages in the interior and selling them into slavery in the Middle East. It was easy therefore for the Europeans to establish their own slave trade. Ships would come from Europe to trade goods for slaves. The slaves were then shipped to the colonies in the Americas where they were sold at a profit. The money then went to buy cargoes of goods to bring back to Europe, setting up a trade triangle. In the eighteenth century philanthropists began campaigning for the abolition of slavery and it was eventually abandoned early in the nineteenth century.

see Abolitionists

CABOT, JOHN (c. 1450–98)

Italian navigator. John Cabot (Giovanni Caboto) chose England's patronage, under the commission of Henry VII, to fund his voyages of exploration. He and his sons based themselves at Bristol and set about constructing a ship called the Matthew. Christopher Columbus had already discovered the Americas in 1492 and Cabot arrived at the other side of the Atlantic Ocean in 1497. Coming ashore at Cape Breton Island, he became the first European to reach mainland America.

CADE, JACK (D. 1450)

English leader of the Kentish rebellion. In 1450 Henry VI's misgovernment of England, most notably high taxes and corruption at court, gave rise to the Kentish rebellion, an uprising against the royal forces at Sevenoaks. The leader of the rebellion was a landowner named Jack Cade, who ultimately died for his cause.

see Henry VI

ASKE, ROBERT [1500–37]

Leader of the uprising known as the Pilgrimage of Grace in 1536–37. In 1532 Henry VIII broke with the Catholic Church, declaring himself head of the new Church of England. His policies, including the Dissolution of the Monasteries, led to rebellion, particularly in the northern counties. Robert Aske, a barrister from a good Yorskhire family, was the key player in the most significant of these, the Pilgrimage of Grace. Despite efforts at conciliation, Henry failed to fulfil his promises and Aske and other leaders were executed.

◆ *see* Henry VIII, Pilgrimage of Grace

PIRACY

Piracy was first practised by buccaneers in the Caribbean. Walter Raleigh (1552–1618) and Francis Drake (1540–96) were two famous British pirates who went on to achieve fame as ocean-going explorers. The heyday of

piracy in the Atlantic fell between the 1650s and 1720s. There may have been as many as 2,000 pirates at any given moment during this period. The British Navy hanged more than 400 pirates between 1716–26.

◆ *see* Sir Francis Drake, Sir Walter Raleigh

▲ *ABOVE: Merchant ships were an easy target for pirates*

DRAKE, SIR FRANCIS (1540–96)

English explorer. The end of the medieval period was marked by
European exploration of the globe. Francis Drake was one of the pioneers
in this field. Drake made a name for himself and became a wealthy man
by his activities as a pirate or buccaneer against the Spaniards in the
Caribbean between 1567 and 1572. When Elizabeth I came to the throne
she sponsored Drake on a voyage round the world in the Golden Hind
(1577–80). Drake became mayor of Plymouth (1581) and fought the
Spanish Armada (1588), but died of dysentery off the coast of Panama.

🔷 *see* Elizabeth I, Spanish Armada

▲ *ABOVE: Queen Elizabeth knights Francis Drake*

RALEIGH, WALTER (1552–1618)

English navigator and pirate. Like Francis Drake, his contemporary, Walter Raleigh (1552–1618) too fell into favour with the Virgin Queen, Elizabeth I. Raleigh made several unsuccessful attempts to establish a British colony in Virginia, North America, between 1584 and 1587. He then made an exploration to the north coast of South America in 1595. He is credited with bringing both the potato and tobacco from the Americas to Europe. He was beheaded for conspiracy by James I.

◌ *see* Elizabeth I, Piracy

▶ *RIGHT: Walter Raleigh*

POOR LAWS (1601)

Series of Acts of Parliament designed to alleviate the suffering of the poor in England. The Poor Law Act was passed in 1601 and was designed to address the problem of dealing with the poor among the British population. Parish overseers were empowered in various ways. They were charged with providing facilities and materials with which to set the unemployed to work. Profits were then used to provide relief for the aged, to apprentice pauper children and to build poorhouses. By 1834 when another Poor Law Act was passed, workhouses had become an established part of British society. The act forbade the granting of poor relief to all able-bodied persons, except those in workhouses. However, conditions in workhouses were kept unpleasant enough to deter all those who actually had any alternative but starvation. Thus the poor were trapped in a vicious cycle.

◌ *see* Elizabeth I

ENCLOSURE ACTS (1603)

Series of Acts intended to limit depopulation of rural areas because of enclosure of common land. Until the fourteenth century most land was treated as common, where anyone had the right to graze livestock or grow food. Then the wealthy began the practice of enclosure: appropriating common land as private property. Enclosure continued through the fifteenth and sixteenth centuries, causing widespread poverty and homelessness. Populations in rural areas fell with the loss of common land, which ultimately led to peasant revolts. The Enclosure Act of 1603 was introduced by government to prevent landowners from depopulating rural areas too much, only to see it sabotaged at local level by the landowners. From 1760 new Enclosure Acts of Parliament were passed to reduce the class of smallholding yeomen to agricultural labourers, thereby denying them a right to own the land they farmed. They were thus forced into the employment of landowners or forced to leave and make a living elsewhere.

CATESBY, ROBERT

Instigator of the Gunpowder Plot. Under the Protestant James I, Catholics were being persecuted in England. In 1605 Robert Catesby hatched the Gunpowder Plot with fellow Catholic conspirators. The plan was to blow up the king and Parliament. The conspiracy was betrayed by an anonymous letter and the conspirators were caught and executed, Catesby among them.

see Gunpowder Plot, Guy Fawkes

PILGRIM FATHERS (1620)

Name given to the Puritans who left England and established the first English settlement in the New World. In 1620 the Mayflower set sail from

Plymouth bound for the New World. On board were 102 people, of whom fewer than 25 were Puritan refugees. The journey became known as the voyage of the Pilgrim Fathers. They landed in North America three months later and founded New Plymouth, Massachusetts.

▶ *see* James II, Mayflower

▲ *ABOVE: The departure of the Pilgrim Fathers*

PLAGUE (1665)

Disease that ravaged England in the seventeenth century. Bubonic plague decimated European populations in the 1300s. In some areas, almost half the population died. It only abated when all of those vulnerable to infection had died. The epidemic earned the name Black Death. In 1665 a new strain of the disease – The Great Plague – hit the shores of Britain. It was not so virulent as the last, but still claimed the lives of a fifth of the population of London.

GREAT FIRE OF LONDON (1666)

Fire that destroyed many of London's finest buildings. On 2 September 1666 a fire began at a bakery in Pudding Lane. Most of the city's buildings were made of timber and a prevailing wind quickly carried the fire to other properties. The Great Fire of London burned for four days. It consumed 13,000 houses over an area of 400 acres, but the disaster had at least cleansed the city of plague-carrying rats.

▶ *see* Plague, Charles II, Christopher Wren

HARRISON, JOHN

English clockmaker who solved the problem of longitude at sea. The great navigational problem with transoceanic voyages during the seventeenth century had been calculating longitude. Knowing how far west or east you were was vital to plotting co-ordinates, as ships could miss their intended landfall by 15 miles, wasting vital time. John Harrison was one of many who submitted designs for ships' chronometers to the British government from 1714, hoping to win a prize. His H4 design was eventually recognised the winner in 1772.

RYE HOUSE PLOT (1683)

Plot hatched against Charles II and his brother, James, Duke of York. The conspirators, who appeared to oppose Charles's resolve that the Catholic James succeed to his throne, planned to intercept them at Rye House, in Hertfordshire, while they were on their way home from the races at Newmarket. Charles and James returned from Newmarket earlier than expected due to a fire at the racecourse and the plot was forestalled.

◆ *see* Charles II, Exclusion Bills, James II

NATIONAL DEBT (1693)

Debt incurred by the government of a country. In Britain the first national debt was owed in 1693 when the government issued stocks to raise £1 million. The Bank of England, under the Treasury, is the body which deals with national debt in Britain. There has been a direct historical relationship between national debt and warfare in Britain, simply because wars cost a lot of money. World Wars I and II pushed the British national debt up considerably. Since then other factors, such as keeping the economy buoyant by overseas borrowing, have increased national debt.

BANK OF ENGLAND

During the reign of William III (1688–1702) Parliament decided to set up the Bank of England. In 1694 the bank was founded as a tool for dealing with the burgeoning trade between the British Empire and the rest of the world, and to deal with the English national economy. National debt, public sector borrowing, monetary policy and foreign-exchange rates all fell within its remit. It also began supervising the overall English banking system.

◆ *see* William III

ABOLITIONISTS (18TH CENTURY)

Group of eighteenth-century philanthropists who campaigned for the abolition of the slave trade. The Abolition Society was formed in 1787 and Abolitionists travelled around to ports investigating the conditions on slave ships and interviewing captains and crews. The slave trade was finally banned in Britain in 1807. The English evangelist, William Wilberforce, was instrumental in the abolition of slavery in British dominions by forcing the Abolition Bill through Parliament.

◆ *see* William Wilberforce

ENLIGHTENMENT (18TH CENTURY)

Name given to the period in the eighteenth century which saw a move towards rational and humanist views. The eighteenth century saw a revolution in many areas, especially in philosophy and science. Britain was at the fore during this period, now known as the Enlightenment. The essence of the Enlightenment was that it believed in liberating the possibilities of rational and scientific knowledge. The social environment was dominated by religion at this time, which was seen by thinkers as an inhibiting agent on the human mind because of superstitious beliefs.

TURPIN, DICK (1705–39)

Highwayman. Richard Turpin was an innkeeper's son from Hampstead Heath, Essex. He turned to highway robbery, gaining notoriety as Dick Turpin. England was not policed at that time in its history, so earning one's keep as a robber was an attractive idea to someone who was not born into privilege. Turpin was also involved with cattle-rustling and smuggling contraband. He was eventually caught, however, and hanged by the neck at York. It is likely that his legendary ride from London to York, on Black Bess, was actually completed by another highwayman, John Nevison (1639–84), in 1676.

▶ *RIGHT: Dick Turpin*

JACOBITE REBELLION (1715–46)

Rebellion in support of the overthrown James II. When James became a Catholic in 1671 he suffered attempts to exclude him from the succession and in 1688 he was deposed and replaced by William of Orange. James came from the Stuart royal house, emanating from Scotland. His supporters were called Jacobites. In 1689, under the leadership of John Graham Claverhouse (1649–89), the Scottish Highlanders rose against the new king of England. Their rebellion was successful for a while, having defeated the loyalist forces at the pass of Killiecrankie. Further rebellions, under the leadership of James Edward Stuart – the Old Pretender – in 1715, and then his son, Charles Edward Stuart – the Young Pretender – in 1745, were both effective at threatening the loyalist monarchy. Everything came to a head, though, in 1746 at the Battle of Culloden, where the loyalists finally defeated their enemy, bringing the Jacobite Rebellion to an end.

SOUTH SEA BUBBLE

Financial crash. In 1711 the South Sea Company was founded. It had a monopoly on trade with South America at the time and proved to be extremely profitable, so profitable in fact that in 1719 it offered to take the British national debt into its own hands in exchange for further trade concessions. The 100 shares it started with quickly grew to 1,000, prompting a frenzy of speculation from investors. However, the South Sea Company grew too quickly and its 'bubble' of success eventually burst in 1720. The effect was like that of a stock market crash, and thousands of investors were financially ruined overnight. Even worse, it exposed corruption in the British Cabinet. Robert Walpole (1676–1745) became the first prime minister as a result, and restored financial confidence.

PAINE, THOMAS (1737–1809)

American republican supporter. Thomas Paine was a left-wing political writer and activist. In 1774 he arrived in America and published a pamphlet entitled 'Common Sense' in 1776, an influential piece of republican propaganda. Paine fought on the side of the colonists during the American Revolution, or War of Independence, won in 1783. He returned to England in 1787 to write The Rights of Man, published 1791. Indicted for treason in 1792, he escaped to France.

BENTHAM, JEREMY (1748–1832)

English philosopher. During the Industrial Revolution in Britain the dramatic changes to the social infrastructure caused people to think about the consequences of their actions. Reacting to the plight of the working class, philosopher Jeremy Bentham published his Principles of Morals and Legislation in 1789. He outlined his theory (now known as utilitarianism) that a regime is ethically right only if it aims to achieve 'the greatest happiness for the greatest number' of the population.

WILBERFORCE, WILLIAM (1759–1833)

British philanthropist. William Wilberforce entered British Parliament in 1780. He had philanthropic sympathies and began to develop reformist ideas on slavery. In 1807 his bill for the abolition of slavery was passed. Slavery was ubiquitous in the British Empire and its practice generated a great deal of profit, so Wilberforce had his work cut out convincing others that slavery should be outlawed. In the year of his death, though, slavery was abolished throughout the empire.

◆ *see* Abolitionists

BOSTON TEA PARTY (1773)

Rebellion in North American colonies against British imposition of taxes. The British decided to impose new forms of taxation on their colonists. In 1773 the East India Tea Company delivered a cargo of tea to the

harbour at Boston, Massachusetts. In protest at having to pay 'tea tax' before they could unload the cargo, a party of Bostonians took matters into their own hands. They disguised themselves as native Americans and boarded the ship in the darkness of night. The tea was then thrown overboard into the ocean. The event became known as the Boston Tea Party.

◆ *see* American Revolution, George III

◀ *LEFT: The Bostonians disguised as native Americans throw tea overboard in protest over taxation*

FRY, ELIZABETH (1780–1845)

English prison reformer. The philanthropic Quaker, Elizabeth Fry, took pity on the plight of female prisoners. She formed an association in 1817 to improve their conditions of imprisonment and, with her brother, compiled a report on prison reform in 1819.

DARWIN, CHARLES (1809–82)

English scientist. Darwin had a curiosity for the natural sciences and was in the privileged position of being able to choose a career as a naturalist. During a voyage on HMS Beagle (1831–36), visiting South America and the Galapagos Islands, a realisation came to him about the way species evolve. Knowing what a furore his theory would cause, he did not reveal it for a further 22 years. By 1858, however, Alfred Wallace (1823–1913) had written to him outlining a similar idea. Darwin was forced to publish his life's work. On the Origin of Species by Natural Selection or the Preservation of Favoured Traits in the Struggle for Life was published in 1859.

▲ *ABOVE: Charles Darwin*

LUDDITES (1811–16)

Members of a movement against the burgeoning revolution in industry. With the Industrial Revolution came the realisation that machines may take away valuable jobs from the people. Between 1811 and 1816 protesters, known as Luddites, organised sabotage attacks to destroy machinery that threatened their livelihoods. The cotton and wool mills of northern England, in particular, were targeted by the Luddites as machines became more and more automated. They claimed to be led by a mythical figure called General Ludd.

LIVINGSTONE, DAVID (1813–73)

Scottish missionary. Livingstone was a missionary who devoted his life to the exploration of Africa. He arrived on African shores in 1841 at the age of 28. In 1849 he reached Lake Ngami. He then travelled the upper Zambezi with his wife, Mary Moffat, and his children, but they fell ill and returned to England. He then explored Loanda and followed the Zambezi to its mouth in 1856, when he discovered the falls he named after Queen Victoria. From 1866 he set out on a mission to discover the source of the Nile, reaching Ujiji in 1871. It was here that Henry Morton Stanley (1841–1904) famously tracked Livingstone down. They went on to jointly explore the north end of Lake Tanganyika before Livingstone died of fever.

▲ ABOVE: David Livingstone

PETERLOO MASSACRE (1819)

Name given to the killing of protestors at a rally (16 August 1819). During an open-air meeting on parliamentary reform at St. Peter's Fields, Manchester, on 16 August 1819, the gathering was suddenly charged by infantry and cavalry. The British government had seen the meeting as a threat and overreacted. Eleven people died and many more were injured in what would become known as the 'Peterloo Massacre', an allusion to the Battle of Waterloo, such was the horror of the British public. The massacre would lead to an attempt to overthrow the government by the Cato Street Conspirators (1820), who planned to murder Viscount Castlereagh and his ministers on 20 February.

◆ *see* Cato Street Conspiracy

▲ *ABOVE: The Peterloo Massacre*

CATO STREET CONSPIRACY (1820)

Plot to murder foreign secretary Robert Stewart, Viscount Castlereagh and Cabinet ministers. Castlereagh was foreign secretary in 1820 when the plot was discovered. The plot was hatched at Cato Street, Edgware Road, London, with the intention of overthrowing the established government and replacing it with a provincial government. The conspirators were caught and executed.

◆ *see* Viscount Castlereagh

▶ *RIGHT: Cato Street*

NIGHTINGALE, FLORENCE (1820–1910)

English philanthropist and medical reformer. In 1854 Florence Nightingale arrived in the Crimea with a staff of nurses to set up a field hospital for the wounded British soldiers fighting in the war there. Conditions were so inefficient and unhygienic that 42 per cent of the injured were dying from infections to their wounds. Nightingale and her team improved the situation so considerably that the death rate fell to a mere two per cent. Florence Nightingale won great praise for her achievements in the Crimea and dedicated her life to raising the status of nursing, receiving the Order of Merit in 1907.

◆ *see* Crimean War

▶ *RIGHT: Florence Nightingale*

METROPOLITAN POLICE (1829)

London's law enforcement. The predecessors to the Metropolitan Police force were the Bow Street Runners, a body of men introduced in 1749 by Henry Fielding. London got its first effective police force, however, in 1829, under Robert Peel as Home Secretary. Bobbies, or peelers, as they were known, proved so successful that they were introduced to other parts of the country from 1856. In 1878 the London Metropolitan Police force established its Criminal Investigations Department (CID) at New Scotland Yard. Members of the CID are specialists at surveillance, detection and forensic science.

SWING RIOTS (1830–31)

Riots against the use of machinery. The Swing Riots occurred in the south and east of England. The Luddites targeted machinery in cotton and wool mills, but the Swing Rioters turned their attentions to wrecking farming machines and attacking the landowners for introducing them. In both cases the riots were protests over rising levels of unemployment due to displacement by technology.

◆ *see* Industrial Revolution

CHARTISTS (1838–48)

Democratic movement intended to improve the lot of the working classes in Britain. With the evolution of the working class during the Industrial Revolution, social politics began to play their part more obviously. The working class comprised the vast majority of the population in Britain by the early 1800s, yet they had little influence over their own civil rights because the upper classes held sway. Between 1838 and 1848 Chartism flourished in Britain. It derived its name from the People's Charter, a document based on six fundamental reforms, which included universal male suffrage, annual Parliaments and the secret ballot. However, prosperity began to take hold in Britain generally and the momentum of Chartism was lost due to poor organisation among its leaders.

FENIAN MOVEMENT (1858)

Irish underground society, forerunner to Sinn Fein. The movement was based in America. It was founded in 1858 and was an Irish-American group. There were many from Irish stock in America and they had the sympathy and money to consider it worthwhile attempting to establish an independent Irish republic, as Ireland was a part of the United Kingdom at that time. Various uprisings (1866–70) failed, however.

◆ *see* Sinn Fein

251

PANKHURST, EMMELINE
(1858–1928)

English suffragette. At the start of the twentieth century women were not allowed to vote in political elections. In 1903 Emmeline Pankhurst founded the Women's Social and Political Union to address the situation. Pankhurst launched the militant suffragette campaign in 1906, involving the organisation of protests, which included hunger strikes by imprisoned campaigners, herself among them. Her daughters, Christabel and Sylvia, were keen supporters of her activities. Women finally received the right to vote in the year of her death.

◆ *see* Suffragettes

▲ *ABOVE: Emmeline Pankhurst is arrested*

EDUCATION ACTS (1870, 1902, 1918, 1944)

Series of Acts of Parliament designed to rationalise and improve the education system. Basic literacy and numeracy education were not made available to the working class in Britain until the early nineteenth century. In 1808 the 'British and Foreign Schools Society' was established, followed, three years later, by the 'National Society for Promoting the Education of the Poor in the Principles of the Established Church'. Both improved the lot of working-class children considerably, and in 1862 the British government made grants available for the education of some children up to 12 years old. Then in 1870 came a breakthrough. Parliament passed the Elementary Education Act (Forster's Act), creating district school boards, and provided education to all children as a basic civil right. The Education Act 1902 saw the evolution of county council-run education authorities. The Education Act 1918 raised school-leaving age to 14 and secondary schooling was introduced by the 1944 Act. Each Act since has brought new educational benefits.

GREENWICH MEAN TIME (1884)

Means of standardising global time. With most of the globe having been charted by the late nineteenth century, it became apparent that the world needed to be divided into standardised longitudinal sectors to avoid navigational confusion. Britain was a leading power at that time so the prime meridian ended up running right through the political heart of England. The Greenwich meridian, as it is called, runs straight through the Royal Observatory at Greenwich, London. Adopted in 1884, it signifies zero degrees longitude. The Greenwich meridian also denotes average solar time in the time zone containing the British Isles, known worldwide as Greenwich Mean Time (GMT).

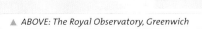

▲ ABOVE: The Royal Observatory, Greenwich

253

SUFFRAGETTES

The Suffragette movement campaigned for votes for women. Between 1886 and 1911 women's suffrage bills were repeatedly introduced and defeated in the British Parliament. They were bills asking for women to be given the right to vote in political elections, for only men were able to vote – such was the air of male chauvinism in post-Victorian society. In 1903 a self-styled suffragette named Emmeline Pankhurst founded the Women's Social and Political Union. By 1906 she had launched a militant suffragette campaign designed to pursue women's right to vote by protest. Suffragettes, who were predominantly middle-class, educated women, made all manner of protests in the name of their just cause. Many suffragettes were arrested and imprisoned for their actions. Their tactic was to go on hunger strike and gain public sympathy to secure release. Eventually the suffragette movement achieved its goal. Women over 30 were given the vote in 1918 and all women over 21 in 1928.

Emmeline Pankhurst, World War I

CRICK, FRANCIS (B. 1916)

British scientist who jointly dicovered the structure of DNA. 1953 was the year that saw science progress into the realm of modern genetics. Much was already known about heredity from breeding experiments with animals and plants, but it took three molecular biologists to finally discover the mechanism responsible for the way genetic information is coded. Francis Crick and American James Watson (b. 1928) determined the structure of DNA (Deoxyribonucleic Acid), helped by the work of Maurice Wilkins (b. 1916).

DEPRESSION

Name given to the years after the 1929 financial crash in which there was a worldwide recession. On 29 October 1929 millions of dollars were wiped off US share values in only a few hours. The Wall Street Crash, as it was dubbed, caused an economic crisis as US overseas investments were recalled. Europe, especially war-torn Germany, was severely affected by this as levels of international trade fell dramatically. Britain, along with other European countries, made a slow recovery over the late 1930s.

▲ ABOVE: Protestors in Washington during the Depression

RATIONING (1939)

Process of limiting food supplies to the public during World War II by the Ministry of Food. The Ministry controlled the procurement, distribution and prices of most foodstuffs, so that people were treated as fairly as possible, regardless of wealth or status. Post-war derationing didn't end fully until 3 July 1954.

▶ see World War II

WELFARE STATE (1945)

In 1942 the Beveridge Report on social security first planted the seed for the idea of a welfare state in Britain. The report committed the wartime coalition government to providing full employment, a free national health service and a social security system in post-war Britain. The Labour government, 1945–51, put the welfare state into effect as far as was practicable. The notion of the welfare state remains an ideal and has been eroded since by changes in political attitudes. Nevertheless, it remains a fundamental characteristic of British society. The welfare state concept has been adopted by several other nations.

NATIONAL HEALTH SERVICE (1948)

Government-run public health service. In 1946, following World War II, the National Health Service (NHS) Act of Parliament was passed, under the Labour government, as a scheme to provide comprehensive free medicine to a beleaguered nation. The NHS was brought into operation in July 1948, with the Ministry of Health assuming direct responsibility for hospital services. Administration was entrusted to regional and local offices. Any British national has the right to free medical attention under the NHS without the need for insurance. The National Health Service is paid for primarily by the tax payer

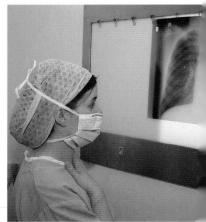

▶ *RIGHT: National Health Service*

LOCKERBIE BOMBING (1988)

On the night of 21 December 1988 tragedy struck the village of Lockerbie, Dumfries and Galloway, south-west Scotland. A Pan Am Boeing 747 airliner, en route to America, was sent plummeting to earth by a bomb which exploded in its cargo hold. The wreckage scattered over several miles, but the main portion of the fuselage came down on the village. Eleven villagers died along with all passengers and crew from the aircraft.

EUROPEAN UNION (1993)

Community of European nations. On 1 November 1993 the European Union (EU) was formed when the Maastricht Treaty came into force. It was a revamping of the existing European Community (EC), of which Britain had been a member since 1973. The European Union not only embraced the old EC but also comprised two intergovernmental 'pillars'; one responsible for covering 'Common Foreign and Security Policy' (CFSP); the other covering 'Co-operation on Justice and Home Affairs'. In 1995 came the EU statement that it wished to commit to the attainment of a single European currency – monetary union – and that the unit of currency would be the euro. The reason for membership of the European Union is that it theoretically bestows cultural and economic advantages on a country, primarily because it allows a collective to function as a whole on the world stage where markets are dominated and largely controlled by America, Japan and other super rich nations. The EU's aims are therefore to expand European trade, reduce competition, remove restrictive trade practices, and improve the flow of capital and labour within the continent, so that theory is put into practice. Culturally the EU works on a liberal philosophy, seeking to encourage the integration of European peoples.

WAR

ROMAN INVASION (AD 43)

Julius Caesar had proved (55 BC) that the Romans could carry out a successful campaign across the Channel. Nearly 100 years later, four legions began to assemble at Boulogne, supported by 20,000 auxiliary troops. They landed at Richborough in Kent, but the Belgae tribe gathered 80,000 men to contest the Roman crossing of the Medway. Using diversionary tactics the Romans outmanoeuvred the British, forcing them to retreat into Essex. Emperor Claudius arrived shortly after Medway and stayed in Britain for 16 days, entering Colchester, with elephants, to accept the surrender of many British tribes. Over the next few years the Romans advanced and subjugated the south-west, the north as far as Lincoln and the north-west to the Midlands. Caratacus, leading a guerrilla war, was finally cornered to the west of the Severn, near Caersws and taken captive. Boudicca (ad 61) rebelled but 10,000 Romans slaughtered her 230,000 strong force. Following the Battle of Mons Grauprus (ad 84) to the north-west of Aberdeen, where 13,000 Romans defeated 30,000 Caledonians, Roman expansion in Britain was nearly complete. By AD 50 England and Wales, up to Carlisle, had been conquered and much of the Lowlands of Scotland by AD 90.

◆ *see* Boudicca, Julius Caesar, Emperor Claudius

HARDRADA, HARALD (1015–66)

King of Norway and Norse warrior. Half-brother to Olaf II, married to the daughter of Yarosalv, Grand Duke of Kiev, he became joint king of Norway (1046). After a war against Denmark he invaded England (1066), supporting Harold II's brother, Tostig. He was killed at the Battle of Stamford Bridge.

◆ *see* Harold II, Battle of Hastings, Battle of Stamford Bridge, William I

NORMAN CONQUEST (1066)

Struggle for the English throne. Harold was shipwrecked in Normandy in 1064 and secured his release by pledging his allegiance to William, Duke of Normandy. When Edward the Confessor died childless, the English Royal Council elected Harold king. With the sanction of Pope Alexander II, William landed his army at Pevensey on 28 September 1066 and defeated Harold at Hastings. He then proceeded to London, brushing aside all resistance and was crowned king on Christmas Day. The Danes supported Saxon rebels in the north but in a series of campaigns the Norman Conquest was complete by 1070.

◆ *see* Battle of Hastings, Norman Dynasty, William I

▲ *ABOVE: Norman Conquest*

STAMFORD BRIDGE, BATTLE OF (1066)

Battle of the Norman Conquest (25 September 1066). Nominally supporting William, Duke of Normandy's claim to the English throne, King Harold Hardrada and Tostig, his ally, invaded Yorkshire with 300 ships and 12,000 men. They enjoyed several successes against local Saxon Lords but were surprised at Stamford Bridge, near York, by Harold II. They were both killed and their army destroyed. Hardrada's son, Olaf, was allowed to sail away with just 24 ships carrying the survivors.

◆ *see* Harold II, Norman Conquest

HASTINGS, BATTLE OF (1066)

Battle for the English Crown (14 October 1066). William of Normandy believed he had no option but to invade England following Harold's coronation. William had two reasons to claim the throne: Edward the Confessor had promised William succession; Harold had sworn allegiance to William. The invasion plan required building ships and as many as 3,000 were used to transport the 2,000 horses and 7,000 men on the 60-mile voyage from St Valery. Harold was heading south from York and his victory over Hardrada when hearing of the Norman landings. He arrived in London (6 October) and marched 58 miles to Battle, arriving on the night of 13 October. Harold drew his 7,500 men along a ridge, facing the Normans in three divisions. William's light troops attempted to break up the English formation with missiles but this had little effect until he launched a full-scale infantry and cavalry attack. In the confusion it appeared that William had been killed and the Normans retreated. Revealing himself by taking off his helmet, William rallied his cavalry and annihilated the English pursuers. For eight hours the English line withstood attacks until Harold and his brothers were killed and the remaining English army scattered.

◆ *see* Harold II, William I

BOUVINES, BATTLE OF (1214)

Decisive victory (27 July 1214) by the French king, Philip II, over the Holy Roman Emperor Otto IV, King John of England and Ferdinand of Portugal. The two armies collided south-east of Lille with the French recording a major triumph that propelled France into European dominance and resulted in the downfall of King John.

◆ *see* King John

BARONS' WARS (1263–67)

Series of rebellions against Henry III, led by Simon de Montfort. Following Henry III's attempts to amend the Magna Carta, which had been adopted by the nobles in 1258 to curb his excesses, Louis XIV of France arbitrated the dispute. In 1263 he decided in favour of the king and the nobles resorted to arms. Henry's troops were defeated at the Battle of Lewes in 1264 and de Montfort, the Earl of Leicester, became virtual ruler. He summoned parliament in 1265 but on 4 August Henry's troops were led by his son, later Edward I, and defeated the barons at the Battle of Evesham, where de Montfort was killed.

see Henry III, King John, Magna Carta, Simon de Montfort

EVESHAM, BATTLE OF (1265)

Last battle of the Barons' War (4 August 1265). The barons' troops, some 5,350 under Simon de Montfort, were taken by surprise, believing Prince Edward's 8,000 Royalists were in fact their own reinforcements. De Montfort was killed and his troops scattered, leaving the coast clear for the restoration of Henry III.

see Barons' Wars, Henry III, Simon de Montfort

▲ *ABOVE: Simon de Montfort is killed in the battle of Evesham*

FALKIRK, BATTLE OF (1298)

Battle between the English and Scots (22 July 1298). Intent on ensuring Scottish independence, William Wallace captured mary English castles north of the Forth and at the Battle of Stirling Bridge on 11 September 1297 he annihilated an English army crossing a narrow bridge. In 1298 an 8,500-strong English army under Edward I defeated Wallace's 10,000 at Falkirk and forced him into hiding. He fled to France, returned to Scotland, was captured, taken to London, tried for treason and executed.

◆ see Edward I, William Wallace

BANNOCKBURN, BATTLE OF (1314)

A battle between the Scots and English, 24 June 1314, during the Scottish War of Independence. A 40,000-strong Scottish army under the command of Robert Bruce, king of Scotland, intercepted Edward II's 60,000 troops marching to the relief of Stirling Castle. The English launched a mass attack but these troops blundered into concealed pits and were slaughtered by the Scots. The English lost 10,000 men and Scottish independence was won. The battle remains the most celebrated victory of the Scots over the English to this day.

◆ see Robert Bruce, Edward II

ARBROATH, DECLARATION OF (1320)

Declaration of Scottish independence. The Declaration of Arbroath in 1320 asserted Scotland's independence following Robert Bruce's victory over the English at Bannockburn in 1314. Composed by the Scottish Parliament in Arbroath Abbey and sent to the pope in Avignon. After one further invasion in 1320, the English signed a 13-year truce.

◆ see Robert Bruce, Edward II

BERWICK, SIEGE OF (1333)

Siege during the war between Edward III and the Scots. After the death of Robert Bruce, Edward Balliol laid claim to the Scottish throne. He was a friend and ally of Edward III; the latter decided to set an example and punish the Scots for forcing his friend to flee. On 12 April 1333 Edward laid siege to Berwick Castle. With an army of 13,000 Scots about to arrive Edward hanged his hostages and marched to face a Scottish army to the south.

see David II, Edward III, Battle of Halidon Hill

HALIDON HILL, BATTLE OF (1333)

Battle between Archibald Douglas's Scots and the English under Edward III and Edward Balliol (19 July 1333). Positioned defensively Edward's professional army slaughtered the Scottish warriors attempting to march up the hill through a swamp. Over 4,000 Scots were killed, including Douglas, after they were broken and pursued by English knights and bowmen.

see Siege of Berwick, David II, Edward III

HUNDRED YEARS' WAR (1337–1453)

Longest war in history. The Hundred Years' War raged through the reigns of five English and French kings. Henry I was the Duke of Guienne in south-west France and had allegiance to Philip VI, the French king. He was intent on destroying the power of his Dukes. Edward III claimed the French Crown because his

▶ *RIGHT: Hundred Years' War*

265

mother was the sister of the French king and Philip VI was only a cousin. The French declared the Crown could not be inherited through a woman. There were economic reasons for the war. In 1336 Philip V arrested all English merchants in Flanders. The Flemish towns revolted and allied with England. Edward III landed in Normandy with 10,000 men (July 1346) and defeated the French at Crécy, then at sea at Sluys and captured Calais (September 1347). In 1355 the English marched in southern France and the Black Prince and his English longbowmen slaughtered the French at Poitiers (1356).

A treaty was signed in 1360 but when Charles V took the French crown in 1369 he broke the treaty, taking the English possessions except Calais and Bordeaux. In 1415 Henry V defeated the French at Agincourt and the Treaty of Troyes (1420) decreed that after Charles VI's death Henry should be king of France and England. Henry died in 1422, followed by Charles. Two new monarchs, Henry VI and the future Charles VII disputed the treaty. Joan of Arc raised the English siege of Orleans and crowned Charles VII. She was captured and executed by the English but French nationalism had been awoken. By 1453 only Calais was left. The war had lost the English their continental possessions despite numerous victories and France was free from foreign interference.

◆ *see* Battle of Crecy, Edward III, Battle of Poitiers

SLUYS, BATTLE OF (1340)

Naval battle (24 June 1340) during the Hundred Years' War. Under the command of Sir Robert Morley and Richard Fitzalan, the 200-strong English fleet attacked 70 French ships commanded by Hugues Quieret in Sluys Harbour. Quieret was killed and his whole fleet captured or destroyed. England was now safe from French invasion.

◆ *see* Hundred Years' War

CRÉCY, BATTLE OF (1346)

Major battle (26 August 1346) between the English and French during the Hundred Years' War. When Edward III invaded France for the second time he was blocked in northern France by a 40,000-strong army led by Philip VI and King John of Bohemia. The English deployed their 19,000 men on the slope of a hill. When the French attacked, the English longbowmen decimated them. After 16 assaults the French were left with 1,500 dead. English casualties were negligible.

🔹 *see* Hundred Years' War

POITIERS, BATTLE OF (1356)

Battle (19 September 1356) of the Hundred Years' War. A 6,000-strong English army under Edward, the Black Prince, had positioned themselves in vineyards and were attacked by an army of 20,500 French, under King John. The French cavalry charged into heavy fire from the English bowmen. The English charged and routed the French army. The French lost 4,500 men and King John was captured. English losses were small; they were able to safely retreat towards Bordeaux.

🔹 *see* Edward III, Edward the Black Prince Hundred Years' War

BERWICK, TREATIES OF (1357 AND 1586)

Series of agreements between Scotland and England. As a border town, Berwick-upon-Tweed has changed hands between England and Scotland a total of 13 times. Perhaps the most significant treaties include one in 1357 when David II, king of Scotland, agreed that should he have no male heir, then the heirs to the English throne should succeed to the Scottish throne. In 1560, two years after Elizabeth I became queen, Protestant Reformers north and south of the border signed a treaty to expel French Catholics from Scotland. This was the turning point in the religious conflict between the two countries. In 1586 Elizabeth I and James VI of Scotland signed another Treaty of Berwick, acknowledging that James VI was heir to the English throne. In signing this treaty with his cousin, James succeeded Elizabeth in 1603 as James I, the first Stuart king of England, uniting the two countries.

⬧ *see* David II, Elizabeth I, James VI

AGINCOURT, BATTLE OF (1415)

Battle fought on 25 October 1415 during the Hundred Years' War, in which a small and battle-weary force of Englishmen under the leadership of Henry V defeated a superior French army.

Following the English capture of Harfleur, Henry V's army was retreating back towards Calais, severely weakened by hunger and disease, planning to return to England. The 25,000-strong French army under the Constable of France, Charles d'Albret, intercepted the smaller 6,000-man English force. An English request for a truce was rejected and they deployed on a narrow front in driving rain. The French troops,

▲ *ABOVE: Henry V fighting the French in the Battle of Agincourt*

mainly heavily armoured cavalry, thundered towards the more mobile English archers and quickly became immobile in the mud. Hundreds were slaughtered. The English advanced, dispatched the stricken cavalry and successfully attacked the French infantry. Over 500 members of the French nobility were killed, including d'Albret, amongst their 5,000 dead. English losses numbered only about 200 men. After the battle England dominated most of France until the middle of the fifteenth century.

see Henry V, Hundred Years' War

ROUEN, BATTLE OF (1419)

Henry V's last major battle (19 January 1419). Henry V besieged the city in 1418 but Rouen held out until January of the following year before the garrison was forced to surrender. The city paid Henry a massive 300,000-crown ransom. In completing this campaign Henry had gained all the provinces he desired in France and, after difficult negotiations, married Catherine in May 1420. The peace was short-lived, however, and he returned to France to extend English power.

see Hundred Years' War

WARS OF THE ROSES (1455–85)

Struggle for the English throne between the Yorkists and Lancastrians. The Houses of York (White Rose) and Lancaster (Red Rose) were both descendants of Edward III. The Lancastrians had been in power since 1399 but civil disorder, heavy taxes and losses during the Hundred Years' War, and the temporary insanity of Henry VI, brought Richard, Duke of York, to prominence. The Yorkists won the first battle at St Albans (22 May 1455) but were beaten at Ludford Bridge (12 October). After their victory at Northampton (10 July 1460), Henry was forced to name Richard as his successor. Henry's wife, Margaret of Anjou, now disinherited, beat

◀ LEFT: Rival Houses York and Lancaster

the Yorkists at Wakefield on 30 December and again at St Albans on 17 February 1461. Richard's son Edward, defeated the Lancastrians at Mortimer's Cross on 2 February 1461, was proclaimed Edward IV on 4 March and beat Margaret again at Towton on 29 March. The Lancastrians fled the country and Edward did not face another rebellion until 1469 when he again drove them out of England. In September 1470 Margaret, with the support of the French, restored Henry VI and Edward fled. Allying with Charles the Bold, Duke of Burgundy, he returned in 1471 and beat the Lancastrians at Barnet (14 April) and Tewkesbury (4 May). After Edward died (1483) Richard III seized power and the Yorkists turned to support Henry Tudor, a Lancastrian. He beat Richard at Bosworth (22 August 1485) and ended the wars by marrying Elizabeth of York in 1486.

◆ *see* Battle of Bosworth, Lancastrian Dynasty, Yorkist Dynasty

BOSWORTH, BATTLE OF (1485)

Decisive battle that brought an end to the War of the Roses. The protracted fight for the English throne between the houses of York and Lancaster came to a bitter end in Leicestershire on 21 August 1485. Richard III's troops took up position on Ambien Hill but, unknown to him, two of his allies, Lord Stanley and Henry Percy, had agreed to support the rebel Henry Tudor. At the crucial moment they turned on their king and Richard's army was routed. Richard preferred death to capture and fell on the field of battle, leaving Henry Tudor to become Henry VII.

◆ *see* Henry VII, Richard III, Wars of the Roses

FLODDEN, BATTLE OF (1513)

Battle (9 September 1513) of the Anglo-Scottish Wars. When Henry VIII refused to cease his wars against France, James IV of Scotland invaded England at the head of 100,000 men. By the time his army reached Northumberland desertions had reduced his army to about 30,000. It was here that the English army, under the command of the Earl of Surrey, faced him. Fierce fighting ensued, claiming the lives of 10,000 Scots, including King James, the Archbishop of St Andrews, 12 earls and hundreds of leaders of Scottish clans. English losses were about 4,000.

◆ *see* Henry VIII, James IV

SOLWAY MOSS, BATTLE OF (1542)

Invasion of England by James V of Scotland. James V was Henry VIII's nephew and when the Scots had defeated the English at Haddon Rig he sent an army to face him. James marched with nearly 20,000 men into Cumbria and encountered an English border force of about 800. Caught in the swamp and without clear direction, the Scots were routed and 1,200 prisoners were taken. James died a fortnight later after the Battle of Linlithgow.

◆ *see* Henry VIII, James V

SPANISH ARMADA (1588)

Attempted Spanish invasion of England by the Spanish. Under the Roman Catholic Spanish king, Philip II, a massive armada of 130 ships carrying 30,000 men was ordered to the Netherlands. Philip's intention was, at a stroke, to suppress the Protestant revolt in the Netherlands, that had been simmering since 1566, and was supported by Protestant England. He proposed that the fleet should invade England, seize Elizabeth I's throne and convert the English to Catholicism. The fleet was sighted off the English coast on July 29, and in a series of running battles off Plymouth and the Isle of Wight, the English attempted to break up the armada. When the armada anchored at Calais, awaiting the arrival of the invasion force to embark, Lord Charles Howard attacked, on August 8, and scattered the Spanish. Many were forced to sail around Scotland and Ireland to return to Spain and only 67 arrived home.

◐ *see* Elizabeth I, Philip II of Spain

FAIRFAX, THOMAS, 3RD BARON OF CAMERON (1612–71)

Scottish Parliamentarian general. Fairfax first served in the Parliamentarian army in Yorkshire and became commander-in-chief in 1645 with Oliver Cromwell as his lieutenant general. He helped win the Battle of Naseby and besieged Colchester in 1648. He presided over the trial of Charles I in 1649 but resigned, disagreeing with the death sentence. He resigned his commission in 1650 but came out of retirement in 1659 to lead the commission to visit Charles II at The Hague to ask him to take the British throne.

◐ *see* English Civil War

BISHOPS' WARS (1639 AND 1640)

Two brief campaigns involving the Scots against Charles I. Charles attempted to strengthen control of the Scottish Church by the English bishops with the imposition of the English Book of Common Prayer in 1637. In 1638 the Scots pledged themselves in the National Covenant to restore Presbyterianism. The General Assembly of Scottish Churches abolished the bishop's power and the first war ended by the Pacification of Berwick without a single battle having been fought. Charles conceded that the Scots had a right to a Free Church assembly and parliament. Charles managed to raise another army but was unable to prevent the

Scots from invading England and occupying Northumberland and Durham, largely due to the refusal of his Short Parliament to grant him money to fight the war. A peace treaty was signed in October 1640 at Ripon and Charles promised to pay the Scots an indemnity that necessitated his calling a Long Parliament.

◆ *see* Charles I, William Laud, Long Parliament, National Covenant, Short Parliament

EDGEHILL, BATTLE OF (1642)
First battle of the English Civil War (23–24 October 1642). Indecisively, this battle pitched 14,000 Parliamentarians under the Earl of Essex against a similar number of Royalists led by Charles I. Royalist cavalry broke the Parliamentarians, who lost many men in the disorganised pursuit. Essex abandoned the battlefield and the Royalists marched on London.

Charles I, Oliver Cromwell, English Civil War, Battle of Marston Moor

▲ *ABOVE: Prince Rupert at the Battle of Edgehill*

273

ENGLISH CIVIL WAR (1642–48)

War between Parliament and Charles I. The roots of the war lie in Charles's tyrannical attitude and determination to be governed by no man. The subsequent rebellion led to years of battles between Royalist and parliamentary forces, both sides aided intermittently by the Scots. The Parliamentarians eventually won the day and the Commonwealth was established under Oliver Cromwell after the king was executed in 1649. The Republic lasted 11 years until the Restoration of Charles II in 1660.

◗ see Charles I, Oliver Cromwell, Battle of Edgehill, Eleven Years' Tyranny

▲ *ABOVE: Oliver Cromwell*

MARSTON MOOR, BATTLE OF (1644)

Royalist defeat in the north (2 July 1644). 27,000 Parliamentarians and Scots under Thomas Fairfax and Oliver Cromwell attacked 18,000 Royalists under Prince Rupert. Rupert's cavalry were soundly beaten by Cromwell's Ironsides, although the Parliamentarian right was crushed. Under Cromwell's command the Royalists were driven from the field, losing 4,000 men. Parliament now had control of the north. Rupert's attempt to relieve York had failed; the Royalists were reduced to a handful of beleaguered garrisons in the north.

◗ see Charles I, Oliver Cromwell, Battle of Edgehill, English Civil War

NASEBY, BATTLE OF (1645)

Battle of the English Civil War (14 June 1645). After sacking the city of Leicester, the Royalist army was chased and cornered near Market Harborough by 13,000 Parliamentarians under Fairfax. The 9,000

Royalists under Charles I and Prince Rupert broke the Parliamentarians but Cromwell meanwhile had overwhelmed their infantry. The Royalists lost 5,000 men and all their artillery.

◆ *see* Oliver Cromwell, English Civil War

DROGHEDA, SIEGE OF (1649)

Siege (3 September 1649) during Cromwell's campaign in Ireland. Oliver Cromwell's 10,000 Parliamentarian troops laid siege to Drogheda, held by The Marquis of Ormonde's 3,000-man garrison. The first assault was repulsed; the town was stormed and the garrison put to the sword. Over 4,000 are reputed to have been killed.

◆ *see* Oliver Cromwell

DUNBAR, BATTLE OF (1650)

Battle (3 September 1650) during Cromwell's Scottish campaign. David Leslie's 22,000-strong Scottish Royalists faced Cromwell's 11,000 near Dunbar. Foolishly, Leslie left his advantageous position on the heights and marched to meet Cromwell. He was promptly routed, with 3,000 killed and 10,000 taken prisoner. Cromwell's losses were comparatively small.

◆ *see* Oliver Cromwell, English Civil War

CHURCHILL, JOHN, DUKE OF MARLBOROUGH (1650–1722)

English general, considered one of the greatest military commanders in British history. By 1682 Churchill had become a colonel and received his peerage. Churchill was second-in-command of the forces facing Monmouth's Rebellion in 1685, ending the campaign a major-general. At this time he split with James II, who intended to make Roman Catholicism the state religion. When William of Orange landed in 1688, James promoted him to lieutenant-general, sending Churchill to fight against William. Churchill deserted to William's cause and after his coronation was made privy councillor and Earl of Marlborough. In 1702 he became the first Duke of Marlborough after a succession of victories over the French. He is remembered for winning the battles of Blenheim (1704), Ramillies (1706) and Oudenarde (1708). He fell out of favour in 1711, moving abroad, but regained recognition when George I became king.

◆ *see* Blenheim Palace, War of the Spanish Succession

◀ *LEFT: John Churchill, Duke of Marlborough*

ANGLO-DUTCH WARS (1652–54, 1664–67, 1672–74, 1780–84)

Series of wars between the English and the Dutch over control of the seas and expansion of empire. The wars saw control of the seas change hands several times throughout the seventeenth and eighteenth centuries. By the conclusion, the final war, England had regained control.

As the English and the Dutch were the two leading maritime trading nations in the world in the second half of the seventeenth century, their intense commercial rivalry soon became a reason for armed conflict. Between 1650 and 1652 the British passed three Navigation Acts that effectively excluded the Dutch from their trade. The first war culminated in English control of the seas by the summer of 1653, severely damaging Dutch business. Luckily for the Dutch, the Stadtholderless Dutch Republic managed to regain control. The second war began when Charles II declared war on the Dutch on 4 March 1665. A plague broke out in England in 1667, forcing them to scale down the conflict. However, when the third war broke out in 1672 England gained the upper hand until naval defeat and public opinion forced them to quit the war in 1674. The final war culminated in Dutch defeat off Ostend in June 1784, having been sparked off by Dutch trading with the rebellious American colonies, despite England being allied to the Dutch for 100 years after the Dutch king, William of Orange, had become king of England. The Dutch fleet was completely destroyed with a loss of over 2,000 men.

▶ RIGHT: English and Dutch fight for control of the sea

NINE YEARS' WAR (1688–97)

War between England and France. This war is also known as either King William's War or the War of the Grand Alliance. William of Orange became William III of England in 1688. He hoped to make England an active ally in his struggle against France. The French Louis XIV supported James II, the Roman Catholic claimant to the throne. The war saw Louis XIV supporting James II in numerous attempts to regain the throne. The Grand Alliance was aimed at forcing France back to borders that had been agreed as early as 1648. While the Anglo-Dutch reigned supreme at sea, Louis won three battles in the Netherlands but could not make any progress in Germany. It soon became clear that neither side would achieve a victory and the Peace of Ryswick was signed in September 1697. The peace did not deal with the problems of North America where the French and the English had fought alongside their respective Native American allies and included an unsuccessful English attempt to take Quebec. This was the first of a series of wars fought between England and France to control the continent, otherwise known as the French and Indian Wars.

▲ *ABOVE: The siege of Londonderry*

LONDONDERRY, SIEGE OF (1689)

Battle of the War of the English Succession (19 April–30 July 1689). The forces of James II besieged 30,000 Ulster Protestants defended by 7,000 armed citizens under Major Henry Baker. Failing in successive assaults the besiegers withdrew, having lost 5,000 men against the garrison's 3,000. Major Baker was one of the casualties.

🔹 *see* Battle of the Boyne, Glorious Revolution, James II, William III

DUNKELD, BATTLE OF (1689)

Battle (21 August 1689) during the Jacobite Rebellion. A force of Highlanders under Colonel Canon attempted to dislodge the Cameronian Regiment under Colonel Clelland, who had occupied the house belonging to the Marquis of Athol. Canon was killed in the action and the Highlanders were forced to retire without their leader.

🔹 *see* Jacobites

BOYNE, BATTLE OF THE (1690)

Key battle (1 July 1690) that secured the throne for William III over the exiled James II. Intent on preventing the former king of England, James II, from regaining the throne, the new king, William of Orange, recently crowned William III, moved swiftly to intercept the exile and his troops. James was resting with his 21,000 men on the banks of the River Boyne when the 35,000-strong loyalist army attacked him. James's troops were soundly beaten, losing over 1,500 men to William's 500. James returned to exile in France and William's position was secured by this prompt action. Since 1795, Protestant Orangemen have celebrated the victory.

◆ *see* James II, William III

▲ *ABOVE: William III at the Battle of the Boyne*

279

SPANISH SUCCESSION, WAR OF (1701–14)

King Louis XIV's attempts to extend French power. On behalf of his son by a second marriage, Archduke Charles (who would later become Charles VI), Louis XIV claimed succession to the throne of the Holy Roman Empire. Although the French and imperial forces began fighting in Italy, the general war began in 1702 with France, Spain, Bavaria, Portugal and Savoy against the English, Dutch and the German states. The Duke of Marlborough enjoyed considerable success (1702–03) but the French missed their chance to take Vienna in 1703, finding themselves defeated at Blenheim by the Duke of Marlborough in 1704. The English also captured Gibraltar. In 1706 the French evacuated Italy and Marlborough beat them again at Ramillies to force them out of the Low Countries. In 1708, in partnership with Eugene of Savoy, Marlborough drove the French back into France and took Lille after the Battle of Oudenarde. Peace negotiations failed but the French were defeated again at Malplaquet in 1709. Meanwhile in North America the conflict known as Queen Anne's War saw the English and French, both with Native American allies, fight many bloody battles. With the death of Joseph I, the Holy Roman Emperor, Charles VI took the throne in 1711. The Peace of Utrecht (1713)

concluded the war as far as France, England and Holland were concerned. Charles VI continued the war, defeating Eugene in 1712 but finally he consented to peace in 1714, signing the Treaties of Rastatt and Baden.

◪ *see* Queen Anne, Treaty of Utrecht

▲ ABOVE: *English capture Gibraltar during the war of Spanish succession*

BLENHEIM, BATTLE OF (1704)

Famous victory of John Churchill, 1st Duke of Marlborough and Eugene of Savoy in the War of the Spanish Succession, fought 13 August 1704. 52,000 English and Austrian troops faced a 60,000-strong French army drawn up behind the Nebel River, near Blenheim. Whilst Eugene mounted a strong diversionary attack, Marlborough advanced across the river and swept Tallard's French army into the Danube. Tallard was taken prisoner, along with 13,000 men. The allies lost 12,000 and the French 18,000. The battle saved Vienna from the French and finally dispelled the myth that the French army was irresistible.

◆ *see* John Churchill, War of the Spanish Succession

UTRECHT, TREATY OF (1713–14)

Series of international treaties ending the War of the Spanish Succession. These treaties aimed to prevent France and Austria from dominating the Spanish empire. Philip V, grandson of Louis XIV of France, became King of Spain but renounced his claim to the French throne. Austria received Milan, Naples, Sardinia and the Spanish Netherlands. Britain acquired Gibraltar, Minorca, Nova Scotia, Hudson Bay, Newfoundland and St Kitts. France agreed not to support Jacobite claims to the English throne. Prussia was given three provinces and the Duke of Savoy was given Sicily. Britain emerged as a great colonial commercial and naval power.

◆ *see* Queen Anne, War of the Spanish Succession

CLIVE, ROBERT, BARON OF PLASSEY (1725–74)

Founder of British India. From a humble position as a clerk in the East India Company, Clive was posted to Madras in 1744. After the city's capture by the French he joined the British army in 1747. In 1751, with just

500 men, he captured Arcot and raised the Siege of Trichinopoly. He defended Arcot for 11 weeks. In 1753 he came back to England as a hero, returning to India in 1756 and, recapturing Calcutta, forced the French out of India and defeated Siraj-ud-Dawlah's 50,000 men with less than 3,000 of his own. He was knighted in 1764.

◆ *see* Battle of Plassey, Seven Years' War

CORNWALLIS, CHARLES, 1ST MARQUESS (1738–1805)

General and statesman during the American Revolution. Defeated by Washington at Trenton (26 December 1776) and Princeton (3 January 1777). Cornwallis won victories at Brandywine Creek (September) and Camden (16 August 1780). He was forced to retreat to Yorktown after the bloody battle at Guildford Court House (March 1781) where he was later compelled to surrender on 19 October.

◆ *see* American Revolution, Battle of Yorktown

JENKINS' EAR, WAR OF (1739–41)

Struggle that grew out of the commercial rivalry between England and Spain. When Robert Jenkins, master of the ship, Rebecca, had his ear cut off by Spanish coastguards in 1731, the ear was later shown to the House of Commons in 1738, forcing Sir Robert Walpole to declare war.

◆ *see* War of the Austrian Succession

AUSTRIAN SUCCESSION, WAR OF (1740–48)

Series of battles over rights to leadership of the Hapsburg Empire. Much of Europe was drawn into the conflict, which dragged on for eight years. Peace was finally concluded with the Treaty of Aix-la-Chapelle in 1748.

The war began after the accession of Maria Theresa as ruler of the Hapsburg Empire. Charles Albert, the elector of Bavaria, claimed the throne, as did Philip V of Spain and Augustus III of Poland and Saxony, and Frederick II of Prussia claimed part of Silesia. Frederick allied with France, Spain, Bavaria and Saxony and defeated Maria's Austrians at Mollwitz in 1741. The Prussians agreed a truce in exchange for most of Silesia but the armistice was broken. The English had been at war with Spain since 1739 and allied with Austria to defeat the French at Dettingen in 1743. Following the English defeat at Fontenoy, George II suggested a peace compromise that would lead to the Treaty of Aix-la-Chapelle. Maria Theresa's troops were defeated at Hohenfriedburg and Kesselsdorf, forcing her to sign the Treaty of Dresden with Prussia in December 1745. However, throughout 1746–48, the war continued in Northern Italy, the Low Countries and North America, and peace was not restored until the treaty was signed in 1748. By then Maria Theresa had secured an alliance with Russia but the other states – Austria, Great Britain, Holland and Sardinia against France and Spain – were weary of the war.

see Treaty of Aix-la-Chapelle, Battle of Dettingen, George II

DETTINGEN, BATTLE OF (1743)

Battle that took place on 27 June 1743 during the War of the Austrian Succession. The allies, 40,000 strong under George II, found their retreat cut by 60,000 French under de Noailles and 23,000 under de Grammont. George II led a charge that broke the French – the last British monarch to lead his troops into battle.

see War of the Austrian Succession, George II

▶ *RIGHT: George II at the Battle of Dettingen*

CALCUTTA, BLACK HOLE OF (1746)

Airless cell in Fort William, Calcutta. On 20 June 1746 Siraj-ud-Dawlah, the Nawab of Bengal, took the fort from the British East India Company and imprisoned 146 Britons, locking them up in the dungeon overnight. Accounts vary but it is believed that only 23 were found alive the following morning. Other accounts say that 64 were held and 21 survived. Contemporary Indian historians claim that the incident never took place. There was great outrage at the time and the British exacted harsh retributions.

◇ *see* Robert Clive, Battle of Plassey

CULLODEN, BATTLE OF (1746)

Last battle (16 April 1746) of the second Jacobite Rebellion. Charles Edward Stuart, the Young Pretender, and James II's grandson landed in Scotland in July 1745. Having taken Edinburgh and fought three battles in Scotland and invaded England as far as Derby, he was forced to retreat into north-eastern Scotland. His army of 5,000 Highlanders were cornered at Drummoissie Muir or Culloden Moor and routed by 9,000 British regulars under the Duke of Cumberland, George II's son. Charles fled to France and 1,000 nobles that had supported him were condemned to death. For his atrocities Cumberland was named The Butcher.

◇ *see* Bonnie Prince Charlie, Jacobite Rebellion

AIX-LA-CHAPELLE, TREATY OF (1748)

Treaty which ended the War of the Austrian Succession in 1748. It awarded Silesia and Glatz to Prussia and gave Parma, Piacenza and Guastalla to the Spanish. Great Britain continued to have control of slave transportation to Spanish America and important trade agreements with the Spanish colonies. Significantly, the treaty also recognised Protestant succession in England. Prussia emerged as a major European power and the Hapsburgs began to look to the east in order to develop their state.

◆ *see* War of the Austrian Succession

SEVEN YEARS' WAR (1756–63)

European world rivalry. When Frederick the Great seized the Austrian province of Silesia in 1740 he triggered off the War of the Austrian Succession. In 1756 Maria Theresa attempted to recapture Silesia for the third time; thus began the Seven Years' War. England sided with Prussia and France supported Austria but the real struggle between France and England, the old enemies, would rage further and take place on three continents. The French-Indian Wars secured North America for the British and in India the French were defeated at Plassey (3 June 1757). In Europe, after some initial French victories, the British and their allies won at Rossbach (5 November 1757), Leuthen (5 December), Crefeld (June 1758), Minden (1 August 1759), and a planned French invasion of England was headed off at the Battle of Lagos, off Portugal (August 1759). After further French defeats at Quebec (September 13), Wandiwash (22 January 1760) and Pondicherry (January 1761), the French had lost both India and North America. The Treaty of St Petersburg (5 May 1762) ended the war between Prussia and Russia and the Treaty of Fontainebleau (3 November 1762) and later the Treaty of Paris (10 February 1763) assured Britain's ascendancy over France.

◆ *see* George II

▶ *RIGHT: The Seven Years' War*

PLASSEY, BATTLE OF (1757)

Battle for control of Bengal (23 June 1757). Following the recapture of Calcutta in January 1757, Robert Clive, the British commander, allied himself with disaffected local leaders. He attacked a huge Bengali army under Siraj-ud-Dawlah with little more than 3,000 men and routed them, securing control of Bengal and ultimately India.

◆ *see* Robert Clive, East India Company

NELSON, ADMIRAL HORATIO (1758–1805)

British Admiral during the Napoleonic Wars. Nelson joined the Royal Navy at the age of 12 in 1770 and was a captain by 1778. When the French Revolutionary Wars broke out in 1793, he began his distinguished naval career by defeating the Spanish at Cape St Vincent (1797) and crushed the French fleet in Abukir Bay (1798). He crippled the Danish fleet at the

Battle of Copenhagen (1801) and by this time he had lost the sight of one eye (1794) and his right arm (1797). Nelson was by now a baron and a viscount. In 1803 Nelson blockaded the French at Toulon but they escaped and united with the Spanish fleet. At the Battle of Trafalgar (21 October 1805) he cornered these navies but was killed, not before knowing of his victory, and uttering the immortal 'England expects that every man will do his duty'. Nelson had saved Britain once more.

◆ *see* Napoleonic Wars, Battle of Trafalgar

▲ *ABOVE: Nelson boarding a captured ship during the battle of St Vincent*

HMS VICTORY (1759–1812)

Lord Nelson's flagship. Designed by Thomas Slade, construction began in Chatham on 23 July 1759. She was launched on 7 May 1765 and commissioned in 1778. She became the most successful 104-gun first-rate ship of the line. Prior to Nelson using her as his flagship at Trafalgar, she had been the flagship of Admirals Keppel, Kemperfelt, Howe and Jervis. She completed her active career on 7 November 1812. She is a major heritage attraction in Portsmouth dock.

◆ *see* Napoleonic Wars, Admiral Nelson

▲ *ABOVE: HMS Victory*

WELLINGTON, DUKE OF, ARTHUR WELLESLEY (1769–1852)

British General and prime minister. Commissioned into the British army (1787), he became an Irish MP (1790). In 1796, as a Colonel, he went to India and took part in several battles, including Assaye (1803) against the Marathas. He returned to England (1805), was knighted and became a British MP. During 1805–1807 he fought against France in

◀ *LEFT: The Duke of Wellington*

Hanover and Denmark and commanded the British forces in Portugal (1810). During the Peninsular War (1808–14), he beat the French at Talavera (1809), Salamanca (1812), Vitoria (1813) and Toulouse (1814). He was made first Duke of Wellington (1814). In June 1815 he decisively defeated Napoleon at Waterloo and was given a cabinet post in 1818. He became commander in chief of the British Army in 1827 and prime minister in 1828. He resigned in 1830 but was reinstated in 1834, made Foreign Minister 1834–1835 and commander in chief again in 1842.

◆ *see* Napoleonic Wars, Battle of Waterloo

AMERICAN REVOLUTION (1775–83)

Conflict between Great Britain and members of the 13 British-owned colonies in North America. The revolution (or American War of Independence) eventually resulted in the British losing these colonies and the setting up of an independent United States.

Following the Treaty of Paris, which had brought the Seven Years' War to an end in 1763, Britain found itself in possession of vast territories. In order to recoup the costs of the long conflict, harsh economic and financial measures brought intolerable burdens to the 13 British colonies. The Sugar Act was introduced in 1764 and the Stamp Act in 1765. The Townshend Duties further increased burdens on commodities such as glass, tea and paper. In 1774 the first American Congress passed the Declaration of Rights. In April the following year General Gage, aiming to seize rebel munitions and agitators in Lexington, sparked off the first battle. On 15 June 1775 George Washington was appointed commander in chief and fought the successful action at Bunker Hill. On 1 January 1776 Washington hoisted the colonial flag and on 4 July Congress proclaimed the Declaration of Independence. Now facing General Howe, Washington was forced to undertake a series of battles against veteran British troops.

By 1778 the French, under Admiral d'Estaing, had arrived to support the Revolutionaries. The next year saw a series of indecisive battles in the north, but after Cornwallis was defeated by Washington at Camden, the British became entrenched at Yorktown. With the French fleet blockading the harbour, Cornwallis was forced to surrender on 19 October 1781. In 1783 Britain recognised the former colonies as an independent nation and the new American constitution was ratified in 1789.

 *see* Charles Cornwallis, George III, Battle of Yorktown

BUNKER HILL, BATTLE OF (1775)
First major battle of the American Revolution (17 June 1775). In an attempt to force the British to evacuate Boston, some 1,200 rebel troops, led by Colonel William Prescott, occupied and fortified Breed's Hill on 16 June. Preceded by a naval bombardment, 2,200 British troops, under

General Howe, launched three successive and costly assaults on the hills. By now another 300 rebels had joined them and although the British eventually captured both hills, they suffered 1,000 casualties. The rebels lost 400. During the battle British shells hit Charlestown, burning it to the ground.

 *see* American Revolution

▲ *ABOVE: The Battle of Bunker Hill*

YORKTOWN, BATTLE OF (1781)

The last of the campaigns of the American Revolution. After General Cornwallis had failed to subjugate Carolina, he moved his troops north to occupy Yorktown and fortify it against the rebels. A rebel army, 8,000 strong, under General La Fayette, besieged the force whilst a French fleet under de Grasse blockaded the harbour. Under continual bombardment the British held out, hoping for reinforcements from New York where Clinton was refitting his troops. La Fayette was reinforced by Washington and Rochambeau who had marched south. Cornwallis was forced to surrender on 19 October, thus securing for the rebels American independence.

◆ *see* American Revolution, Charles Cornwallis

VERSAILLES, TREATY OF (3 SEPTEMBER 1783)

British recognition of American independence (3 September 1783). Following the end of the war between American Revolutionaries and Great Britain (1775–83), American independence was recognised and boundaries fixed. The treaty went further in dealing with possible problems by giving Florida to Spain and Minorca and Senegal and Tobago to France. The American negotiators included Benjamin Franklin

and John Jay. The treaty, also known as The Treaty of Paris, was followed by British evacuation of New York (5 November 1783).

◆ *see* American Revolution, George III

◀ *LEFT: The signing of the Treaty of Versailles*

NAPOLEONIC WARS (1803–15)

Campaign waged by Europe against Napoleon's expansionist policies. Distrust between Britain and France sparked off a series of wars dragging most European states into conflict.

Napoleon's armies would fight from Portugal to Moscow. The Treaty of Amiens that aimed to restore lost territories after the French Revolutionary Wars required England to return Malta to France. England refused and war broke out. The English captured many French colonies but Napoleon aimed to cut off English trade with Europe and invade England. In 1804 Napoleon was crowned Emperor and proclaimed himself king of Italy annexing some Austrian territory, bringing Austria into the coalition against France, along with Britain and Russia. Spain allied itself with France. Threats of French invasions were halted by Nelson's victory at Trafalgar (21 October 1805) but Napoleon had defeated the Austrians and Russians at Ulm (20 October) and Austerlitz (3 December). In 1806 Napoleon created the Confederation of the Rhine, uniting the German states. From 1806–12 the Russo-Turkish War raged, the Turks siding with the French. Prussia joined Russia and declared war on France (6 October 1806) but they were defeated six days later at Jena; the French captured Berlin. On 21 November the Berlin decree blockaded British trade with Europe.

After defeats in 1807 Russia and Prussia allied with France and occupied Portugal. In 1808 the British invaded Portugal, driving the French out of the country and Spain. In 1809 Austria allied with Britain, losing two battles, forcing them out again. In 1812 Napoleon invaded Russia and by 1813 most of Europe was against him. He won his last battle at Dresden (27 August 1813) but now Europe was poised to invade France. He abdicated on 11 April 1814 and was exiled to Elba.

He returned for 100 days, culminating in the Battle of Waterloo and his final defeat. The Treaty of Paris (20 November 1815) formally ended hostilities.

◆ *see* Battle of Trafalgar, Battle of Waterloo, Duke of Wellington

TRAFALGAR, BATTLE OF (1805)

Naval battle (21 October 1805) of the Napoleonic Wars. The French Admiral Villeneuve, commanding 40 ships, was ordered to slip out of Cadiz to land troops in Southern Italy on the night of 19 October. Admiral Nelson, commanding 31 vessels, intercepted the Franco-Spanish fleet on the morning of 21 October, leading the attack himself aboard HMS Victory. The battle took place off Cape Trafalgar, on the southern coast of Spain. By the afternoon 20 Franco-Spanish vessels had been destroyed or captured and Villeneuve had been taken prisoner. This action ended Napoleon's plans of an invasion of England and claimed 14,000 Franco-Spanish lives. Nelson was mortally wounded and 1,500 British were killed. Most of the captured ships were lost in a storm but the British had gained naval supremacy that they would keep for over a century. On the same day Napoleon was winning the battle of Ulm against the Austrians under General Mack.

◆ *see* Admiral Nelson, Napoleonic Wars

WATERLOO, BATTLE OF (1815)

End of the Napoleonic Wars (18 June 1815). Two months after escaping from Elba, Napoleon mobilised 360,000 men and moved them towards the Franco-Belgian border, intent on destroying the Prussian army (16,000) and the Anglo-Dutch (93,000) while they were still separated. Crossing the border on 15 June he fought an inconclusive battle against the Prussians. The following day French General Ney attacked

Wellington's Anglo-Dutch army at Quatre-Bras. Intent on stopping the Anglo-Dutch retreat to Brussels, Napoleon attacked Wellington. Stubborn resistance and the Prussian arrival in the afternoon sealed Napoleon's fate. French casualties were around 40,000, Anglo-Dutch 15,000, Prussians 7,000. Napoleon's downfall was complete.

◆ *see* Napoleonic Wars, Duke of Wellington

▶ *RIGHT: Victory at the Battle of Waterloo*

AFGHAN WARS (1839–42, 1878, 1919)

Three wars between Afghanistan and Britain caused by the threat of increasing Russian influence in British India. The First Afghan War began when the Afghan ruler Dost Mohammed refused an alliance with Britain (1838). Britain invaded and replaced Dost Mohammed with Shah Suja; two years later the British envoy in Kabul was murdered and Akbar Khan, Dost Mohammed's military leader, demanded British withdrawal. Britain complied but were attacked by the Afghans along their route. A British force arrived at the Khyber Pass, defeating the Afghans twice before burning Kabul. Dost Mohammed was reinstated in 1842.

In 1878 a Russian mission arrived in Kabul, sparking off the Second Afghan War, which saw the British regain control of Afghanistan. In 1879 the British envoy was murdered and the Afghan ruler, Amir Yakoub Khan, dethroned. At Maiwand and Kandahar the British again asserted their control of the country.

The Third Afghan War took place between May and August 1919, after Afghan forces invaded British India. The outcome was inconclusive, but Afghanistan gained full independence by terms of the peace treaty.

▶ *RIGHT: Corporal Philip Smith winning the Victoria Cross during the assault in the Redem*

KITCHENER, LORD HORATIO HERBERT (1850–1916)

Military commander and statesman. Kitchener joined the Royal Engineers in 1871 and was promoted in 1883 to captain for his service in Palestine, Egypt and Cyprus. In 1884 he served in the abortive attempt to relieve Khartoum. He was governor general of Eastern Sudan (1886–88) and became commander in chief of the Egyptian Army in 1892. He successfully invaded Sudan in 1895 and defeated the Khalifa at Omdurman in 1898. Kitchener was promoted to major general in 1896 and baron in 1898. He served in the Boer War and was made commander in India (1902–09), during which time he was promoted to field marshal. He became consul general in Egypt in 1911 and was made Earl of Broome in 1914. From 1914–16 he held the position of secretary of state for war and recruited the Volunteer British Army. Kitchener was lost at sea on 5 June 1916 when the cruiser, Hampshire, hit a mine and sank.

◆ *see* Boer War, Kitchener's Army, World War I

FRENCH, FIELD MARSHAL SIR JOHN DENTON PINKSTONE (1852–1925)

British commander at the beginning of World War I. A distinguished cavalry commander during the Boer War, French relieved Kimberley and occupied Bloemfontein. He served as chief of the Imperial general staff in 1912 but resigned in 1914 in opposition to troops in Northern Ireland. He was supreme commander of British troops on the Western Front in 1914 and at the first Battle of Ypres stopped the German thrust towards Calais. He resigned in December 1915 following criticism about the huge numbers of casualties suffered under his command.

◆ *see* Boer War, World War I

CRIMEAN WAR (1853–56)

War that began as a quarrel between Russian Orthodox monks and French Catholics over Jerusalem and Nazareth; fought between England, Turkey, France and Sardinia against the Russians. The work of Florence Nightingale in the Crimea revolutionised nursing practice.

Russia occupied Turkish Moldavia and Walachia in July 1853. The Turks declared war and in March 1854 England and France declared war on Russia, followed by Sardinia in January 1855. The allies began by driving the Russians out of Moldavia and Walachia but it was decided that the Russian naval base at Sevastopol presented a threat to security in the region. In September 1854 allied troops landed in the Crimea with the intent of capturing Sevastopol, which was heroically defended until September 1855. Military operations were marked by stubbornness, gallantry and incompetence.

As the allies marched southwards to invest Sevastopol, the Russians unsuccessfully tried to prevent the allies from crossing the River Alma. The Russians twice tried to relieve Sevastopol but were beaten at Balaclava and Inkerman. The winter of 1854–55 brought great misery to both the allies and the Russians. The British discovered their supply situation was grossly incapable of supplying the men. Through the work of Florence Nightingale mortality rates of the British wounded at the hospital in Scutari were drastically cut. In early 1856 Sevastopol finally fell and the war was brought to a conclusion by the Peace of Paris. This was the only European war that Britain fought between the ending of the Napoleonic Wars in 1815 and the beginning of the Great War in 1914.

◆ *see* Battle of Balaclava, Charge of the Light Brigade, Florence Nightingale

BALACLAVA, BATTLE OF (1854)

Battle between 30,000 Russians under Prince Mentschikov and the British under Lord Raglan, 25 October 1854. The Russians drove the Turks from their redoubts at Kadikoi and entered the valley of Balaclava, where they were driven back by the heavy cavalry brigade under General Scarlett. Although particularly famous for Lord Cardigan's Charge of the Light Brigade, it was the Highland

▲ ABOVE: Battle of Balaclava

Brigade who distinguished themselves when they repulsed the Russian cavalry. British losses were slight except for the Light Brigade.

↻ *see* Charge of the Light Brigade, Crimean War

CHARGE OF THE LIGHT BRIGADE (1854)

Disastrous cavalry charge led by Lord Cardigan during the Battle of Balaclava. Due to a misunderstanding, the Light Brigade charged the Russians at the head of a valley, were shelled from all sides and forced to retire with heavy losses. The event was immortalised by Tennyson's poem of the same name and General Bosquet's remark 'It's magnificent but its not war'.

↻ *see* Battle of Balaclava, Crimean War

SEVASTOPOL, SIEGE OF (1854–55)

Siege that took place during the Crimean War. The Anglo-French army, under Canrobert and Raglan, besieged a large force of Russians commanded by Prince Mentschikov. The city was under continual bombardment for nearly a year until the French stormed the southern defences. Over 54,000 Russians died.

◆ *see* Crimean War

BADEN-POWELL, LORD ROBERT STEPHENSON SMYTH (1857–1941)

British soldier and founder of the Boy Scouts. Baden-Powell joined the 13th Hussars in India in 1876 and between 1888 and 1895 served in India, Afghanistan, Zululand and Ashanti. During the British campaign in Matabeleland (1896–97) he was chief staff officer. After Mafeking (October 1899–May 1900) he was promoted to major general. He organised the South African Constabulary and became inspector general of cavalry in 1903. He was knighted in 1909 and founded the Boy Scouts and Girl Guides.

◆ *see* Boer War, World War I

HAIG, GENERAL SIR DOUGLAS (1861–1928)

British Commander. Haig, having served on the general staff in India was made lieutenant-general and given command of the First Army Corps of the British Expeditionary Force when war broke out in 1914. Later he was made a full general and after huge British losses at Loos-en-Ghelle in 1915, replaced French as supreme commander. His handling of the major campaigns on the Western Front came under criticism, particularly from the prime minister, David Lloyd George. British casualties were severe in 1916 on the Somme and at Passchendaele in 1917. Many blame Haig for the wasteful loss of life and poor tactical understanding.

◆ *see* Battle of the Somme, World War I

ZULU WAR (1879)

British expansion in Africa. In December 1878 Sir Henry Vartle Frere, the British High Commissioner in South Africa, had decided that the strong and independent Zulu kingdom to the north represented a threat to British expansion in the region. He demanded that the Zulu king, Cetshwayo, disband his army and submit his country to British guidance. Under Lord Chelmsford three British columns entered Zululand in January 1879. On 22 January the centre column was attacked and virtually wiped out by the Zulus at Isandlwana. Zulu warriors then crossed into Natal but were beaten off by a company of British regulars at Rorke's Drift. The two remaining columns were left exposed and simply had to dig in and wait. British reinforcements were quickly sent to the area to relieve the two other columns. The Zulus were defeated at Khambula and KwaGingindlovu and a column under Sir Evelyn Wood had almost been wiped out at Hlobane on March 28. On 1 June Louis Napoleon, Prince Imperial of France, was killed in a skirmish. The British continued to advance towards Ulundi, the Zulu capital, where on 4 July the Zulus were again defeated and the capital burned. Cetshwayo was captured and sent into exile.

◖ *see* Battle of Rorke's Drift

RORKE'S DRIFT, BATTLE OF (1879)

Battle (22 January 1879) of the Zulu War. Zulu troops, flushed with their success at Isandhlwana, where they had wiped out over 1,000 British soldiers, descended on the outpost held by one company of the 24th Regiment. Under the command of Lieutenants Chard and Bromhead, the 139 men beat off the 4,000 Zulus who were compelled to withdraw into Zululand, leaving 400 dead. British casualties were 25 killed and wounded and eight Victoria Crosses were awarded.

◖ *see* Zulu War

LAWRENCE, T. E. (1888–1935)

English soldier. During World War I, English soldier Thomas Edward Lawrence was assigned to the military intelligence department in Cairo, Egypt, as a translator. In 1916 he became involved with negotiations for an Arab revolt against the Ottoman Turks. He became a guerrilla leader with a genius for tactics, combining sabotage raids on Turkish communications with organising the Arab revolt. His success earned him such a reputation that he became known as Lawrence of Arabia.

see World War I

MONTGOMERY, FIELD MARSHAL (1887–1976)

British military leader. Montgomery joined the army in 1908 and served as captain during World War I. He replaced Auchinleck in 1942 as commander of the British Eighth Army in Africa. He defeated Rommel in the second Battle of El Alamein, Cyrenaica and Tripolitania and Battle of the Mareth Line, 1943. He became field marshal and was involved in the D-Day invasion of June 1944. He also masterminded Operation Market Garden in September of the same year. Later viscount and chief of the imperial general staff and served as deputy supreme commander of NATO (1951–58).

see World War II, Battles of El Alamein

TRIPLE ENTENTE (19TH–20TH CENTURIES)

Diplomatic and military alliance between Britain, France and Russia. Originally designed as a countermeasure against the Triple Alliance of Germany, Austria-Hungary and Italy. A Franco-Russian military pact, signed in January 1894; in the following year a more comprehensive alliance was agreed. The French, smarting from defeat by the Germans in 1870–1871, opened negotiations with Britain. It was not until 1904 that traditional rivalries were put aside. Britain and Russia concluded an agreement in 1907, completing the Triple Entente. The tension between the Triple Entente and the Triple Alliance culminated in the outbreak of World War I.

◄ *see* Allies, World War I

BOER WAR (1899–1902)

Series of conflicts between the Transvaal and the Orange Free State in South Africa and Great Britain. Throughout the nineteenth century ill feeling had mounted between the Dutch Afrikaaners – or Boers – and British settlers. The Boers had already migrated north to avoid becoming subject to the British colony of the Cape of Good Hope. Gradually the new Boer republics were annexed by Great Britain and when gold brought thousands of British miners to the area, it seemed clear that the Boers and the British were on a collision course. Paul Kruger, the president of the South African Republic, demanded the withdrawal of the British troops from the Transvaal borders in October 1899. This was not forthcoming and although the Boers were initially successful in trapping British forces at Ladysmith, Natal, Mafeking and Kimberley, fresh British troops soon arrived and the main Boer army under Piet Cronje was forced to surrender in February 1900. Following further defeats, President Kruger fled to Europe but the peace was short-lived. New guerrilla warfare erupted, led by Louis Botha and Jan Christiaan Smuts, and continued until peace negotiations began on 23 March 1902, culminating in the signing of the Treaty of Vereeniging on 31 May. During this

▲ *ABOVE: During the Boer War the 91st Highlanders advance over the veldt*

guerrilla period the British were under the command of Lord Kitchener and followed a policy of laying Boer lands to waste and putting civilians into concentration camps. The British suffered around 28,000 losses during the war but the Boers, although only losing 4,000 men, had lost 20,000 civilians from disease and starvation.

◖ *see* Robert Baden-Powell, Lord Kitchener

WORLD WAR I (1914–18)

Worldwide conflict claiming 30 million casualties. There are many reasons why World War I broke out between the allies and the central powers of Germany, Austro-Hungary and the Ottoman Empire. The main act was the assassination of Austrian Archduke Francis Ferdinand (28 June 1914) by Serbian nationalists. Germany supported demands to suppress Serbian militants. Despite negotiations Austria declared war on Serbia (July 28). European powers mobilised their armies.

On August 1 Germany declared war on Russia and marched into Luxembourg. On August 3 they declared war on France, forcing Britain to declare war on them (August 4). The British Expeditionary Force (BEF) under the French began landing at Le Havre (August 7). The Russians invaded from the east on August 13 and threw the Austrians into confusion. Three attempted Austrian invasions of Serbia in August, September and November failed. The Germans continued through Belgium, defeating the French and Belgians at Charleroi (August 22) and the BEF at Mons (August 23–24). Hindenburg defeated the Russians at

▲ *ABOVE: The 98th Yorkshire Regiment cut German wires*

Tannenberg (August 26–29) and Mazurian Lakes (September 9–14). German advances on the western front were checked at Marne (September 5–9). On the eastern front they continued to make ground against the Russians. At Ypres (October 30–November 24) the BEF held against the Germans but an allied offensive in December failed. The Gallipoli Campaign failed to knock the Turks out of the war. On the western front throughout 1915 both the Germans and allies failed to make headway despite huge casualties. On May 23 Italy declared war on Austro-Hungary and in September British and French offensives faltered. German attacks at Verdun began 21 February 1916, continuing for a year but gaining little ground.

In May 1916 the British fleet defeated the Germans at Jutland and in June the Russians launched a new offensive. Throughout July and November the Battle of the Somme raged, seeing the first use of tanks. The British advanced from Egypt and in three battles occupied Palestine and later Mesopotamia. The US declared war on Germany on 6 April 1917 after submarine attacks on their ships. New allied offensives in April and May gained some ground. In October the American Expeditionary Force arrived but in November the Russians began negotiations for an armistice. In 1918 the German spring offensive gained 40 miles; a second 15 miles; a third was stopped by US troops. In August the allied offensive saw victories against the Germans at Amiens, Arras and the Somme. The last allied offensive broke the Hindenburg line and armistice talks began 28 September. The Austro-Hungarians signed an armistice 3 November 1918 and, following the collapse of the German government and mutinies, the Emperor abdicated. The Germans signed the armistice on 11 November 1918. The Treaty of Versailles imposed harsh terms on the Germans.

◼ *see* BEF, Dardanelles Campaign, Gallipoli, Kitchener's Army, Battle of the Somme, Battles of Ypres

ARRAS, BATTLES OF (1914–18)

Series of battles in World War I. In the first battle of the campaign German troops occupied the town of Arras from September 1–18, losing it to French forces. The 1915 battle saw 113,000 French deaths with similar German losses. In April and May 1917 Sir Douglas Haig cleared the Germans from the Vimy Ridge. In March 1918, 15 German divisions attacked Arras; they were beaten back with huge losses. On 26 August 1918 British and Canadian forces attacked east Arras, and despite German counterattack, captured nearly 19,000 prisoners and 2,000 guns.

▷ *see* World War I

BRITISH EXPEDITIONARY FORCE (BEF)

British standing army that went to France at the beginning of World War I and World War II. The Haldane Reforms of 1908 recognised that Britain's treaty obligations required larger units of the British army to be trained and organised so that they could be mobilised as an expeditionary force. In 1914 the BEF consisted of six infantry divisions and one cavalry division. Of these all except two went to France at the beginning of the war. The BEF again went to France in 1939 but was brought back to England via Dunkirk in 1940 when France fell in the May offensive.

▷ *see* Kitchener's Army, World War I, World War II

KITCHENER'S ARMY (1914)

Name given to the volunteers for the army at the beginning of World War I. At the outbreak of war, Horatio Herbert Kitchener, one of Britain's foremost generals, was made secretary of state for war (the first serving British officer to hold the post). Reliant upon a volunteer army, Kitchener used extensive rallies and advertising to expand the British army from 20 divisions to 70 in a relatively short period of time. The campaign had overwhelming results and over one million men had signed up by Christmas 1914. The momentum continued for some months but eventually conscription had to be introduced (1916).

◖ *see* Lord Kitchener, World War I

YPRES, BATTLES OF (1914–1918)

Four battles in Belgium during World War I. The first battle was the last major one of 1914. The Germans attacked the BEF and advanced several miles, but were halted by French and Belgian reinforcements. The British counterattacked and the Germans launched another assault in rain and snow. About 80 percent of the BEF died. The second battle is notable for being the first time the Germans used chlorine gas (24 April 1915). The Germans attacked the British salient but the front was held with the introduction of Canadian reserves. The third battle, also known as Passchendaele, opened with a ten-day artillery bombardment by the British, including Australians and Canadians, advancing two to five miles. By the end of the five months' fighting, allied losses were approaching 300,000, the costliest of all British offensives. The last battle saw significant German advances, being unable to break the Ypres salient despite heavy fighting.

◖ *see* World War I

DARDANELLES CAMPAIGN (1915–16)

Unsuccessful allied invasion of Turkey (25 April 1915–8 January 1916). The campaign was proposed and devised by the British to relieve Turkish pressure on the Russians and to gain control of Istanbul and the Black Sea. Naval operations in February 1915 had failed due to mining. The amphibious landing began in April and was met with heavy Turkish resistance. Hamilton, the British commander, seemed overcautious and as a result little headway was made from the beaches. In August the Allies launched another offensive but due to the inspired leadership of Mustafa Kemal this attack also failed. Allied troops were withdrawn in December and January.

◆ *see* Gallipoli, World War I

GALLIPOLI (1915–16)

Allied land invasion of Turkey (25 April 1915–10 January 1916). Initially 145,000 men were landed on the Gallipoli Peninsular, but due to indecision and incompetence, little progress was made. By the time the troops were withdrawn the British had lost 205,000, the French 47,000 and the Turks around 300,000. Despite the fiasco, the Turks were sufficiently weakened to allow the British to take Palestine in 1917 and for the Germans to cancel their planned offensive in France in 1915.

◆ *see* World War I

SOMME, BATTLES OF THE (1916, 1918)

Two major battles in north-east France during World War I. Seeking to relieve German pressure on Verdun, General Haig and French General Joffre launched a series of attacks against the German defences commanded by Von Hindenburg and Von Ludendorff. Little ground was made despite 500,000 allied casualties and 450,000 German killed and wounded. The allied advance amounted to seven miles along a 20-mile front. In the last year of the war the Germans successfully broke through the allied lines

▲ *ABOVE: Machine gunners in gas masks during the Battle of the Somme*

in the Somme, driving them back 40 miles. Again, Von Ludendorff commanded the Germans but when General Foch took over command of allied troops in the area, he managed to halt the offensive. By then 180,000 Germans and 200,000 allied soldiers had been killed. At one stage in the last battle the Germans were within two miles of the Paris railway. This was the first battle of the last German offensive.

 see World War I

PASSCHENDAELE (1917)

Third battle of Ypres (31 July–10 November 1917). After the British took the village of Messines overlooking the German lines on June 7 a major offensive was planned. Persistent rain and artillery barrages made the battlefield a swamp. As the attacks went in the Germans slaughtered thousands with their machine guns and mustard gas. After months the Canadians captured Passchendaele. At a cost of 250,000 men the allies had gained just eight kilometres.

 see World War I

CONSCRIPTION (1939)

Compulsory military service. Although most of the major powers during World War I had conscripted military service it was not until 1916 that Britain resorted to conscription. Before then they had depended on volunteers. In May 1939 the Conscription Act was brought into force and adopted on 3 September, requiring all males between 18 and 41 to serve compulsory military service. The Emergency Powers Defence Act further reinforced this in May 1940 and extended conscription in order to fully mobilise all the human resources of the country. After the war conscription in the form of National Service continued until the 1950s.

 see World War I, World War II

WORLD WAR II (1939–45)

Worldwide conflict between the allies and axis powers. Hitler came to power in Germany (1933) and began re-arming. In March 1938 he annexed Austria and in September took Sudetenland from Czechoslovakia. On 1 September Germany invaded Poland; two days later Britain and France declared war on them. Poland was defeated by 22 September and on 30 November the Russians invaded Finland. In April 1940 the Germans invaded Denmark and Norway and launched their offensive against the Netherlands, Luxembourg, France and Belgium (10 May). The Netherlands were conquered (14 May) and Belgium surrendered (28 May). The BEF and French forces evacuated from Dunkirk on 4 June. By 22 June France had sued for peace, overrun by the Germans. In August, whilst the Italians had started their offensive in Africa, Britain was winning the Battle of Britain. Italian invasion of Egypt (September) was met with a counteroffensive that swept the Italians back into Libya.

Axis forces turned to the Balkans; Yugoslavia surrendered (17 April 1941), Athens was captured (27 April) and Crete (31 May). German submarines were sinking hundreds of allied ships but the US lend-lease programme provided the allies with urgent munitions. Under Rommel, the German offensive in North Africa was launched (April 1941), driving the British back to Egypt. On 22 June Germany invaded the USSR, rapidly advancing towards Leningrad, Moscow and Kiev. By December the Russians had counterattacked and the offensive was halted. In North Africa the British had launched a counteroffensive driving the Germans back. A Russian winter offensive forced the Germans to withdraw west.

On 7 December the Japanese attacked the US Pearl Harbor, forcing America to declare war on them and their allies, Germany and Italy. The Japanese overran British, French and American colonies in the east and threatened India. In 1942 the Japanese were defeated at Midway and

America now went on the offensive. The German's June offensive in the east gained ground but the USSR began counterattacks. In the Far East America had regained Japanese conquests and in Africa the Battles of El Alamein drove the Germans back into Libya. US forces landed in Algeria (8 November), capturing thousands of Germans at Stalingrad on the Russian front (2 February 1943). By May the Germans had been cleared from Africa. The allies invaded Sicily (10 July) and the new Russian offensive pushed westward. The Americans had captured more Japanese-held islands and in September the allies invaded the Italian mainland; Italy surrendered on September 3. On 6 June 1944 the allies landed in France whilst the Russians overran Romania (24 August), Bulgaria (8 September) and Yugoslavia (20 October). By 25 August the allies were in Paris and reached the German border by 11 September. A last German counterattack in the west failed and, with Russia advancing from the east, the allies launched their last offensive, culminating in the Russian capture of Berlin (2 May). Hitler had committed suicide. Japan now faced the full might of the allies but it took two atomic bombs to force their surrender (14 August).

 see Winston Churchill, D-Day, Dunkirk

DUNKIRK (1940)

Allied evacuation from France (26 May 1940). After the Germans had captured Boulogne and Calais, British withdrawal from France under the code name Operation Dynamo began from Dunkirk at 6.57 p.m. With the French 16th Corps and the British Expeditionary Force holding the perimeter, 338,266 men, including 120,000 French, were brought back to Britain by an armada of 860 small ships of which 240 were sunk. They still left one million allied troops to become prisoners of war.

 see World War II

BLITZ, THE (1940–41)

Series of intense air raids against British civilian targets during World War II. In order to prepare the way for a German invasion of Great Britain, initially German air attacks were focused on British shipping and then Royal Air Force airfields. Then, in September 1940, the Germans shifted their emphasis to attacks on London and other major cities, with the intention of breaking the British spirit. From 7 September London was attacked on 57 consecutive nights. The air attacks continued until May 1941, by which time they were largely centred on London. The winter of 1940–41 saw the greatest ferocity of attacks and during March and April 1941 nearly 10,000 German sorties were flown, although the Germans had largely switched to night-bombing attacks. Facing mounting casualties, German air operations began to decline, despite notable devastation to Coventry, London and Liverpool.

◖ *see* World War II

BRITAIN, BATTLE OF (1940)

Germany's air war against Britain as a prelude to invasion. In July 1940 Hitler ordered Goering's Luftwaffe to seize control of the Channel and destroy the Royal Air Force. He had 3,000 aircraft at his disposal against about 600 RAF fighters. In early August the attacks centred on the Channel ports and airfields. On 15 August 1940 German aircraft hit targets further north. In the crucial two-week period from 24 August to 6 September, the RAF lost 25 per

▶ *RIGHT: Battle of Britain*

cent of its pilots, the Germans twice as many. On 7 September the Germans launched the first of their daylight air raids; huge losses forced a switch to night attacks. By 12 October, with losses mounting, Hitler abandoned Operation Sealion, his invasion plan, and the hitherto invincible German armed forces had suffered their first defeat. The Battle of Britain gave rise to Winston Churchill's famous statement to the nation: 'Never in the field of human conflict was so much owed by so many to so few.'

�«ℂ *see* Winston Churchill, World War II

HOME GUARD (1940–45)

Winston Churchill's local defence volunteers. On 14 May 1940 it was established for men that were too young, too old or in reserved occupations. Expecting 150,000 volunteers, within a month 750,000 had joined and one million by June. The Home Guard was to delay a German invasion force, giving the regular army time to reach the location.

�«ℂ *see* World War II

ALLIES, THE (1941)

Term describing the nations that opposed the Axis Forces of Germany, Italy and Japan during World War II. In the first two years of the war this referred to the British Commonwealth and Western European states. Both the USSR and the USA were neutral. The Japanese attack on Pearl Harbor in 1941 brought the Americans into the war on the side of the Allies. Eisenhower favoured the Europe-first approach, and so the combined efforts of the United States, Canada, Great Britain, the USSR and France turned on Germany before facing the Japanese threat in the East.

�«ℂ *see* World War II

EL ALAMEIN, BATTLES OF (1942)

Two battles (1 July and 23–24 October 1942) in North Africa during World War II. General Auchinleck managed to stop the oncoming German and Italian assault on Egypt. He was replaced by Field Marshal Montgomery who commanded 200,000 men and 1,100 tanks. In October he launched a counteroffensive that claimed nearly 9,000 axis casualties, 30,000 prisoners and a pursuit of 1,500 miles across North Africa to Tunis. The second battle was one of World War II's most decisive.

◖ *see* Field Marshal Montgomery, World War II

ARNHEM, BATTLE OF (1944)

Largest paratrooper action in history. On 17 September 1944, in an attempt to outflank the Siegfried Line, two American and one British airborne divisions were dropped to secure the bridges from Nijmegen to Arnhem. The intention was to capture the Ruhr region – the industrial heartland of the Axis forces. Ordered to hold the bridges until land forces arrived, the airborne troops withstood vicious German counterattacks. Bad weather and ground troops' slow progress led to defeat at Arnhem itself and the overall plan, Operation Market Garden, was only partially successful.

◖ *see* Allies, World War II

D-DAY (1944)

Allied amphibious and airborne landings in Normandy (6 June 1944). On D-Day British, Canadian and US troops established five bridgeheads on the Cotentin Peninsular in Northern France along a 30-mile stretch. The Americans landed on Omaha and Utah beaches and the Anglo-Canadian forces at Sword, Juno and Gold. Simultaneously, American paratroopers were dropped behind the German lines and numerous small-scale commando raids were launched. This was all preceded by an intensive naval and airborne bombardment, coupled with extensive sabotage by the French resistance. By midnight the Utah beach troops had penetrated nine miles inland but those at Omaha, where 3,000 Americans had been killed, had only managed one mile. At Gold, Arromanches and Bayeux had been taken; Sword had failed to capture Caen and the Canadians at Juno had swept seven miles inland. By 12 June the bridgehead was 80 miles long and 10 deep. The D-Day battle had been won.

🔲 *see* World War II

▶ RIGHT: *Allied landings in Normandy*

YALTA CONFERENCE (1945)

Allied conference on military and political strategy. US President Franklin Roosevelt, British prime minister Churchill and Russian Premier Stalin agreed to 'destroy German militarism and Nazism and to ensure that Germany will never again be able to disturb the peace of the world'. They agreed to partition Germany; how Europe would appear after the war and how to collect reparations. This high point of allied unity was aimed to deal with a number of political problems.

🔲 *see* Winston Churchill, World War II

FALKLANDS WAR (1982)

War between Argentina and Britain over ownership of the Falkland Islands. The Argentinians took the island in April 1982 and Britain responded in kind. After two months of fighting the Argentinians surrendered. The Falklands became a separate British dependent territory in 1985 but it was not until 1990 that diplomatic links between the two Argentina and Britain were re-established. The Argentinians have not renounced their claims over the islands.

◆ *see* Margaret Thatcher

GULF WAR (1990–91)

Conflict between Iraq and an international coalition (2 August 1990–3 March 1991). By 1990 Iraq owed $80 billion and demanded that Kuwait, its neighbour, cancelled their part of the debt and helped with repayments. Iraq also accused Kuwait of overproducing oil, thus contributing to the depression of the price of oil, Iraq's main export. Negotiations and mediation failed. Just after midnight on 2 August 150,000 Iraqi troops crossed the border and overwhelmed Kuwait's 20,000-strong army. Four days later the UN Security Council imposed an economic embargo on Iraq; the latter responded by annexing Kuwait on 8 August. A week later a large, international force gathered in Saudi Arabia; some 400,000 US troops backed by 200,000 from Great Britain, South Korea and New Zealand. On 29 November the UN issued an ultimatum that Iraq must leave Kuwait by 15 January 1991. They failed to do so and in the weeks after the deadline 100,000 sorties by coalition aircraft pounded Iraqi targets. On 24 February the coalition invaded south-west Iraq, moving north then east to encircle Iraqi forces in the south and Kuwait. By February 28 Iraqi resistance had collapsed and a ceasefire declared. On 3 March Iraq accepted the ceasefire conditions. 100,000 Iraqis were killed; the coalition lost 240 dead, 776 wounded.

▶ *RIGHT: Forces attack during the Gulf War*

313

▲ *LEFT: The civil wars in Yugoslavia tore apart formerly close-knit communities.*

WARS IN THE FORMER YUGOSLAVIA (1991–1995)

The civil war between the rival republics of multi-ethnic Yugoslavia had long been inevitable. Its trigger was an attempt at breakaway in 1991 by Slovenia and Croatia. However, the central government still had clout and joined with Serb guerrillas to prevent it. Bosnia Herzegovina struck the next blow at Yugoslav unity in 1992, by declaring independence, but soon lost more than two thirds of its territory to the Bosnian Serbs, aided by Serbia. The horrors of the 'ethnic cleansing' that followed recalled the Nazi genocides of World War II. Peacemaking efforts by the UN European Community foundered on Bosnian Serb defiance and their refusal to give up any captured territory. Then, the Serbs went too far. In 1995, they seized 350 UN peacekeepers and committed more atrocities in Muslim Srebrenica where they massacred hundreds of civilians. With this, the US virtually arm-twisted the Serbs to the conference table at Dayton, Ohio where they were obliged to make peace with the Croats, Muslims and other ethnic groups on 21 November 1995.

THE WAR IN IRAQ (2003)

The Gulf War of 1991 left unsolved problems with regard to Saddam Hussein and his brutal regime in Iraq. The most pressing was his suspected stockpiling of weapons of mass destruction. Late in 2002, US President George W. Bush began to push for action to put a stop to Saddam's activities. Despite a UN resolution and several warnings, Saddam failed to comply. On 19 March 2003, despite world-wide anti-war protests, a coalition of American, British and Polish forces attacked Iraq. The war, which lasted three weeks, was grossly unequal. Coalition air power ruled the skies – not one Iraqi aircraft appeared in combat – and coalition aircraft were able to bomb Baghdad with near-impunity. On the ground, British forces surrounded the city and port of Basra by 22 March and by 9 April, the Americans had secured Baghdad. Iraqi resistance, such as it was, was greatly hampered by mass desertions. Once the fighting was over, several important members of Saddam's government – though not Saddam himself – were either captured or gave themselves up.

◆ see Gulf War

▲ ABOVE: The American forces raced to Baghdad in record-breaking time.

BIBLIOGRAPHY

Ball, S. J., *The Cold War: An International History, 1947–1991*, London, 1998

Black, C. F., Greengrass, M., Howarth, D. et al, *Cultural Atlas of the Renaissance*, Oxford, 1993

Blair, P. H., *Roman Britain and Early England, 55 BC–AD 871*, 1963

Chandler, David, *The Dictionary of Battles*, London, 1987

Darvill, T., *Prehistoric Britain*, London, 1987

Eliade, Mircea, *A History of Religious Ideas*, Chicago, 1984

Fussell, P., *The Great War and Modern Memory*, London, 1975

Gilbert, Martin, *Second World War*, London, 1989

Goodman, A., *The Wars of the Roses, Military Activity and English Society, 1452–1497*, London, 1981

Greene, D. M., *Greene's Biographical Encyclopedia of Composers*, London, 1996

Hart, L., *The History of the Second World War*,

Herrin, J., *The Formation of Christendom*, Oxford, 1987

Hobsbawn, E. J., *Industry and Empire*, London, 1990

Holmes, George (ed.), *The Oxford Illustrated History of Medieval Europe*, Oxford University Press, Oxford, 1988

Hughes, Robert, *The Shock of the New*, London, 1991

Keen, M., *The Pelican History of Medieval Europe*, London, 1968

Langmuir, Erika and Norbert, Lynton, *The Yale Dictionary of Art and Artists*, Yale University Press, 2000

Ling, Trevor, *A History of Religion East and West*, London, 1977

Lloyd, T. O., *The British Empire, 1558–1995*, Oxford, 1996

Mayr-Harting, H., *The Coming of Christianity to Anglo-Saxon England*, London, 1972

Morgan, Kenneth O. (ed.), *The Oxford Illustrated History of Britain*, Oxford, 1997

Morillo, S., *Warfare Under the Anglo-Norman Kings, 1066–1135*, Woodbridge, 1994

Norwich, John Julius (ed.), *The Oxford Illustrated Encyclopedia of the Arts*, Oxford University Press, Oxford, 1984

Pakenham, T., *The Scramble for Africa, 1876–1912*, London, 1991

Pollard, A. J., *The Wars of the Roses*, London, 1988

Radway, R., *Britain, 1900–1951*, London, 1997

Rolleston, T. W., *Celtic*, London, 1995

Salway, P., *Roman Britain*, Oxford, 1981

Savage, A. (trans.), *The Anglo-Saxon Chronicles*, London, 1982

Smout, T. C., *A History of the Scottish Peoples*, London, 1969

Taylor, A. J. P., *English History, 1914–1945*, Oxford, 1965

Treasure, Geoffrey, *Who's Who in British History*, London, 1997

Tucker, S. C., *The Great War*, London, 1998

Wood, Jack, *Union for Recovery the Failure and Rise of British Industry*, Wembley, 1986

Young, John, W., *Britain and the World in the Twentieth Century*, London, 1997

AUTHORS

ERIC EVANS (Introduction) Eric Evans is Professor of Social History at the University of Lancaster. He has edited and contributed to numerous studies on the history of the British Isles, as well as writing many of his own titles, including *The Birth of Modern Britain* and *The Complete A–Z 19th and 20th Century British History Handbook*.

GERARD CHESHIRE (Industry and Society) Gerard Cheshire is a prolific writer. He has written and contributed to many books on a wide range of subjects, including science, social history and technology as well as magazine articles and partworks.

DAVID HARDING (Politics) David Harding is an experienced journalist. His specialist subject is political history and current affairs, but he also writes on subjects as diverse as sport and war.

LUCINDA HAWKSLEY (Culture) Lucinda Hawksley is a freelance writer and editor. She studied art history and has published several books on art, including *Pre-Raphaelites*.

BRENDA RALPH LEWIS (Royalty) Brenda Ralph Lewis has been writing on historical subjects for 35 years, specialising in the history of the British royal family. She has written or contributed to nearly 100 books on the subject and also writes BBC television programmes.

JON SUTHERLAND (War) Jon Sutherland is an experienced writer and lecturer in business studies. He has written and contributed to over 100 books and encyclopedias on a wide range of subjects. His specialist area is military history.

HELEN TOVEY (Religion) Helen Tovey completed a degree in History at the University of Exeter. Since then she has been working as a writer and editor, specialising in British and European social history, religion, art and architecture.

PICTURE SOURCES

The Art Archive: British Library: 5, 165; London Museum/ Eileen Tweedy: 222; Musee de Versailles/Dagli Orti: 158-159; Museum of London: 224; Pitti Palace, Florence/Dagli Orti (A): 199; Royal Leicestershire Regiment/Eileen Tweedy: 295; Windsor Castle: 194

Image Select: 221

Impact Photos: 99; Philippe Achache: 101; Mohamed Ansar: 126; John Arthur: 118; Piers Cavendish: 120; Debay/Ernoult: 3·3; David Freeman: 46; Philip Gordon: 71; Alex Macnaughton: 256; Tony Page: 12, 16, 139, 253; Christine Porter: 28; Aerial Portraits: 19; Simon Shepheard: 34; Jacqui Spector: 233

Mary Evans Picture Library: 6, 10-11, 15, 21, 22, 23, 24, 27, 29, 31, 36, 37, 39, 44-45, 49, 52, 55, 56, 57, 59, 60-61, 64, 66, 68, 79, 89, 92, 94, 97, 103, 107, 109, 113, 124-125, 137, 145, 150, 151, 154, 161, 162, 167, 175, 180, 182, 183, 186 (t & b), 188, 192, 195 (b), 200, 201, 203, 207, 208, 209, 210, 213, 214, 215, 216, 218-219, 230, 231, 232, 234, 235, 238, 239, 241, 246, 247, 248, 249 (t & b), 250, 252, 254, 255, 258-259, 263, 265, 268, 273, 274, 276, 277, 278, 279, 280, 283, 285, 286, 287 (b), 289, 293, 296, 300, 301, 307, 309, 312; Edwin Wallace: 8, 160, 229, 261; Institution of Civil Engineers: 7, 54, 176, 244; National Portrait Gallery: 41

Topham Picturepoint: 13, 26, 33, 38, 43, 47, 50, 58, 69, 74, 80, 83, 87, 91, 112, 116, 117, 121, 122, 123, 131, 135, 141, 143, 148, 153, 171, 172, 177, 178, 184, 187, 190, 195 (t), 196, 204, 205, 211, 217 (t & b), 220, 223, 237, 270, 287 (t), 290, 299, 303, 305, 314, 315

INDEX